WITHDRAWN
UTSA LIBRARIES

Development Dilemmas

It is widely believed that economic development in much of the world is not happening quickly enough. Indeed, the standard of living in some parts of the world has actually been declining. Many experts now doubt that the solution can be purely technical and economic – it must also be political and moral.

This book brings together contributions from leading authorities on economics and political philosophy to survey current barriers to growth, including problems with policy and problems with concepts and thinking. Getting policies right, the contributors stress, is a complicated task in itself, but it also may not be enough; instead, people in both the developed and developing worlds may also need to reconsider basic and time-worn beliefs about facts, values, the measurement of data, rights, needs and the nature of government.

Of interest to economists and policy makers, *Development Dilemmas* is a long-awaited addition to the debate over economics and political philosophy in the developing world.

Melvin Ayogu is Professor of Economics at the University of Cape Town and Associate of the Chartered Institute of Bankers. He has written numerous articles and book chapters in the areas of international finance, public finance, corporate finance, political economy and economic development. **Don Ross** is Professor of Philosophy at the University of Alabama, Birmingham, AL and Professor of Economics at the University of Cape Town. He has published several books and numerous articles on the foundations of behavioural science, game theory and strategic dynamics in international trade.

Routledge studies in development economics

1 **Economic Development in the Middle East**
   Rodney Wilson

2 **Monetary and Financial Policies in Developing Countries**
   Growth and stabilization
   Akhtar Hossain and Anis Chowdhury

3 **New Directions in Development Economics**
   Growth, environmental concerns and government in the 1990s
   Edited by Mats Lundahl and Benno J. Ndulu

4 **Financial Liberalization and Investment**
   Kanhaya L. Gupta and Robert Lensink

5 **Liberalization in the Developing World**
   Institutional and economic changes in Latin America, Africa and Asia
   Edited by Alex E. Fernández Jilberto and André Mommen

6 **Financial Development and Economic Growth**
   Theory and experiences from developing countries
   Edited by Niels Hermes and Robert Lensink

7 **The South African Economy**
   Macroeconomic prospects for the medium term
   Finn Tarp and Peter Brixen

8 **Public Sector Pay and Adjustment**
   Lessons from five countries
   Edited by Christopher Colclough

9 **Europe and Economic Reform in Africa**
   Structural adjustment and economic diplomacy
   Obed O. Mailafia

10 **Post-apartheid Southern Africa**
   Economic challenges and policies for the future
   Edited by Lennart Petersson

11 **Financial Integration and Development**
   Liberalization and reform in Sub-Saharan Africa
   Ernest Aryeetey and Machiko Nissanke

12 **Regionalization and Globalization in the Modern World Economy**
   Perspectives on the Third World and transitional economies
   Edited by Alex F. Fernández Jilberto and André Mommen

13 **The African Economy**
   Policy, institutions and the future
   Steve Kayizzi-Mugerwa

14 **Recovery from Armed Conflict in Developing Countries**
   Edited by Geoff Harris

15 **Small Enterprises and Economic Development**
   The dynamics of micro and small enterprises
   Carl Liedholm and Donald C. Mead

16 **The World Bank**
   New agendas in a changing world
   Michelle Miller-Adams

17 **Development Policy in the Twenty-First Century**
   Beyond the post-Washington consensus
   Edited by Ben Fine, Costas Lapavitsas and Jonathan Pincus

18 **State-Owned Enterprises in the Middle East and North Africa**
   Privatization, performance and reform
   Edited by Merih Celasun

19 **Finance and Competitiveness in Developing Countries**
   Edited by José María Fanelli and Rohinton Medhora

20 **Contemporary Issues in Development Economics**
   Edited by B.N. Ghosh

21 **Mexico Beyond NAFTA**
   Edited by Martín Puchet Anyul and Lionello F. Punzo

22 **Economies in Transition**
A guide to China, Cuba, Mongolia, North Korea and Vietnam at the turn of the twenty-first century
Ian Jeffries

23 **Population, Economic Growth and Agriculture in Less Developed Countries**
Nadia Cuffaro

24 **From Crisis to Growth in Africa?**
Edited by Mats Lundal

25 **The Macroeconomics of Monetary Union**
An analysis of the CFA franc zone
David Fielding

26 **Endogenous Development**
Networking, innovation, institutions and cities
Antonio Vasquez-Barquero

27 **Labour Relations in Development**
Edited by Alex E. Fernández Jilberto and Marieke Riethof

28 **Globalization, Marginalization and Development**
Edited by S. Mansoob Murshed

29 **Programme Aid and Development**
Beyond conditionality
Howard White and Geske Dijkstra

30 **Competitiveness Strategy in Developing Countries**
A manual for policy analysis
Edited by Ganeshan Wignaraja

31 **The African Manufacturing Firm**
An analysis based on firm surveys in Sub-Saharan Africa
Dipak Mazumdar and Ata Mazaheri

32 **Trade Policy, Growth and Poverty in Asian Developing Countries**
Edited by Kishor Sharma

33 **International Competitiveness, Investment and Finance**
A case study of India
Edited by A. Ganesh Kumar, Kunal Sen and Rajendra R. Vaidya

34 **The Pattern of Aid Giving**
The impact of good governance on development assistance
Eric Neumayer

35 **New International Poverty Reduction Strategies**
Edited by Jean-Pierre Cling, Mireille Razafindrakoto and François Roubaud

36 **Targeting Development**
Critical perspectives on the millennium development goals
Edited by Richard Black and Howard White

37 **Essays on Balance of Payments Constrained Growth**
Theory and evidence
Edited by J.S.L. McCombie and A.P. Thirlwall

38 **The Private Sector After Communism**
New entrepreneurial firms in transition economies
Jan Winiecki, Vladimir Benacek and Mihaly Laki

39 **Information Technology and Development**
A new paradigm for delivering the Internet to rural areas in developing countries
Jeffrey James

40 **The Economics of Palestine**
Economic policy and institutional reform for a viable Palestine state
Edited by David Cobham and Nu'man Kanafani

41 **Development Dilemmas**
The methods and political ethics of growth policy
Melvin Ayogu and Don Ross

Development Dilemmas
The methods and political ethics of growth policy

Edited by Melvin Ayogu and Don Ross

LONDON AND NEW YORK

First published 2005
by Routledge
2 Park Square, Milton Park, Abingdon, Oxon OX14 4RN

Simultaneously published in the USA and Canada
by Routledge
270 Madison Ave, New York, NY 10016

Routledge is an imprint of the Taylor & Francis Group

© 2005 Selection and editorial matter, Melvin Ayogu and Don Ross;
individual chapters, the contributors

Typeset in Times by Wearset Ltd, Boldon, Tyne and Wear
Printed and bound in Great Britain by MPG Books Ltd, Bodmin

All rights reserved. No part of this book may be reprinted or
reproduced or utilized in any form or by any electronic, mechanical
or other means, now known or hereafter invented, including
photocopying and recording, or in any information storage or
retrieval system, without permission in writing from the publishers.

British Library Cataloguing in Publication Data
A catalogue record for this book is available from the British Library

Library of Congress Cataloging in Publication Data
A catalog record for this book has been requested

ISBN 0-415-33105-6

In memorium: Professor Jean-Jacques Laffont 1947–2004

Contents

List of contributors	xiii
Acknowledgements	xvi
Introduction DON ROSS AND MELVIN AYOGU	1

PART I
General perspectives — 13

1. **Finance for development** — 15
   JOSEPH STIGLITZ

2. **Globalization: less than meets the ear?** — 30
   ROBERT H. BATES

3. **Philosophical foundations of normative economics** — 40
   DANIEL M. HAUSMAN

4. **Development theory and the philosophies of science** — 62
   HAROLD KINCAID

5. **The political economy of statistical evidence: economic data problems in developing countries and their impact on empirical research** — 80
   HASHEM DEZHBAKHSH

PART II
Special problems and applications   103

6 **Regulation, enforcement and development**   105
   JEAN-JACQUES LAFFONT

7 **Good ideas and human welfare: Big Pharma versus the developing nations**   125
   ALEX ROSENBERG

8 **The WTO, unfair trade and development**   144
   DON ROSS

9 **The 'new (global) economy' and inequality in South Africa**   170
   NICOLI NATTRASS AND JEREMY SEEKINGS

PART III
New critical perspectives   191

10 **The political philosophy of needs and weak states**   193
    LAWRENCE HAMILTON

11 **Modelling human behaviour: a biological perspective on the African prospect**   215
    MIKE BERGER

    Afterword   246
    MELVIN AYOGU AND DON ROSS

    Index   252

Contributors

Melvin Ayogu is Professor of Economics, University of Cape Town, and Associate of the Chartered Institute of Bankers. He has authored and co-authored several articles, book chapters and technical reports in the areas of international finance, public finance, corporate finance, political economy and economic development. With Augustin Fosu, he edited a volume on privatization and corporate governance published by Oxford University Press in 2002.

Robert H. Bates is Eaton Professor of the Science of Politics in the Department of Government and Faculty Fellow of the Center for International Development at Harvard University. He focuses on the political economy of development, particularly in Africa. Among his most recent publications are 'Organizing Violence', *Journal of Conflict Resolution* 2002 with Smita Singh and Avner Greif and *Prosperity and Violence* (W.W. Norton 2001).

Mike Berger was formerly Professor and Head of the Department of Chemical Pathology at the (then) University of Natal Medical School. He is a Fellow of the Royal College of Pathologists, UK, the College of Pathologists, South Africa and the American Heart Association and Council on Arteriosclerosis, Thrombosis and Vascular Biology. After retirement from his formal position at the end of 1996, his academic interests centred on the broad interdisciplinary domain between the basic biological sciences and those disciplines concerned with human collective behaviors and structures. He is currently a senior honorary lecturer in the Department of Human Biology at the University of Cape Town and is preparing the Fifteenth Annual Jacob Gitlin Memorial Lecture on the topic of anti-Semitism and related intractable xenophobias.

Hashem Dezhbakhsh is Faculty Fellow of Economics and Director of Economics Undergraduate Studies at Emory University. He was the chairman of the Emory University Economics Department from 1998 through August 2001. Dr Dezhbakhsh has published in such specialty areas as Econometrics and Statistics, Political Economy of the Budgetary Process, Law and Economics, and Financial/Macro Economics. Dr Dezhbakhsh is the recipient of several teaching awards including Emory University's Williams Distinguished Teaching Award and the Ohio State University's Outstanding Graduate Student Teaching Award. He has appeared as an expert on many radio talk shows as well as on CNN, FOX News Channel, and ABC, NBC, CBS and FOX affiliates in Atlanta. He has also worked as an economic consultant.

Lawrence Hamilton is Senior Lecturer in Political Science at the University of KwaZulu-Natal, Durban, South Africa. He was previously Mellon Research Fellow at Clare Hall, Cambridge, UK. He researches within political philosophy, the history of political thought, and political economy, in particular on needs, rights, constitutions, imperialism, land reform and the history of natural rights philosophies. His most important recent publications include *The Political Philosophy of Needs* (Cambridge University Press, 2003) and '"Civil society": critique and alternative', in *Global Civil Society and Its Limits*, eds S. Halperin and G. Laxer (Palgrave, 2003).

Daniel M. Hausman is the Herbert A. Simon Professor of Philosophy at the University of Wisconsin-Madison. After graduating from Harvard in 1969, where he studied biochemistry and then English history and literature, he taught public school and received a MAT degree from New York University. He then did a second BA in philosophy at Cambridge University before receiving his PhD from Columbia in 1978. His dissertation (later published as *Capital, Profits and Prices*) addressed questions in philosophy of science raised by economics, and his research has focused on economic methodology, ethics and economics, and causation. He co-founded the journal *Economics and Philosophy* and co-edited it from 1984 to 1994 with Michael McPherson. Recent books include *The Inexact and Separate Science of Economics, Economic Analysis* and *Moral Philosophy* (with Michael McPherson), and *Causal Asymmetries*.

Harold Kincaid is Chair of the Philosophy Department and Director of the Center for Ethics and Values in the Sciences at the University of Alabama, Birmingham, AL. He is the author of *Philosophical Foundations of the Social Sciences* (Cambridge University Press, 1996) and *Individualism and the Unity of Science* (Rowman and Littlefield, 1997) and numerous articles in the philosophy of science and philosophy of economics.

Jean-Jacques Laffont was Professor of Economics at the Universite des Sciences Sociales de Toulouse and J.E. Elliott Chair in Economics at the University of Southern California. His research interests included public economics, information economics, regulation and economics of development. He passed away before this book was published.

Nicoli Nattrass is a Professor in the School of Economics and Director of the Centre for Social Science Research at the University of Cape Town. Her research interests include unemployment, inequality, economic policy and AIDS.

Alex Rosenberg is the R. Taylor Cole Professor of Philosophy at Duke University. He is the Co-Director of the Duke in Geneva Program and also co-director of the Centre for Philosophy of Biology. His interests focus on the problems of metaphysics, mainly surrounding causality, and the philosophy of social sciences, especially economics and the philosophy of biology.

Don Ross is Professor of Philosophy at the University of Alabama, Birmingham, AL and Professor of Economics at the University of Cape Town. He has published several books and numerous articles on the foundations of behavioral science, game theory, and strategic dynamics in international trade. The first volume of his *Economic Theory and Cognitive Science* will appear in 2005. He is Director of the SABITA Infrastructure Development Assessment Project in South Africa.

Jeremy Seekings holds a joint appointment in the Department of Sociology and the Department of Political Studies at the University of Cape Town. In 1999 and 2002 he was a visiting professor at Yale University. He is also the director of the Social Survey Unit in UCT's Centre for Social Science Research. His research interests include the politics of redistribution in post-apartheid South Africa, democratization and the transformation of urban politics, the political economy of welfare policy in South Africa and South African political history.

Joseph Stiglitz is Professor of Economics and Finance at Columbia University. After serving as a member of the Council of Economic advisors during the Clinton administration, he was Chief Economist and Senior Vice President of the World Bank from 1997 to 2000. He is the co-founder and Executive Director of the Initiative for Policy Dialogue. In 2001, he was awarded the Nobel Prize in Economics. His most recent book is *The Roaring Nineties* (2003).

Acknowledgements

As this book developed out of a conference, and would not have come into being without it, we have two sets of people to thank: those who helped us get the conference off the ground, and those who pitched in on the book itself.

So, first: The conference was entitled 'Development Issues in the New Economy', and took place at the University of Cape Town in March 2002. It was made possible by grants from the International Development Research Center, Ottawa, Canada, the Rockefeller Foundation, and Trade and Industrial Policy Strategies (TIPS), South Africa. We thank Akin Adesina, Resident Representative of the Rockefeller Foundation in Southern Africa, Vongai Kandiwe, Program Office, the Rockefeller Foundation, Diery Seck of the Secretariat for Institutional Support for Economic Research in Africa, who connected us to IDRC, and Rashad Cassim of TIPS. We hope they deem that the present product partly justifies their investment. (Needless to say, nothing said in this book should be taken as expressing the views of these institutions.)

Global Conferences of South Africa did a superb job of organizing the conference, especially as represented by Karen Deiderichs, who might possibly be the most efficient person on earth. Having watched Karen work, we feel quite sheepish about referring to ourselves as the conference's 'organizers'. Thanks also to GC's founder, Brian McDonald, for taking on a project so much smaller than the company's usual brief, yet treating it thoroughly seriously in every way.

All of the authors of chapters here of course merit thanks, but two deserve special mention for accepting commissions to fill what we perceived as thematic gaps, despite having missed out on the attractions of the conference itself. These are Mike Berger and Harold Kincaid.

Thanks to Dan Hausman for suggesting the book's title.

Our most important debt of gratitude is to Rian Wall, who served as Editorial Assistant and did far more hard work than we can claim to have. Her efficiency and conscientiousness gave the famous Karen (see above) a run for her money, and was a tribute to the value of the project that sponsored Rian's employment, the Department of Foreign Affairs and International Trade Youth International Internship Program and the Center for International Business Studies, Memorial University of Newfoundland.

Thanks to Terry Clague at Routledge for supporting the book project.

Introduction

Don Ross and Melvin Ayogu

1 The subject and basis of this book

There is a widespread conviction, crossing ideological boundaries, that the developing and least developed countries are not closing the wealth gap between themselves and the OECD nations quickly enough. Indeed, many people, especially those disposed to deep distrust of global economic institutions and multinational corporations, claim regularly in the popular media that the gap between the richer and poorer parts of the world is in fact widening.

Because the concepts of international economic equality and national wealth are imprecise ones, subject to a plethora of different measurement conventions, there is presently no consensus among economists as to whether, in general, it is more reasonable to regard the developed and developing worlds as converging or diverging. Many economists and institutions are busy gathering new data and running econometric tests of new hypotheses. This book does not represent another effort at surveying or adjudicating the results of these efforts. It is, instead, about some of the underlying conceptual and evidential questions that make analysis of the problem so difficult.

There *is* rough consensus on a few highly *general* facts. The so-called 'Asian tigers' – Hong Kong, South Korea, Singapore, Taiwan, Thailand, Malaysia – have, despite the turmoil of 1998–99, clearly converged dramatically with North America, Western Europe and Australasia on most leading measures of growth. Two of the world's largest developing countries, China and India, have seen their per capita GDPs and per capita incomes grow faster than the OECD average for a number of years, though inequality within China has probably increased, as has the difference in wealth between urban and rural India. Most of Latin America has careered between years of optimism and rising expectations, and other years of political crises linked to financial retrenchments and widespread loss of confidence in economic progress. Most Eastern European countries had to navigate over upsurges of poverty during the transition from central planning; those now entering the EU have probably weathered the worst of this, while others continue to face uncertainty. Most of the Middle East has been at best stagnant for some time. Two areas of the world, Sub-Saharan Africa and central Asia, have certainly fallen short of global growth averages, and a number of countries in these regions have, by any reasonable measure, become poorer over the past decade.

These differences from region to region are part of the reason why one cannot justify simple generalizations about whether development policies, either national or international, are 'succeeding' or 'failing'. We must ask, as our broadest question, one intended to elicit less sweeping answers: Which baskets of development policies and processes have succeeded in which circumstances, and why?

One might suppose that, once we have got our question right, our task in answering it then simply consists in gathering, organizing and interpreting the right facts. Obviously, this is a preponderant *part* of the task. However, as the chapters assembled in this book attest, it turns out that ambiguities in the central concepts associated with development encourage us to continue questioning our own questions as we gather data – indeed, to keep asking ourselves which data are really (relevant and true) *data*. That is to say: the project of understanding and assessing development policies and processes has a philosophical dimension as well as an economic one.

Most people are likely familiar with the idea that philosophy is relevant to development economics by way of the ethical dimension. While a few economists still hold out for the view that policy-relevant economics can be a value-free 'positive' science, this perspective is now clearly that of a shrinking minority. Several chapters in this book – those by Hamilton, Rosenberg and Ross – are indeed about the relationship between development policies or institutions and ethics. Hausman's chapter directly addresses the question of how this relationship itself should be understood. And over half the chapters in total – including the contributions of Stiglitz, Bates, Laffont, and Nattrass and Seekings – are indirectly about the roles of particular value questions in policy formation and evaluation.

However, the relevance of philosophical analysis goes beyond the ethical dimension in the narrow sense. One of the main branches of philosophy is epistemology – the study of how and to what extent people can and do justify the factual beliefs they come to hold on particular topics. Epistemological questions tend to become especially complex when they interact strongly with ethical ones, since there is overwhelming psychological and historical evidence that people systematically bias their epistemic standards – goodwill notwithstanding – when the answers to questions under investigation are highly normatively charged. Indeed, under such circumstances the very process of accumulating data and deciding what should count as data often becomes problematic. In this book, the chapters of Hausman and Kincaid are as much concerned with epistemological issues as with ethical ones, and issues surrounding data gathering are the direct topic of Dezhbakhsh's chapter.

Finally, questions about the ways in which people try to understand their own behavioral patterns, about how they go about integrating – as they somehow must – normative and factual judgments, through processes of cultural transmission, have strong philosophical aspects. Bates's chapter here is about ways in which political issues around development are driven by the way in which the concept of 'globalization' is culturally troped, and about how this produces normative 'spin' on processes that goes beyond or ignores alternative factual emphases. Is a description of development convergence as 'globalization' a report of a fact, or a value judgment, or both? Do descriptions of globalization as 'cultural imperialism' and 'spreading cosmopolitanism' report one fact under different spins, or two complementary facts, or two competing factual possibilities? Bates's chapter takes note of some aspects of cultural responses to development that prevailing spins push into the background. Berger's chapter, reflecting a recent wave of research in the evolutionary dynamics of human cultural transmission, seeks to explain why certain spins tend to triumph over others that might do equal justice to facts. Berger's work here also connects this issue directly back to the ethical ones by asking how knowledge of these very dynamics can help us to make more desirable development outcomes more probable.

We have just been describing the main ways in which this book brings philosophical analysis to bear on issues in the political economy of development. However, our approach in assembling the book was *not* to simply ask professional philosophers to deploy their disciplinary training and methods on the topic. We proceeded from the assumption that the best, most useful and informed, philosophy is continuous with the contributions of less abstract and more situated inquiry. Where subjects in the domains of behavioral and social sciences are concerned, theoretical discussions amongst psychologists, sociologists, political scientists and economists should shade imperceptibly into philosophical dimensions, rather than being presented as though some artificial methodological line establishes a division of labor. Much of the best philosophical discussion, in the areas of both physical and behavioral-cognitive-social sciences, has been produced by people in specific science departments rather than by people in philosophy departments. And some major contributions to scientific understanding have emanated from professional philosophers.

Thus, this book brings together practitioners from several disciplines. Dezhbakhsh, Laffont, Nattrass and Stiglitz are economists. Hausman, Kincaid and Rosenberg are philosophers. Ross is both a philosopher and an economist. Bates, Hamilton and Seekings are political scientists, and Seekings is also a sociologist. Berger is a medical scientist. We think it is testimony to the truly interdisciplinary nature of the issues that we don't find a tight correlation between these disciplinary affiliations and the

4   *Introduction*

distributions of topics and methods in the chapters here. Thus the book is organized according to a thematic logic, rather than by reference to disciplinary perspectives.

In this, it follows the organizing principles of the conference that gave rise to it. On 25–27 March 2002, the School of Economics at the University of Cape Town hosted 'Development Issues in the New Economy'. The original versions of most of the chapters here – those of Berger, Kincaid and Ross having been commissioned later – were presented there. After the conference, the participants traveled together within South Africa, continuing their discussions and debates while surrounded by the colorful energy – and the poverty – of a middle-income developing country. They then reconsidered their papers in light of the conference deliberations to produce the chapters gathered here. As a consequence of the locale where these themes were initially aired, we think this book makes a contribution to the development debate that is less distorted by a first-world-centered perspective than is much of the current conversation. The conference audience included academics, politicians, bureaucrats, journalists and businesspeople from South Africa and from elsewhere in that wonderful but challenging continent. They were not hesitant in asking tough questions after the papers, from their own hard-earned points of view. We hope that their involvement has had a substantive influence on the contents of this book, and we thank them.

2 The contents of the book

The book opens with Joseph Stiglitz's criticism of the development policy framework that has been pursued under the terms of the so-called 'Washington Consensus'. Readers of Stiglitz's 2002 book *Globalization and Its Discontents* will not be surprised that the Washington Consensus policies, and some of the institutions that promoted them, especially the United States Treasury Department and the International Monetary Fund, here come under a strongly jaundiced gaze. Stiglitz's chapter is not philosophical in character. He takes for granted that the point of development policy is to improve the welfare of as many people as quickly as possible and with as much stability and permanence as possible in the improvements. He also takes for granted that economic analysis can find and guide implementation of such policies. However, his critique is partly ethical, since some policies are criticized for being ineffective, while others are attacked as unfair. Stiglitz's sweep is wide and comprehensive, and his chapter provides a fitting overture to the rest of the book by making clear how much is at stake, for so many people, in our doing the work that is necessary, empirical, conceptual and normative, to choose policies that might be both fair and effective.

A reader who has been left feeling a bit indignant by Stiglitz's tone might find some basis for relief in Bates's chapter, which comes next.

Bates's topic, like Stiglitz's, is the whole broad area of the 'new political economy' of globalization. However, whereas Stiglitz emphasizes the dislocations that globalization threatens in the absence of wise policies, Bates reminds us that globalization *per se* is not something dangerous. (Of course, as he would agree, *anything* as large as globalization in its social and economic effects can have adverse consequences if the policies for managing them are botched badly enough.) For most of the history of modern political thought, at least in the West, *cosmopolitanism* has been regarded as something to be welcomed and celebrated. To what extent should globalization be regarded as the beckoning of a true cosmopolitan spirit, rather than as a form of imperialism? As with most elegant writing, Bates's chapter is deeper in its content than its simple conversational style suggests. It at once offers a criticism of the conceptual tyranny over our thinking that can be wielded by a simplistic idea – 'globalization' itself, with the associations it has attracted by political accident – and applies economic logic to the market for cultural values that globalization, interpreted as cosmopolitanism, enriches.

Bates's chapter shares an important characteristic with all of those in the book, one remarked upon in the first section of this Introduction. That is, it interrogates the experience of globalization from *inside* the perspective of the developing world, rather than from the detached distance of the wealthier societies. Many who have watched young, idealistic demonstrators on the streets of Seattle, Genoa, Quebec City and elsewhere, who believe they are representing the interests of the poor, have felt more than a little uneasy as they saw causes promoted – stricter environmental protection, higher labor standards, more efficient regulation of business – that might be perceived in Africa, Asia or Latin America as luxuries to be afforded *after* one has become affluent. There are indeed important aspects of economic and cultural life in the developing world that are more guessed at than known by most people living in the OECD. We think it ethically and pragmatically essential to try to view development from the perspective of the places where it matters most.

Continuing our opening focus on the most general themes, the third chapter is by a leading philosopher of economics, Daniel Hausman. His chapter addresses the extent to which the problems of development are best understood through the lenses of professional economics. Like all scientists, economists have had to develop special methodologies and restrictions on their conceptual framework in order to impose the kind of discipline on their own conversation that allows for accumulation of evidence and progressive expansion of conceptual knowledge. However, development is not, in the first place, a topic for disinterested speculation and slow accretion of scholarly wisdom. It is something happening to people – or, as the case may be, *not* happening to people – whose immediate needs are urgent. The needs are also ethically complicated, both as regards matters of universal concern, like material poverty, and questions that have varying salience in different cultural value systems. The track record of economists in allowing these sorts of concerns to reach the forefront of policy concern leaves much to be desired. Hausman doesn't much concern himself with the *history* of this. Instead, he focuses directly on the working assumptions built into economic theory, from which development problems are addressed. His conclusion is not that we should *stop* taking an economic perspective on development, in the narrow sense of 'economic' he describes and criticizes, but that we should recognize its limitations so that we do not mistake it for the whole view. When we receive the advice of economists, Hausman argues, we need to do so with a clear understanding of what economic analysts are trained to *ignore*, so that we take care to involve others in the debate who are not trained to impose special limitations on themselves.

Harold Kincaid, another leading philosopher of economics, and of social science in general, continues to explore this theme in the next chapter. Kincaid does not agree with Hausman that there is such a thing as a monolithic theoretical perspective to be associated with 'economics'. Instead, he traces significant divergences amongst the ways in which different groups of economists think about development to deep, and generally un-noticed, philosophical assumptions they make about which kinds of studies can unearth useful discoveries about causal relationships in complex systems like national economies. Though still philosophical in its point of departure, Kincaid's chapter is focused closer to the bedrock of actual and specific policy initiatives than is Hausman's. This represents a general organizing principle of the book, which opens with very broad themes, at both the policy and philosophical levels, and progresses steadily to more specific issues and problem-settings – while referring back to the wider context in which these are focused. (In Part III, the focus broadens out again, but now to pick up on unorthodox perspectives that are anticipated at several points in earlier chapters.)

Kincaid challenges the extent to which it is useful to try to *theorize* development in an overly general way, as opposed to rolling up our sleeves, gathering good information and a tool kit of argument patterns, and then getting on with our efforts pragmatically and opportunistically. He is also worried about the extent to which we distort data by insisting on squeezing it into preconceived models. Economist Hashem Dezhbakhsh's chapter, which comes next, is concerned with an even more basic epistemological problem: to what extent can we acquire accurate and relevant data for measuring development in the first place? Dezhbakhsh's chapter is more factual than argumentative, and the facts it records are sobering. There is a real extent to which we may be busily engaging in policy debates and prescriptions *without really knowing what we're talking about.* In this connection, we reiterate something said in the opening paragraphs of this Introduction: here we are, talking in sophisticated terms about development imperatives, while we do not even know whether, in all sorts of specific senses, things are getting better or worse! Fortunately, Dezhbakhsh provides some practical advice, based on his direct experience as someone who puts economic and econometric data on development to work, on how we could try to do better. We hope that participants in the development debate from all the concerned academic disciplines and policy desks will take the problems Dezhbakhsh identifies here seriously enough to pay close attention to his institutional recommendations.

Dezhbakhsh's chapter closes Part I of the book, on general perspectives about development problems as they are theorized within the 'mainstream' framework of political economy. We then move, in Part II of the book, to questions about some specific applications, still within this mainstream, before turning in Part III to perspectives that tread on less familiar intellectual territory.

The first chapter in Part II is by economist Jean-Jacques Laffont, and concerns the subject of corruption. Few discussions of development policies and frustrations fail to touch, sooner or later, on this subject. We think it fair to say that everybody, regardless of their theoretical or ideological backgrounds, agrees that the existence of effective institutions, both public and private, is among the basic prerequisites for successful development. In turn, a key component of effectiveness is relative freedom from corruption. Of course, developed countries have no shortage of graft or selfish rent-seeking – witness Enron, Parmalat and the running hijack of the global agricultural market by subsidized OECD farming interests. Nevertheless, one of the things developed countries can afford that developing countries often cannot are sophisticated regulatory bureaucracies, whose staffs can be well enough paid to make betrayal of the public interest less tempting for them. Furthermore, where there are thriving private sectors and wide availability of credit, there are more reliable ways for people to accumulate wealth than abusing positions of trust. The straightened circumstances of developing and least-developed countries in these respects give rise to a chicken-and-egg situation. If a country needs effective institutions to achieve development, but must have achieved development to install and grow effective institutions, how is it possible to get the show rolling at all?

Laffont, one of the worlds' leading authorities on incentives, here models *part of* the problem of corruption – the tendency for holders of public contracts with informational advantages to exploit those advantages to the maximum – and its solution, as a technical issue in supplying a public good. Perhaps, instead of wringing our hands about chickens and eggs, or hoping that moral exhortation will change entrenched cultural practices – again, did two decades of incessant discourse on business ethics in America keep executives at Enron and other large companies away from cookie jars? – we should simply try to determine what needs to happen to levels of investment in anti-corruption enforcement during early stages of development. Laffont argues that this investment curve will typically be humped. That is, there will be some period during early development during which proportional investment in anti-corruption enforcement needs to increase – while incentives for corruption are rising faster than public or private wealth – before decreasing with affluence. Here, then, technical economic analysis may help us to see something that has gone wrong on the ethical front in previous development initiatives.

The next chapter, by philosopher Alex Rosenberg, builds very naturally on this platform by turning to another hot issue in the development debate that centers around questions of incentives. Developing countries frequently complain that protection of patents in medicines, as required under the terms of the WTO regime, severely harms their prospects by making vital drugs unaffordable or, even worse, by incentivizing first-world drug companies to shelve patents that could not be sold for high enough profits in the relevant (impoverished) markets for them. To many people, the ethical trade-off between patent protection and the deaths of poor people looks, as Rosenberg says, 'like a no-brainer'. Philosophers, however, are regularly in the business of showing us that our conclusions often go wrong just where unexamined intuitions seem clearest. Rosenberg's chapter here is of this kind: he produces a partly ethical, partly economic argument for the very strong conclusion that patents *must* not be violated. However, he then develops an original proposal for institutional design that might relieve us of the whole dilemma in the first place. There is a sting in the tail, however. Rosenberg notes that in order for his proposal to work, it might be necessary to restrict a fundamental freedom, and one strongly associated with Bates's cosmopolitan interpretation of globalization, namely, the right of geographical movement of people. He concludes by suggesting that the need to face this cruel issue is not peculiar to his particular problem here, but generalizes across the whole field of development. Well, it has been some time since anyone thought that development was going to be easy – either economically or ethically.

New obligations with respect to intellectual property are just one aspect of a more general issue that arises for developing countries as they try to converge on first-world wealth by integrating with that world and its institutions. Whatever benefits it brings, there can be no question that for a poor country, joining the WTO imposes costs. It is a constant refrain of anti-globalization factions throughout the world that these costs are unethically high, given the current policy and institutional framework of the WTO. Some of these arguments are quite similar in their tone and flavor to those of Stiglitz's that open this book. In the next chapter in Part II, philosopher and economist Don Ross surveys some of these arguments in light of the way that developing countries actually confront WTO negotiations on a strategic basis. While there is no question that the multilateral bargaining process is 'unfair' in a very abstract philosophical sense, Ross criticizes the tendency of both populist critics and political philosophers to think that it constitutes useful policy advice to simply call for greater 'democracy', 'transparency', and 'broader values' in the institution. He explains important *reasons* why the WTO is structured as it is, and why any envisaged reforms in pursuit of greater fairness will need – for the sake of developing countries' interests – to bear these reasons in mind. Unfortunately, few of the existing normative critiques even take notice of them. Ross also gives grounds for doubting that there is substance to the common complaint that the WTO process increases the power of multinational corporations relative to that of governments. That view entirely depends, he argues, on whether governments are considered as institutions *one at a time*, or collectively as a sector. He also discusses the extent to which the WTO can justifiably be regarded as insufficiently democratic, in the context of philosophical questions about what 'democracy' might realistically *mean* at the global level. All of this leads to a concluding policy section, in which Ross describes some institutional reforms that have actually been put on the table in WTO and World Bank publications, and shows how this more incremental agenda would better address existing unfairness than would any direct application of abstract moral criticisms.

The concluding chapter in this part is a country case study. Fittingly, in light of the location of the conference that gave rise to the book, the country in question is South Africa. Economist Nicoli Nattrass and political sociologist Jeremy Seekings have spent their careers studying the changes in South Africa's political economy, especially in its labor market, as it has opened itself to global competition and adopted policies explicitly intended to raise the formerly disenfranchised majority of its population towards the status of the global middle class. Their analysis is a seamless blend of social-political and economic analysis, one that well encapsulates the interdisciplinary pragmatism of the book as a whole. As parts of the population acquire real stakes in the restructured South African economy, they seek to protect those stakes through the institutions of organized labor, and through supporting policies that favor growth in skills-intensive sectors. Nattrass and Seekings give strong empirical grounds for fearing that this unsurprising behavior has the unintended consequence of retarding the campaign against poverty. The process, they suggest, is complemented by the Government's need to signal policy stability and credibility to international investors, which leads it to often resemble a 'poster child' for the very Washington Consensus measures so sharply criticized by Stiglitz at the beginning of this book. Another, larger thematic epicycle in the structure of the book's organization is thereby brought to closure, though of a distinctly ambivalent kind.

In this general development of its themes, the book implicitly raises its most general philosophical question (one that Kincaid's chapter poses *explicitly*): what, both economically and ethically, ought 'development' to *mean*? Does it mean increasing affluence of *countries*, in a national accounting sense, or increasing affluence of *most people within countries*? Does the first of these things generally imply the second, by some sort of reliable causal logic? Assessing the extent to which development is 'working' crucially depends on trying to answer this question.

We certainly do not pretend that this book answers it. However, we think that it makes significant progress in showing us how to pose it in the rich context of real institutional processes and conceptual problems. To complete the grounds for this claim, it is important that we consider reflections on development that are less constrained within 'mainstream' terms of debate. We thus conclude the book with Part III, comprising two chapters that interrogate the topic at a more radically critical level than is typical of either the economic or the philosophical literatures on it.

The first of these chapters, by political scientist Lawrence Hamilton, defends an ethical perspective according to which the very assumption that the developing world should seek to 'converge' with the developed world is a mistake. The prevailing notion of development, Hamilton argues, is one in which people are led to develop an endless proliferation of new 'wants', which no one is ever asked to democratically justify by reference to 'needs', but which ensure that neither satisfaction nor deliberative, collective control of outcomes can ever be achieved. Hamilton argues that a prerequisite for development that might be both successful *and democratic* – something he takes to be analytically *part of* the criteria for 'success' – is for the developing nations themselves to adopt new institutional processes for assessing their own policy goals. If this entails their getting off the 'development bus' as that vehicle is generally understood in the developed world, then, Hamilton concludes, so it should be.

More mainstream commentators might worry that Hamilton's prescriptive stance pays insufficient attention to issues of incentive-compatibility in institutional design. How, one might wonder, will the kinds of deliberative processes he urges control for people's incentives to promote their 'wants' into 'needs', once it is agreed that development should seek to meet the latter rather than the former? Questions of this sort take us deep into the terrain of human nature itself, and its implications for the kind of world it is possible to try to build at the global level.

This is the ground onto which South African medical scientist Mike Berger steps in his chapter that concludes the book. Evidence from evolutionary psychology and anthropology shows us a great deal about the extent to which people evaluate their own lives and their social structures *positionally*, that is, by reference to how their roles, status and material opportunities compare with those of others. Every successful politician is familiar with the strength and importance of this force at the level of the domestic political entity. What will or could it make of policies and efforts intended to make the whole world wealthier at once? In his chapter, Berger examines the evidence on the ways in which people situate themselves as members of national and ethnic groups, and on the extent to which identification dynamics in such groups depend on constructions of rivalry with other groups. He suggests that development is both spurred on in some ways, and hindered in others, by these dynamics. Thus many people in poorer countries conceptualize development as a kind of 'revenge' against the developed world – partly revenge just against the standing insult to their status and dignity that it might seem to present, partly as revenge for real and imagined material transgressions such as colonialism, past slavery and forced exploitation of labor and natural resources. As Berger documents by reference to everyday political discourse in developing countries, this conceptualization encourages a complex emotional interplay of envy and resentment, currently finding widespread expression in a level of hostility to the government and corporations of the United States (in particular) that is difficult to regard as altogether rational. It is not Berger's purpose to regret or to seek to shame such attitudes into remission. Rather, he aims to *understand* them, on grounds that we are unlikely to find a successful set of development policies, a set not swamped by unintended consequences of the kinds of forces that economists are trained to ignore and analytic philosophers to deplore, if we do not.

The book ends with some closing reflections by the editors. We will not aim to anticipate those here, either by describing them or offering further general comments now that we have outlined the themes to come.

Part I
General perspectives

1 Finance for development

Joseph Stiglitz

The subject of my chapter is certain aspects of finance for development. The key question is the following: How can developing countries attain finance for development given the high costs of capital and the higher risk premium they face? In other words how can they compete?

All around the world one repeatedly hears countries complaining that they cannot compete. The US, for instance, cannot compete because of cheap wages; small countries are sceptical about their ability to compete with large countries – every country seems to entertain the view that it is disadvantaged relative to others.

But this, as a matter of logic, cannot be true. Every country has a comparative advantage *somewhere*, and therefore, every country can attract capital. Low wages, for instance, can offset high costs of capital. The key issue is the right exchange rate. If one has the right exchange rate, certain sectors of the economy will be able to attract investment and thus provide the basis for economic growth. Furthermore, the right economic framework can make it easier to attract investment. Consequently it will lead to a better exchange rate and eventually to greater economic prosperity.

I am now going to describe some of the elements of that economic framework. I will argue that the main elements stressed by the Washington Consensus such as macro-economic stability, privatisation and liberalisation are only part of the right framework. If they are taken to the extreme, however, they can impede development. I will argue that there are some other important ingredients one needs to think about as well. For example, attracting capital to developing countries does not lie at the core of the issue. What is really important is the creation of domestic savings.

1 The shortcomings of the Washington Consensus

Economic policy should be oriented towards development and development transformation rather than economic stability alone. The Washington Consensus, however, mainly focuses on macro-economic stability, with a strong emphasis (within macro-economic stability) on inflation control. Furthermore, it stresses the importance of privatisation and liberalisation.

However, each of these measures, when given too absolute or pre-emptive a weight in policy determination, may have an adverse effect on economic development. An overly narrow focus on macro-economic stability can stifle economic growth and increase inequality. In a large number of countries, an excessive focus on macro-economic stability and inflation control have led to very high interest rates. High interest rates, in turn have led to increased levels of unemployment and this has been a major source of continuing poverty. Privatisation, when carried out in the wrong way as it was under the sponsorship of the IMF in Russia, can lead to asset stripping rather than wealth creation.

The interaction of misguided policies can have disastrous consequences. High interest rates, for instance, increase the return to asset stripping. As managers in transition countries like Russia realised that they could not afford the high interest rates and could not access capital, they also realised that they could not easily restructure their enterprises into more productive ones. That made it all the more profitable for them to engage in asset stripping. Thus there is an interrelationship between macro-economic policies and the failures of privatisation. Similar problems have been found elsewhere in the developing world.

It is increasingly acknowledged today that what is going on in a country is not independent of the political economy of that country. One aspect of this is the legal structure – the rule of law. The importance of institutions is undisputed. However, macro-economic policies combined with privatisation and resulting in asset stripping in Russia have significantly undermined the political support for the rule of law. There were more people occupying key managerial roles within Russian society who gained from asset stripping and the absence of the rule of law than there were people in such roles who gained from its creation. Thus, if we start thinking about institutions as being endogenous results of the policies themselves, we recognise that some of the policies put into place as part of the Washington Consensus not only ignored fundamental aspects of political economy but also undermined the creation of institutions that might have facilitated the successful transition of countries like Russia. That differs considerably from the view put forward by Andrei Shleifer (Shleifer, 1994; Shleifer and Boycko, 1994; Shleifer and Vishny, 1994; Shleifer *et al.*, 1995; Barberis *et al.*, 1996; Shleifer and Blasi, 1996; Shleifer, Boycko and Vishny, 1996; Shleifer and Vasiliev, 1996), that privatisation by itself could have created political support for the rule of law.

On the whole we can say that the Washington Consensus has not created the kind of framework that is conducive to investment. Focus on particular elements brings this out clearly. One of the central aspects of the Washington Consensus mantra has been that capital market liberalisation will make a country more attractive for the inflow of capital. It has been argued that if a country does not liberalise its capital markets, it will not be able to attract capital. Both parts of this proposition are false.

Finance for development 17

The country among the emerging markets that has been most successful in attracting capital is China. China has also had the most rapid economic growth within the developing world. The magnitude of its success is reflected in the fact that if one treated the various provinces of China as separate data points, twenty of the fastest growing countries would lie in China.[1]

Another way of putting it is that if one considers the world's low-income countries, a disproportionate fraction of the growth among them occurs in China.[2] So if one wants to study economic growth, one should study China. However, China has succeeded in becoming the largest attractor of FDI both in the developing countries and in the developed world[3] even though it has not liberalised its capital markets. Thus the argument that one has to liberalise capital markets in order to attract investment is simply wrong.

In fact, the argument goes the other way. Capital market liberalisation is associated with higher levels of economic volatility. Higher levels of economic volatility make a country less attractive for investment and have adverse effects on poverty. Thus, capital market liberalisation can create an economic environment that is adverse both to domestic and foreign investment.

What I have been stressing is not only the importance of the political risk associated with the change in policy environment and incentives to corruption. More particularly I have been stressing the risks associated with misguided macro-economic policies and forms of liberalisation that are bad for economic growth. There are a number of other elements of an economic framework that are important but have been under-stressed in the Washington Consensus. One of these is the importance of human capital or a good workforce, which has been one of the crucial ingredients to the success of East Asia. But around the world the advocates of the Washington Consensus have put an emphasis on labour market flexibility – a cold term for falling wages and the elimination of worker protections – rather than on improving the work environment for workers that would be likely to lead to higher productivity.

2 Financial institutions

What is important for investment is not just the issue of interest rate policy that I mentioned earlier. What is also crucial is the ability of a country to channel capital to where it is needed – and this requires appropriately equipped and incentivised financial institutions. These financial institutions must be geared to provide capital for small businesses and micro-credit facilities.

Under the WTO regime there is an increasing emphasis on openness to foreign banks. The concern is that these foreign banks are less interested in lending their money to domestic small businesses, let alone to micro-credit institutions, than to large multinational firms. If that is the case, then small businesses will have to disproportionately bear the risk associated with capital scarcity. In that sense attracting foreign banks may be adverse to long-term economic growth.

This issue is of increasing concern in many developing countries. It was a key issue in the recent sad economic history of Argentina. One of the reasons that Argentina was given an A-Plus rating by the IMF during the period 1996–98, before it fell from grace, was that the country opened up its capital market to foreign banks. Foreign banks took over almost all financial institutions. Unfortunately they were not eager to provide credit to Argentinean firms, particularly to small businesses. The government recognised the problem and tried to set up a special ministry to channel funds to small businesses; however, it did not succeed in doing this effectively. Thus, the opening of the capital market to foreign banks actually contributed to the stifling of economic growth in Argentina and was one of the major factors that pushed the country into economic crisis in late 2001.

Interest rate policy is, of course, still important. High interest rates, as I said before, affect the cost of capital. Firms that cannot access capital cannot grow. Furthermore, high interest rates in a country with open capital markets can lead to higher exchange rates. Many countries have found that these high interest rates combined with high exchange rates have a further adverse effect on economic growth and development.

3 Taxes and tariffs

While appropriately organised and incentivised financial institutions are crucial, concerns about the level and structure of taxes and tariffs play an important role as well. Standard textbooks, like my own textbook in public finance, talk about the virtues of VAT. They praise it as a uniform tax that causes less distortion than others do. They also talk about the disadvantages, such as the fact that VAT is not progressive but proportional and therefore has undesirable distribution consequences. The IMF has been pushing the adoption of VATs in country after country without being too concerned about their negative distribution effects. But it has not understood why VAT is efficient in the developed world. VAT is efficient in developed countries because it taxes all sectors uniformly. However, in developing countries VAT is typically collected on only a fraction of GDP.[4] The reason for that is that much of the GDP in a typical developing country is in the informal sector. This means that VAT is effectively a tax on the formal sector of the economy. But it is precisely the formal sector of the economy that one is trying to encourage in order to promote development.

When VAT is imposed on a global level, one sees some further general equilibrium effects. One of the striking things that has occurred in the past decade is worth mentioning. The prices of the goods exported by developing countries, particularly agricultural goods, have been decreasing relative to the prices of manufactured goods. There have been adverse terms of trade effects to the developing world. As has been noted, these effects began after World War II and the trend, after a short interruption, has continued. This is surprising because the rate of innovation in manufacturing during the post-war period has been very rapid. With that rapid pace of innovation one might have thought that the prices of manufactured goods would come down relative to the prices of agricultural goods. One reason that explains why the reverse has happened is the following: If the people in developing countries are encouraged to go into the informal sector, they are also encouraged to produce those goods that are used as input to the developed countries and discouraged from producing goods that might compete with the output of the developed countries. Under the WTO regime developing countries are, for instance, discouraged from producing textiles but are encouraged to produce raw materials for consumption by the developed countries.

When VAT is applied across all the countries of the world, it has a similar effect. By distorting the structure of the formal sector of the economy it encourages the informal sector – and the informal sector disproportionally produces the kinds of goods that are production inputs for the developed world.

A similar issue arises with respect to the structure of tariffs. Let me give an example that is likely to illustrate a more general principle. When Intel Corporation was considering investing in Costa Rica it strongly emphasised the importance of getting customs clearance within one hour. So if a part in the factory broke on a Tuesday afternoon, they could call up their US supplier, get the part on the plane on Tuesday night, bring it down to Costa Rica Wednesday morning, get it through customs clearance by 6 am and load it immediately into the factory. Thus work could continue before significant delays would occur. Long delays in customs function like tariff-barriers. But they are dissipative tariff-barriers: the country does not get any revenue but the delays interfere with the movement of goods. Costa Rica not only promised to fulfil Intel's demand for a one-hour customs clearance but also met this promise. As a result it got a ship factory worth $500 million which is now the second largest export industry within the country.

4 Trade liberalisation

It used to be a standard part of the economic dogma expressed in the Washington Consensus that trade liberalisation is good for economic growth. People would cite the statistics from the influential paper written by Jeffrey Sachs and Andrew Warner (1995) to illustrate that countries that liberalised more would grow faster than those that did not. More recently, a book published by the World Bank (2002) talks about how the 'globalisers' – the countries that got more integrated into the global economy – have grown faster than other countries. From this it is inferred that if one wants to grow faster, one should obviously liberalise trade.

Looking more carefully at what those statistical studies actually show, however, will lead one to recognise that things are far more complicated. The so-called 'globalisers' were the countries in East Asia, which have had enormous export volumes. But during their periods of rapid growth these countries were not liberalising quickly, but gradually. It is true that China and most of the other East Asian countries have now taken down their tariffs to a very large extent but this happened over a long period of time.

Rodriguez and Rodrik (2001) have looked at the statistical studies that supposedly support the argument that reduced tariff-barriers lead to economic growth. However, there is simply no compelling evidence for that. We can now work with a decade of data concerning alternative strategies for economic growth. The continent where the debate has been most crystallised is Latin America. For three decades – the 1950s, 1960s and 1970s – the Latin American countries pursued import substitution strategies (ISS). In the eighties these strategies collapsed, largely due to the debt crisis. Towards the end of the eighties debt-forgiveness was followed by a reform of economic policy and strong liberalisation, and in the 1990s Latin America experienced renewed growth. The growth that occurred in the early 1990s was partly the kind of growth one always expects to see after a period of stagnation – but it was not sustained. If we compare the decade under reform with the three decades of pre-reform, the numbers we get are quite startling. During the two decades of the 1960s to the 1980s average growth was 5.6 per cent. In the 1990s it dropped to 3.2 per cent! Apparently growth slowed down significantly during the decade of reform compared to the decades of the 'failed' ISS. I do not doubt that there were very good reasons for abandoning import substitution strategies. But we have to learn from both the failures of ISSs and the failures of reform strategies. We have to try to find out why and when each of these strategies work and why and when they fail.

Tariffs do cause distortions, but all forms of taxation are distortionary. The key question is how to use the distortions associated with taxation to promote development rather than to arrest it. As pointed out before, part of the problem is that VAT strategy that has been pushed by the IMF has actually worked to impede development. It has forced more and more firms to go into the informal sector. Firms that have left the formal sector cannot secure credit from formal financial institutions and thus have difficulties in securing finance. This is – again – exactly what happened in Argentina.

5 Foreign investment

The subject of this chapter is 'Finance for development'. As we have seen, the question that many countries have been focusing on is how to attract foreign investment. This focus rests on two assumptions: a) that which separates less developed from more developed countries is their lack of capital and b) that developing countries can solve the problem of development if they overcome this lack of capital. This view is nicely reflected in the designation of the international institutions providing assistance to developing countries. One is called the World Bank – a bank because the key thing that has been taken to be needed is finance. And that is what banks are supposed to provide.

Thinking about development has changed and with it thinking about the role of finance. Finance is an important factor – but absolutely not the only one – and if it is provided in the wrong way it can actually impede other factors.[5]

Keys to long-term economic growth include measures like employment creation. But if it is the case that countries in their attempt to attract foreign investment pursue macro-economic policies that make it impossible to create employment, they will not grow economically. Treating the attraction of (foreign) capital as an end in itself is a fatal confusion. Attracting capital needs to be balanced against other development factors if one wants to promote economic growth.

The obsession with attracting foreign investment has partly originated from the observation of the increased importance of private capital flows relative to development assistance. From 1990 to 1997, before the global financial crisis, private capital flows increased by six to seven times. At the same time public capital flows to developing countries were basically stagnant or slightly decreasing. Thus, by the end of the decade private capital flows were five to six times as great as the public capital flows. That led many to the conclusion that if you want to be successful you have to focus on private capital flows. But these data did not stress the fact that only a small number of countries were receiving most of these capital flows and that the capital only went to specific sectors of their economies. Capital flows did not go into education and they did not go into health.

Countries were told that they had to get the right policy mix in place. The right policy mix should include the opening of capital markets, privatisation and the attraction of FDI. But as I mentioned before, the country that attracted the most foreign investment – China – not only did not liberalise its capital market but also did not privatise. It focused primarily on the creation of new firms rather than on restructuring old ones. In the African context we observe that even countries that have put in place *sound* macro-economic policies, that have reduced inflation rates to zero and that have balanced their budgets and even maintained economic growth of 3 to 6 per cent have failed to attract FDI. That is, of course, one of the challenges the continent is facing.

There are a few countries that have managed to attract FDI. But if one looks more carefully, one recognises that much of it is not the kind of FDI that promotes sustainable growth. A great part of this FDI has gone into natural resources. But one often finds that countries that are rich in natural resources have, in general, not grown very well. Countries like Nigeria have seen their income fall by two-thirds to three-fourths over the last two decades – $250 billion in oil revenues disappearing into nowhere! Yes it is true – you can attract FDI into natural resources if you give them away, in particular if you give them away at a low enough price and especially if some of the money that you have given away comes back to the politicians engaged in rapid privatisation. But this money does not lead to strong economic development.

It is also necessary to differentiate between FDI and portfolio flows. When FDI is not going into natural resources but into manufacturing, it tends to create employment, brings with it technologies, access to markets, and, if well designed, training.[6] Portfolio investment brings none of these advantages. In fact, it often has deleterious effects. The inflow of funds can lead to exchange rate appreciation. This, in turn, can make exports more difficult, inhibit job creation and lead to higher unemployment rates. This is the well-known phenomenon called 'the Dutch disease'.

Recently, the chief advisor of the Russian President has been discouraging portfolio capital flows on the grounds that it has an adverse effect on the exchange rate and therefore on economic growth. It was only after the lowering of the exchange rate following the 1998 crisis that Russia was able to begin growing at all. Moreover, portfolio investment, particularly short-term portfolio investment, is very unstable and that instability leads to increased risk. That, in turn, leads to lower economic growth.

These problems also arise with longer-term portfolio investment, because longer-term loans themselves eventually become short term. Inevitably, countries that have relied heavily on foreign borrowing have found that they have lost a significant part of economic sovereignty. When the foreign banks that are so anxious to get into the country suddenly turn away and the country has to ask the IMF for help, economic policies begin to be dictated by the financial markets and by the IMF.

The bottom line here is that for countries to rely on foreign borrowing is a mistake. If one looks around the world, one sees crisis after crisis. Banks are fair weather friends; they are willing to lend when the economic situation is good. But the moment that times turn bad, banks want their money back and thereby exacerbate the economic downturn. Many countries in the developing world were told that they had to open up their capital markets in order to achieve greater economic stability, but all the evidence points clearly to the contrary.

The point is of particular importance in the context of East Asia. In

East Asia there was no need to open up the capital market for the reason of needing more money. Countries already had savings rates of 30 to 40 per cent. They were having problems investing this money appropriately. One of the miracles of East Asia is that they succeeded in investing their huge savings reasonably well. What advantage could they have gained from opening their capital markets? They certainly did not need increased capital flows. They were told that they should open their financial sectors because doing so would stabilise their economies: if their economies should decline they would be able to get funds from abroad. But even when that story was told, the evidence was all to the contrary: banks simply do not like to lend to people who are in trouble. I have increasingly come to the view that countries should not rely on foreign borrowing.

They should work to attract FDI that promotes economic development. But they should not try to attract portfolio investment, particularly not the kind of short-term portfolio investment that leads to economic instability. The adverse effects of this kind of portfolio investment are even greater than those I have already described. I would like to highlight this by illustrating my point with respect to short-term capital flows.

One cannot build factories on the basis of money that can flow in and out of a country overnight. The instability associated with such short-term flows has currently led to the view that countries have to hold reserves equal to their short-term foreign borrowings in dollars or euros in order to protect themselves. Countries that hold reserves less than their short-term foreign borrowings face a higher probability of having a crisis. Think about what this means for a poor developing country. If a firm within that developing country borrows $100 million from an American bank at 18 or 20 per cent interest, this means that it has to send to the US $20 million every year. For *prudential reasons*, the government of that country has to put $100 million into reserves. Typically, the government holds these reserves in US treasury bills. What does it mean to hold reserves in US treasury bills? It means that the country is lending the United States $100 million. But the interest the country gets for lending the United States $100 million is currently a little less than 2 per cent. This means the country is borrowing $100 million from the United States and is lending $100 million to the United States. But it is paying 18 to 20 per cent on what it borrows and gets back only 2 per cent on what it is lending. Thus, it is sending something like 16–18 million dollars net to the United States. That is clearly good for the United States – and as Americans we appreciate the foreign aid from the poor African countries. It is also quite understandable now why the US Treasury is so enthusiastic about capital market liberalisation. However, it is hard to see how that is going to help the African countries to grow. They could use the money they are putting into reserves in far more productive ways.

Let me reiterate. I think that economic policies that are primarily focused on the objective of trying to attract foreign portfolio flows into a country are likely to stifle economic growth. To encourage economic growth countries should attempt to promote domestic savings.

The success in East Asia was largely based on high savings rates. High savings were secured through a variety of mechanisms such as savings institutions and compulsory savings. The success in East Asia was not based on an attempt to attract portfolio investment but on the promotion of savings within countries and the attraction of job-creating FDI.

6 The outflow of capital and the issue of transparency

Within the context of Africa it is also important to stress the necessity of limiting the outflow of capital. Some of this outflow of capital has to do with corruption. The international community has helped people like Mobutu to move money out of his country by the creation of secret offshore banking centres.

In the aftermath of the East Asian crisis there was a great deal of discussion about the importance of transparency.[7] As the discussion proceeded a consensus was developed in the international community that it had to be comprehensive; it had to apply to hack-funds and offshore banking centres. But amazingly the US Treasury changed its mind. Transparency, according to it, was important in the developing world but not in the developed world. People like Lawrence Summers came forward with arguments saying that if we allow too much openness, then people will not have an incentive to seek information. The OECD fortunately recognised that there was a real problem. They drafted an agreement that would limit secrecy in the offshore banking centres. Until 11 September 2001 the US Treasury vetoed the OECD initiative, claiming that secrecy is obviously good. Only after 11 September did they seem to have made the discovery that secret offshore banking centres have facilitated terrorism, drug trafficking and corruption; now they have changed their tune slightly.

The reason why I am talking so much about this is the following. The secrecy that provides safe haven for terrorists and money laundering is also safe haven for corruption and is to a large part responsible for the capital outflow from the African continent. It is important to do something on the global level to attack the secrecy of these offshore banking centres.

7 Ongoing debates

I am going to talk now about some of the global debates about providing more finance for development. The Monterrey meeting[8] that was recently held focused on finance for development. This meeting was an important initiative for a number of reasons. It brought home the point that finance has implications not just for financial markets. Issues of finance have an effect on everybody in society. Therefore, the people participating in discussions and decisions about finance should not only include finance ministers and central bank governors. The UN meeting managed to bring together a relatively broad spectrum of leaders from the countries of the world. Doing that was of symbolic importance since it made clear that when we are talking about finance we are really talking about development and that discussions about finance have to involve more people.

One of the big issues was the need for more money. To meet the millennium goals such as reducing poverty by half, increasing education, and improving health, there is a substantial need for more money. Within Europe and most of the other developed countries we find a broad consensus to contribute 0.7 per cent of GDP to development assistance. Some countries even contribute 1.0 per cent of their GDP. It is peculiar that the richest country in the world continues to give only a very paltry amount.[9]

One of the issues that is currently under debate in the international community is that of grants vs. loans for development. The issue has certainly attracted more attention than necessary. To my mind it should depend to a large extent on the purposes for which the money is to be given and it has to be looked at from the perspective of the overall aid flows.

8 Innovative proposals

A topic that has not been discussed sufficiently has to do with innovative proposals for finance and development. The trend of globalisation brings with it an increased need for global collective action, which requires more finance. One new proposal has come from Finland, suggesting a global lottery whose proceeds could be used for economic development. Another proposal that has attracted considerable attention in Europe is the Tobin tax, sales taxes on currency trades across borders.[10]

A third proposal is linked to the recognition that there is a large area of global commons, such as the oceans, the sea bed, Antarctica, the atmosphere, etc., that lie outside sovereign boundaries. Managing these global commons is very important and can generate substantial revenues. These revenues could be devoted to the finance of global public goods.

9 SDRs or global greenbacks

There is one more proposal I want to end on. In 1969 the IMF created Special Drawing Rights (SDRs), as a *de facto* international reserve asset to supplement existing official reserves of member countries. The SDR is neither a currency, nor a claim on the IMF. Rather, it is a potential claim on the freely usable currencies of IMF members. It is allocated to member countries in proportion to their IMF quotas. Today the SDR has only limited use as a reserve asset, and its main function is to serve as the unit of account of the IMF and some other international organisations. However, in the current circumstances, SDRs could and should be put to expanded use. Regular emissions of SDRs (or 'global greenbacks' could greatly help to finance economic development.

The current reserve system is both unequitable and unstable. In order to hedge against the volatility of currency and capital flows that come with increased financial integration, developing countries are forced to hold vast amounts of reserves that are estimated at between 1.6 and 2 trillion dollars – and as mentioned before these reserves are extremely costly to them. The additions to these reserves are a subtraction from global aggregate demand. That is to say that every year roughly between 100 and 200 billion dollars is put into these reserves. This means that the money that these countries have is not spent to buy goods – and that creates a downward bias in global aggregate demand. In a way only the US is allowed to continuously spend beyond its income, but even this may not last.

One way of looking at the problem is that there is a basic proposition that the sum of the trade surpluses has to equal the sum of the deficits. Thus, if China and Japan insist on having surpluses, the rest of the world must be in deficit. This means that if one country decides to reduce its deficit, that deficit has to show up somewhere else – deficits are like hot potatoes. That explains in some sense why we have had one crisis after another in recent years. If Thailand and Korea have crises, they want to get rid of their deficits. They get rid of their deficits by turning them into surpluses. But those deficits have to show up somewhere else, because the sum of the surpluses has to equal the sum of the deficits. Thus another country will face a big deficit, tries to turn it into a surplus and passes the deficit on to some other spot in the global system. So what we have is a system with an inbuilt source of instability. That system is characterised by enormous inequity. While there are great costs of the reserves for the developing world, the US reaps the benefit as developing countries provide them with a continuous flow of low-interest loans.

The proposal I would put forward for financing development is a regular issue of SDRs, which could be used to finance global public goods including development. This also would break the instability nexus of the current system and would promote both equity and development. Such a measure would not be inflationary partly because the amounts issued would be relatively small.[11] But it would offset the deflationary bias that the continual push of money into reserves causes. One can think about the proposal as a mutual help arrangement with the reserves representing the amount of goods that a country could acquire from others in times of crisis. If appropriately designed, it could be implemented in a way that would induce all to participate. Not surprisingly, there is one country one could see not liking this idea. How would one get the Americans to go along with it, then? One might, of course, just ignore them. The rest of the world – Europe and Japan – could form a club and let the US go its own way. But that is not the first-best solution. One possibility to induce the United States to join in would be to agree that countries would only hold the currencies of those who are members of the club in their reserves. That would include those who acknowledge that new emissions of SDRs will be used for the purchase of global public goods. Thus, if the US decides that it does not want to co-operate in this global venture, other countries would have to dump their holdings of reserves of US Dollar bonds. That would clearly be adverse to the interests of the USA and would eliminate their incentive for staying out of the club.

10 Conclusion

Part of the responsibility for improving the flow of funds to finance development lies with the developing countries. Developing countries need to adopt better policies. They should only focus on attracting those kinds of funds that will promote economic development. They should not be led by the shibboleth that all funds promote economic growth. But I also believe that part of the responsibility lies with the global community. More ODA (overseas development assistance) is needed and a better reserve system has to be created. The structure of finance to the developing world needs to be re-considered. Although the general theory of risk bearing says that the wealthier countries should bear risk relative to the poor, at present we have the reverse of this. It is the poor that have to bear the risk of fluctuations in real interest rates and exchange rates.[12] That is a major market failure and the international community should do something about it.

I have not talked much about trade. The trade agenda has been very unfair. The Uruguay Round left the poorest region of the world – Sub-Saharan Africa – worse off because of terms of trade effects.[13] However, trade is intimately linked to finance because it is through income generated by trade that countries will be able to create the savings that may enable them to finance development themselves rather than rely on outside funds.

In short: while the provision of finance is certainly an important ingredient of development, we must not focus on it exclusively. If we want to promote economic growth, we also have to keep in mind the broader development objectives. There are economic strategies that can promote finance, particularly domestic finance, and economic development. But these strategies differ widely from many of the strategies that the developing countries have been encouraged to follow in the past.

Notes

1 Most of the provinces in China are larger than most of the countries in Africa.
2 Depending on what period and what numbers are used between 60 and 75 per cent of the total growth of the low-income countries has occurred in China.
3 China's levels of FDI inflow currently compete only with those of the USA.
4 On average, this is one-third to two-thirds of a developing country's GDP.

5 One of the other important factors is the disparity of knowledge. It is not only a disparity of capital but also a disparity of knowledge that separates the developed from the developing countries.
6 A case of well-designed FDI policy can be found in Malaysia.
7 Personally I take the view that a lack of transparency was not the cause of the crisis in East Asia. After all the previous set of crises had occurred in Scandinavia – in the countries that were allegedly the most transparent countries in the world. Thus although I consider transparency to be very important it is not going to inoculate a country against a crisis.
8 'Financing for development', 18–22 March 2002. This UN-hosted conference on key financial and development issues attracted 50 heads of state or government and over 200 ministers, as well as leaders from the private sector, civil society, and all the major intergovernmental financial, trade, economic and monetary organisations.
9 As a result of the Monterrey meeting this amount has increased, but it is still only of the magnitude of 0.5 per cent, as opposed to the 0.7 per cent that the European countries have set for themselves. But the increase is a step in the right direction.
10 It should be noted that James Tobin, the Nobel laureate economist who originally proposed the idea, has himself renounced it.
11 Amounts between 100 and 200 billion dollars are relatively small compared to the global economy amounting to 30 to 40 trillion dollars.
12 That is why they suffered in 1980 when the US raised its interest rates to higher levels.
13 It is a good sign that that the new round of trade talks is going to be called the 'development round'.

References

Barberis, N., M. Boycko, A. Shleifer and N. Tsukanova (1996). How does privatisation work: evidence from the Russian shops, *Journal of Political Economy*, 104(4): 764–790.

Rodriguez, F. and D. Rodrik (2001). Trade policy and economic growth: a skeptics guide to cross-national evidence, in B. Bernanke and K.S. Rogoff (eds), *Macroeconomics Annual 2000*, Cambridge, MA: MIT Press.

Sachs, J. and A. Warner (1995). Economic reform and the process of global integration, *Brookings Papers on Economic Activity*, 1–118.

Shleifer, A. (1994). Establishing property rights, *World Bank: Proceedings of the Annual conference on Development Economics*. April 1994.

Shleifer, A. and J. Blasi (1996). Corporate governance in Russia: an initial look in, in R. Frydam, C.W. Gray and A. Rapaczynski (eds), *Corporate Governance in Central Europe and Russia: Vol. 2 Insiders and the State*, Budapest: Central European University Press.

Shleifer, A. and M. Boycko (1994). Six major challenges, in I.W. Lieberman and J. Nellis (eds), *Efficient Markets*, Washington, DC: The World Bank.

Shleifer, A. and D. Vasiliev (1996). Management ownership and Russian privatisation, in R. Frydram, C.W. Gray and A. Rapaczynski (eds), *Corporate Governance in Central Europe and Russia: Vol. 2 Insiders and the State*, Budapest: Central European University Press.

Shleifer, A. and R. Vishny (1994). Politicians and firms, *Quarterly Journal of Economics*, 109(4): 995–1025.

Shleifer, A., M. Boycko and R. Vishney (1996). A theory of privatisation, *Economic Journal*, 106: 309–319.
Shleifer, A., E. Glaeser and J. Scheinkman (1995). Economic growth in a cross-section of cities, *Journal of Monetary Economics*, 36(1): 117–144.
World Bank Book, The (2002). *Globalization, Growth and Poverty: Building an Inclusive World Economy*, Oxford: World Bank and the Oxford University Press.

2 Globalization
Less than meets the ear?

Robert H. Bates

1 Introduction

It is, of course, natural that economists should stand at the forefront of the debates over globalization. And, as indicated by the contributions of Stiglitz, Laffont, and Nattrass and Seekings to this book, economists have indeed risen to the challenge posed by this topic.[1] There remain aspects of the phenomenon that non-economists can and should address, however, and in this chapter, I tackle three: the impact of globalization on culture, on institutions, and on politics. In addressing the latter two, I should emphasize, I focus on politics at the domestic rather than the global level.

While thus delimiting my discussion, I nonetheless do develop a broader position in the globalization debates. In several key respects, this position dissents from popular orthodoxies. While many see globalization leading to cultural impoverishment and the growing hegemony of the West, I emphasize the ways in which globalization has enriched contemporary culture. Where most see institutional convergence, as competition for investment leads to the choice of 'best practices', I see differentiation and divergence. Where many perceive a race to the bottom, with the destruction of public institutions and the curtailment of public services, I see a race to the top, as governments make costly investments in order to attract foreign investments. Most emphasize the accelerated rate of globalization; I its retardation, as it is slowed by the political conflicts to which it gives rise. And rather than viewing these conflicts as new, as many would do, I instead view them as old: they are the political conflicts that have long characterized the economics of development.

2 The cultural impact

The phrase 'MacDonaldization' highlights the impact of globalization on culture. The phrase refers, of course, to the supposed influence of global communications on the habits of individuals and the values of communities. The ubiquitous presence of MacDonald's franchises, each featuring the same architecture and menus, highlights to many the manner in which cultural variation is being extinguished by the process of globalization. That 'fast food' supplants 'haute cuisine' underscores the magnitude of the loss.

In addressing this loss, some invoke biological analogies: the loss of variety in the cultural 'gene pool', they suggest, reduces the likelihood of species survival. Others see in 'McDonaldization' an echo of imperialism and a re-assertion of Western supremacy through a Gramsci-esque manipulation of the power of culture. Those who seek to serve as the political adjudicators of private taste champion both responses.

There can be no question, of course, that consumer products are now marketed internationally, nor that styles, fashions, and preferences now ramify and re-echo throughout the globe. Nor can there be any doubt but that the majority of fashions – whether for Chicago Bulls' T-shirts or McDonald's hamburgers – originate in the West. To emphasize these truths is to stress but one aspect of a more complex phenomenon, however. It is to stress the gross rather than the net flows of cultural influence. And it is to fail to see that cultural icons are often treated as complements rather than substitutes. These two errors – one of commission and the other of omission – result in a third: an error of measurement. They lead to an over-estimate of the cultural dangers of globalization.[2]

Backed by multi-million dollar advertising budgets, Western products are now sold throughout the globe. Less appreciated is the extent to which products from other cultures flow into the West. I refer not only to goods that are worn on the body and employed to decorate the home, but also – and perhaps more importantly – those that shape the minds and thoughts of people. Young people in the West avidly consume music from other cultures; their cultural heroes include artists and musicians from Africa, the Caribbean, Latin America, and Asia. Western intellectuals seek insights from films, literature, and art that originate from Asia, Africa, and the Middle East. Modern discourse in the advanced industrial nations is pervasively influenced by cultures that they once colonized. Verging on bad taste, some wags speak of the 'Revenge of the Empire', as the Western public tunes into debates sparked and directed by public figures from lands that the West once ruled.

To a marked and important degree, then, the flow of consumption patterns and cultural influences runs, figuratively speaking, from East to West, as well as from West to East. The magnitude and significance of this return flow must be entered into the balance when assessing the overall impact of globalization.

Thus far I have focused on the aggregate level; it is important to focus on the individual level as well. And here we find that in the face of new alternatives, persons do not always replace old practices with new or local practices with those taken from the West. Rather, people often add the new alternative to the old, treating it as a complement to, rather than as a substitute for, traditional practices.

To illustrate, let me refer to some of my acquaintances in West Africa. When donning their finest, they adorn themselves in clothing fashioned by artisans from their hometown. The woven cottons, beautifully dyed, match well the fine watches that encircle their wrists and the briefcases that they bring to their meetings. Among my colleagues number artists who, while taking a break from Beethoven or Bach, work out a new number on drums and stringed instruments, purchased from musicians in their village. Many families span rural homesteads and capital cities in Africa, with sons, daughters, cousins, and uncles dwelling in Paris, Vancouver, and New York. The families of my friends thus draw upon the fabric of their kin to mobilize resources from throughout the globe. Globalization has added to the cultural resources from which they draw, rather than impoverishing them.

In elaborating on this point, it may be useful to let the economists back in. Under the impact of globalization, Western goods may have become more abundant and therefore cheaper in price. Making use of the standard model of consumer behavior, we would predict that utility-maximizing individuals would respond by re-optimizing their consumption bundles. The manner in which they would do so depends upon two factors. One is the shift in relative prices: this shift generates a substitution effect, as people move to consumption of less expensive products. This is the pattern that has attracted the ire and stirred the fears of those who oppose globalization. But with substitution of the lower cost for the higher cost alternative comes another effect. Because they have access to cheaper alternatives, consumers now possess greater real incomes. And if they in fact place a positive value on locally produced objects, they can now increase their consumption of those goods as well. It is this response that leads to behavior largely ignored by the opponents of globalization: the increased expenditure of resources upon the production of local culture.

One implication is that with the spread of markets and the growth of trade, we may expect not only that more people will go to McDonald's but also that more people will wear traditional dress, and spend more on local craftsmen and artists. The spread of Western consumerism should therefore be accompanied by the renaissance, not the extinction, of local cultures. A second implication is that it is precisely those who are most comfortable with the West – i.e., those who consume more of its products – who should also be the champions of local cultures. The result of globalization should thus be one of cultural revival, sponsored by those who in fact participate most actively in global patterns of consumption.

Each reader will have to decide whether these implications of the standard model of consumer choice are consistent with the facts as they know them. As intimated above, I find them consistent with the patterns of the lives of those with whom I have worked and socialized.

3 The variety of institutional forms

Globalization is held to attack not only local cultures, but also local institutions. Implying the opening of economies and the liberalization of markets, globalization, it is argued, implies as well less government, in the sense of less bureaucracy, less regulation, and less interference in markets. In advancing this argument, many allude to the remark attributed to Adam Smith that:

> Little else is required to carry a state to the highest degree of opulence from the lowest barbarianism, but peace, easy taxes, and a tolerable administration of justice; all the rest being brought about by the natural course of things.
>
> (Canon, 1950: xxxv)

and view globalization as leading to this form of government. Others point not to Smith of the eighteenth century but rather to the 'Washington Consensus' of the twentieth (Williamson, 1985) and note its emphasis on the limited role for government in a market economy. Globalization, it is implied, requires a form of political liberalism, in which the government promotes competition, defends property rights, abjures public ownership, and refrains from intervention in markets.

The argument over institutions resembles that advanced over culture, in which globalization is thought to promote uniformity. As in that argument, this one too is subject to rebuttal, both on empirical and on logical grounds.

Empirical evidence shows that governments tend to exhibit major differences in the manner in which they accommodate themselves to the global economy, even though similarly positioned within it. Consider the data regarding the 'Asian Miracle'. The East Asian economies embraced international markets and rode them to near double-digit rates of growth in the 1960s and 1970s. Probing the origins of this 'Miracle', many claimed to have discerned a common set of institutional practices (including the World Bank, 1993). And yet what is striking is not the commonalities among the Asian tigers, but rather the differences.[3] Hong Kong indeed appeared to be governed by an Adam-Smith-like set of political institutions. Singapore, by contrast, was governed by a platonic guardian. In Japan and South Korea, the government promoted the formation of conglomerates; in Taiwan, the government kept firms small. In some countries, the army ruled; in others, civilians, with some being chosen in competitive elections and others anointed in plebiscites.[4] Yet each embraced exports as a way of achieving growth. And within thirty years after the end of World War II, each had departed the ranks of the underdeveloped world.

Clearly, in the case of East Asia, globalization did not take place within a single institutional framework; nor, apparently, has it generated one. The political systems of the Asian Tigers continue to differ.

Of greater relevance to the underdeveloped nations, perhaps, are the experiences of another set of nations: those that have remained agricultural, that lie in the tropical zones bordering the equator, and that depend on coffee exports for the better part of their foreign exchange. The over-twenty major producers face a single market and therefore are subject to the same shocks. These shocks include both precipitate price rises (as when Brazil experiences a frost) as well as price falls (as during the current crisis). And each seeks to use earnings from coffee exports to promote industrial development at home.

During the decades of the mid-1960s to the late 1980s, these countries sought to raise the price of coffee by limiting exports. Most relevant to the arguments of this paper is the extent to which countries so similarly positioned in the global market varied in the way in which they did so. Some limited coffee exports by taxing them; this policy induced a transfer of resources from farmers to the state. Some limited exports by purchasing coffee and stockpiling it at home; such measures resulted in a transfer from taxpayers to export agriculture. Still others over-valued their currency, which resulted in a transfer from exporters to importers, or from agriculture to industry. The different ways in which governments managed the relationship between the domestic and international economy reflected differences in the domestic play of political forces.[5] And the institutional arrangements that they chose resulted in a characteristic distribution of the costs and benefits of trade openness, with the identity of the winners and the losers varying among the different nations.

The empirical record thus reveals institutional variation where the rhetoric would suggest uniformity. The growth of trade can and has led to widely different choices of political arrangements. And, indeed, upon reflection, there is little reason to think that any particular institutional arrangement would prevail. Modern theory views institutions as equilibria: behavior is 'institutionalized' when it becomes self-enforcing.[6] And because the domestic games of politics vary, political practices that might form a self-enforcing equilibrium in one setting fail to do so in another. Given their different patterns of politics, it is therefore natural that even these countries – so similarly situated in the global market – will respond to the challenges produced by that market by devising different institutions.

4 The institutional impact

The argument for institutional uniformity often takes another form. Globalization is held to impose a reduction in the size of government; competition in the global market place spurs a 'race to the bottom'. Capital is mobile, and the owners of capital search for favorable locations in which to invest. Among the advantages they seek are low costs of production, including – or perhaps especially – costs arising from the payment of taxes.

As jurisdictions compete for geographic advantages in the global market, the result, it is argued, is an erosion of public services, as jurisdictions reduce the costs of doing business by curtailing the expenses of government.

This argument too is contradicted by the evidence. Some of these facts have long been known; others result from new research. The common finding is that liberal markets imply not less but more government.

The early evidence came from a small but elegant research program launched within political science in the late 1970s. The researchers focused on the small, open economies of Western Europe: Holland, Switzerland, Austria, and the Scandinavian economies (Cameron, 1978; Katzenstein, 1985). Each of these nations, the researchers found, had created a series of distinctive political institutions. One was a relationship between capital and labor that yielded the flexibility necessary to adapt to the vicissitudes of international markets. Another was a high level of social insurance. In reflecting upon the second finding, the researchers recognized its paradoxical nature: *liberal* trade regimes cohabit with *big* governments. The size of the public sector, they found, rose with the degree of openness to international markets.

Subsequent research has confirmed this finding and deepened our understanding of it. Drawing on the work of Stiglitz and Grossman, Bates, Brock and Tiefenthaler (1991) noted that utility-maximizing agents, when faced with high levels of risk, might well prefer autarchy to trade, regarding the losses incurred from the limitation of trade as a premium paid for insurance. The corollary, they argued, is that in order to achieve higher levels of trade openness, governments might assume the costs of providing insurance.

A return to the original cases confirmed that the differences in the degree of autarchy and trade protection correlated with the degree of price risk in international markets. It also confirmed that, holding the level of price risk constant, as the degree of social insurance increased, the degree of trade protection declined. The greater the degree of openness, the higher the level of internal transfers and insurance premiums borne by the government. These findings have since been extended to a larger sample of countries by Rodrik (1998). By relating the level of autarchy and social insurance to income rather than price risk, Rodrik has also strengthened the arguments.

The critics of globalization often number among its costs a reduction in the role of governments. As argued in this section, however, the evidence strongly suggests liberal trade regimes imply larger, not smaller, governments. To secure openness to international trade, governments appear to mount large and costly programs of transfer payments and social insurance. Only when so sheltered from risk may private agents be willing to specialize in production for markets whose conditions they cannot control.

5 Political resistance

We have already seen evidence that calls into question the thesis that globalization produces 'liberal' – or downsized – governments: private agents that specialize in international trade, it appears, find it attractive to operate in nations with large governments. Not only do businesses seek to socialize the risks arising from international markets. They also seek labor that is educated and trained; security for person and property; public utilities that work; and transport facilities that function. Low costs and high profits are not the same. And businesses appear to prefer locations in which they share the costs of efficient services in preference to ones in which such services are absent.

The standard critique of globalization highlights ideological forms of conflict in which the market is poised against the state. Empirically, however, the two stand as complements rather than substitutes. We must search out alternative sources for the controversies that surround globalization. Given that domestic conflicts from globalization do not derive from the declining quality of public services, as a 'race to the bottom' would imply, we might better locate the sources of such conflict in the rising costs of providing them, as local communities seek to upgrade their facilities in order to attract investment.

One line of conflict runs between political jurisdiction and private investors and focuses on the terms and conditions that govern the public obligations of private capital, and especially the taxation of profits. A second runs within any jurisdiction that competes for foreign investment: it focuses on the allocation of the costs and benefits of the public services necessary for the attraction of capital. Problems of credibility play a major role in both conflicts, virtually giving rise to the one, while intensifying the other.

6 Commitment and bargaining

In the course of negotiations over entry into a foreign market, investors and governments face a common enemy: distrust. For their part, the investors distrust the government's pledges: they naturally fear that once having attracted their capital, the government will then renege on its promises. For their part, governments fear that should they make costly concessions, investors may later defect, moving their plant to a jurisdiction recently rendered more favorable. Lacking a means for binding themselves in negotiating agreements, the two must expend resources on costly acts of signaling. That the costs are high and often borne by persons other than the beneficiaries spawns political conflict.

The contribution by Nattrass and Seekings (Chapter 9) underscores the costs engendered by the inability of governments to commit to promises. At the time of independence, the government of South Africa sought to reverse the policies of protection bequeathed to it by its predecessors and to make South Africa, formerly a pariah state, an attractive venue for foreign investment. The government adopted policies of budgetary restraint, one purpose of which was to provide assurances to foreign capital. As critics of GEAR, the government's program, have stressed, the policies have inflicted high costs on the South African economy, slowing growth and necessitating the postponement of public programs deeply desired and needed by the citizenry. Lacking means for binding itself, the government had instead to signal its commitment, and to do so by adopting measures so severe that only a government sincerely committed to liberal economic policies would choose them.

Given the lack of 'commitment technologies', the dance between governments and foreign capital is slowed by distrust. Agreements become difficult to reach and, if consummated, they are reached at high cost. Adding to the costs of bargaining between governments and investors are conflicts that arise within the polities engaged in a race to the top.

7 Initial challenges

Governments tend to place a greater portion of the costs of the public investments on those who cannot escape them. Those who control factors of production that are of necessity local and immobile – unskilled labor, land, and natural resources – face far greater difficulties in eluding the costs of public improvements than do resources that are mobile, such as capital, and that can therefore escape offshore.

In an effort to develop the local economy and to render it an attractive location for investors, those whose assets are immobile bear a large portion of the costs of upgrading public services – the police, courts, highways, school systems, and utilities – to a global standard and so compete for investments by firms. Being mobile, capital can bargain down its share of the costs. The conflict over cost sharing, and the inequities which it spawns, inevitably become a major source of conflict in countries that are trying to rise in the international economic order. The pattern of conflict is illustrated in the analysis of the South African economy provided by Nattrass and Seekings; it finds its parallel in the economies of Brazil, Colombia, China, and other nations that have sought to develop by opening up their economies.[7]

The conflicts that arise over globalization in the developing world thus tend to revolve around the apportionment of the costs and benefits of attempts to race to the top. These conflicts are important in their own right. They are also important because of their impact on the pace of globalization. Insofar as political tensions are high, they tend to cloud the reputation of political leaders, or at least to call into question their ability to deliver on their promises. The result is that efforts to attract foreign investment may give rise to another stalled-out development program.

Despite the popular rhetoric, the forces of globalization may founder, or at least be significantly slowed, by the politics to which it gives rise.

In a world where credible pledges are needed, it is difficult to signal good intent. The greater the resources expended to entice foreign capital, the greater reason international investors may have to fear subsequent political reversals. The result may be less globalization than its critics may fear and its boosters desire.

8 Conclusion

The topic of globalization has been 'hot' in recent years. Whether on the streets of Seattle or in the boardrooms of Johannesburg, the origins, magnitude, and impact of the phenomenon have dominated political discourse.

In this essay, I have sought to temper the controversy that surrounds this topic by grounding my analysis in realities too often obscured by the surrounding rhetoric. Rather than seeing a race to the bottom, I see a race to the top, as poor countries seek to improve, rather than hollow out, their public services. As with the culture, so too with politics: there are persuasive reasons to expect diversity, rather than uniformity, to emerge. Rather than appearing as a new species, the domestic politics of globalization closely resembles a sub-branch of the normal politics of economic development. Resentment over the magnitude and the distribution of the costs incurred to attract investment render 'development-minded' governments unable or unwilling to adhere to their development programs. The result is less globalization than one might expect, given the magnitude of the controversies that surround it.

Notes

1 For recent notable contributions, see Rodrik (1999); Stiglitz (2003).
2 For a related critique, see Watson (1997).
3 See the research of Amsden (1989); Wade (1990); Kang (2002). See also Fishlow et al. (1994).
4 See the research of Amsden (1989); Wade (1990); Kang (2002). See also Fishlow et al. (1994).
5 See the description and analysis in Bates (1997).
6 See the discussion in Bates et al. (1998).
7 See the contributions in such compendia as Stokes (2001) and Bates and Krueger (1991).

References

Amsden, A.H. (1989). *Asia's Next Giant: South Korea and Late Industrialization*, New York: Oxford University Press.

Bates, R.H. (1997). *Open Economy Politics*, Princeton: Princeton University Press.

Bates, R.H., A. Greif and M. Levi (1998). *Analytic Narratives*, Princeton: Princeton University Press.

Bates, R.H. and A.O. Krueger (1991). *Political and Economic Interactions in Economic Policy Reform*, Oxford: Blackwell.
Bates, R.H., P. Brock and J. Tiefenthaler (1991). Risk and trade regimes, *International Organization*, 45(1): 1–18.
Cameron, D.R. (1978). The expansion of the public economy: a comparative analysis, *American Political Science Review*, 72(December): 1243–1261.
Canon, E. (1950). Editor's Introduction, in A. Smith (ed.), *An Inquiry into the Nature and Causes of the Wealth of Nations*, London: Methuen.
Fishlow, A., C. Gwin, S. Haggard, D. Rodrik and R. Wade (1994). *Miracle or Design? Lessons from the East Asian Experience*, Washington, DC: Overseas Development Council.
Kang, D. (2002). *Crony Capitalism*, New York: Cambridge University Press.
Katzenstein, P. (1985). *Small States in World Markets*, Ithaca: Cornell University Press.
Rodrik, D. (1998). Why do more open economies have bigger governments?, *The Journal of Political Economy*, 106(5): 997–1032.
Rodrik, D. (1999). *The New Global Economy and Developing Nations*. Washington, DC: Overseas Development Council.
Stiglitz, J. (2003). *Globalization and its Discontents*, New York: W.W. Norton.
Stokes, S. (ed.) (2001). *Public Support for Market Reforms in New Democracies*, New York: Cambridge University Press.
Wade, R. (1990). *Governing the Market*, Princeton: Princeton University Press.
Watson, J.L. (ed.) (1997). *Golden Arches East: McDonald's In East Asia*, Stanford: Stanford University Press.
Williamson, O.E. (1985). *The Economic Institutions of Capitalism*, New York: The Free Press.
World Bank (1993). *The East Asian Miracle*, Washington, DC: The World Bank.

3 Philosophical foundations of normative economics

Daniel M. Hausman

Let me begin with an old joke. Brezhnev and other members of the Soviet Central Committee are reviewing a May Day parade in Moscow. Thousands of infantry march by, followed by armored cars, the latest tanks, long range artillery, and progressively larger, sleeker and more impressive missiles. At the end, a battered flatbed truck rumbles by carrying a half-dozen unathletic and bespectacled middle-aged men and women in dirty raincoats sitting around a card table. The crowd is restless and members of the Central Committee are scandalized. One is bold enough to ask Brezhnev what these non-descript civilians are doing in the midst of such a magnificent military parade. Brezhnev replies, 'Ah, those are our economists. You'd be amazed at the damage they can do.'

Like most economist jokes, this one is unkind, but its unkindness should not be exaggerated. It refers to the damage economists *can* do, not to any inevitable harm that they cause. And there is no suggestion that their intentions are evil. Economics can unfortunately do great harm, but I think that it can do good, too. It is a sharp two-edged sword that needs to be mastered and handled with care. Economics has done harm mainly because it has been misunderstood or misused by political and economic interests. There is little that I can do as a philosopher to combat powerful interests who are ready to seize upon any theory – economic, political, even philosophical – to rationalize their ambition and greed. But I can perhaps do something to clarify the interpretation of economic theory and thereby remove confusions and make its ideological misapplication at least a little bit more difficult. Perhaps this chapter can help non-economists to resist purportedly expert policy advice, when it is grounded in misapplication of normative economics. Ultimately one must study the detailed grounds for accepting or rejecting policies, but perhaps an understanding of the contestable assumptions upon which normative economists rely can help prevent people from being buffaloed by confident proclamations of economic 'wisdom'.

In this essay I shall be concerned exclusively with mainstream economics. I focus entirely on mainstream economics, because of its dominance. Mainstream economics is highly individualistic, and in principle it traces economic phenomena – prices, output, incomes, distribution, and so forth – to the rational choices of individuals. Accordingly it includes a 'positive' explanatory and predictive theory of economic phenomena, a theory of rationality, a particular vision of economic methodology, and a normative view concerning the appraisal or the evaluation of economic policies, institutions, and outcomes. My concern in this essay is, more specifically, with theories of economic evaluation or appraisal – that is, with *normative* economics, or, in other words, with the theory of economic welfare. I shall not be concerned with positive theories that aim to show the economic consequences of alternative policies, although, as we shall see, it is not easy to keep positive and normative separate. Theories that purport to predict the consequences of policies are, of course, at least as important to contemporary economic policies as are normative economic theories, but my focus will be on normative economics.

1 A notorious example[1]

Let me begin with a notorious example to illustrate the central features of normative economics and to show why an inquiry into its philosophical foundations is needed. In December 1991, Lawrence Summers, now President of Harvard, then the chief economist at the World Bank, sent a memorandum to colleagues containing the following remarks:

> Just between you and me, shouldn't the World Bank be encouraging more migration of the dirty industries to the LDCs [less developed countries]? I can think of three reasons:
>
> 1 The measurement of the costs of health-impairing pollution depends on the foregone earnings from increased morbidity and mortality. From this point of view a given amount of health-impairing pollution should be done in the country with the lowest cost, which will be the country with the lowest wages.
> 2 I've always thought that under-populated countries in Africa are vastly *under* polluted; their air quality is probably vastly inefficiently [high] compared to Los Angeles or Mexico City. Only the lamentable facts that so much pollution is generated by non-tradable industries (transport, electrical generation) and that the unit transport costs of solid waste are so high prevent world-welfare-enhancing trade in air pollution and waste.
> 3 The demand for a clean environment for aesthetic and health reasons is likely to have very high income-elasticity. The concern over an agent that causes a one-in-a-million change in the odds of prostate cancer is obviously going to be much higher in a country where people survive to get prostate cancer than in a country where under-five mortality is 200 per thousand.

> The problem with the arguments against all of these proposals for more pollution in LDCs (intrinsic rights to certain goods, moral reasons, social concerns, lack of adequate markets, etc.) could be turned around and used more or less effectively against every Bank proposal for liberalisation.
>
> (quoted in *The Economist*, February 8, 1992, 66)

Summers was not seriously proposing a World Bank program to export pollution to the LDCs. Instead, this memorandum is of interest because Summers baldly put into words uncomfortable implications that most economists would prefer not to draw. Their relevance to Africa is obvious.

Air pollution and water pollution lessen health and the quality of life in many ways, yet most kinds of pollution have no market prices. Economists hope to guide choices in such cases by imputing costs, by figuring out what costs *would be, if there were markets* where pollution could be bought and sold. For example, economists may attempt to impute pollution costs by examining housing prices in communities that are much the same, apart from their air quality. Economists have a number of ingenious techniques by which they can estimate how much people in developed countries would be willing to pay to lessen pollution in their environment and how much people in LDCs would have to be compensated in order to be willing to accept more pollution.

Summers argues in addition that these measurements do not derive from ignorance. In his view, the economic costs of the consequences of increased pollution are in fact much lower in LDCs than they are in developed countries. Rational and well-informed people in LDCs *should be* happy to sell pollution rights to people in developed countries for a price that the latter *should be* happy to pay. The willingness to accept more pollution in LDCs does not rest on mistakes about the consequences of doing so.

Suppose that environmental quality could be bought and sold in individual privately consumable units and consider whether rational and well-informed individuals, who live in a particular LDC, L, could strike deals to sell units of 'environmental quality' to rational and well-informed individuals, who live in a developed country, D. If L is one of those 'underpolluted' LDCs Summers refers to, it has a great deal of inexpensive environmental quality, while in D, on the other hand, environmental quality is costly and scarce. So unless the price of a unit of environmental quality is extremely high or extremely low, individuals in both L and D will want to trade.

So if individuals were all rational and well informed, and it were possible for individuals easily to buy, sell, and transport pollution or 'environmental quality', there would be active trading between the developed and less developed nations of the world, and pollution would be pouring out of the developed nations and into the less developed nations. This happy outcome is not feasible, because units of environmental quality cannot be individually appropriated, bought, and sold, and it is hard to transport pollution. Summers laments these barriers to trade, and he thinks the World Bank can enhance world welfare by helping to move pollution to LDCs in return for some measure of compensation.

Merely shifting pollution to LDCs, without paying any compensation could not, of course, be *mutually* beneficial, since the LDCs would be harmed. But it would still result in what economists call a 'net benefit', because the developed countries could compensate the LDCs and still allegedly be better off. I shall discuss the notion of a net benefit and the justification for favoring policies that provide net benefits later.

Why should Summers conclude that it is 'lamentable' that 'pollution is generated by non-tradable industries'? How does Summers reach the conclusion that 'the World Bank [should] be encouraging *more* migration of the dirty industries to the LDCs'? How do normative economists get from claims about how rational and well-informed individuals would choose to claims about *welfare* and from claims about welfare to claims about what the World Bank ought to do? What is the logic of Summers' argument?

Here is one way to spell it out:

1 For some compensation, all rational and well-informed individuals, whether in developed countries or in LDCs, would prefer to transfer pollution from a developed country to an LDC (premise).
2 Whatever well-informed and rational individuals prefer makes them better off (premise).
3 So exporting pollution to LDCs from developed countries and paying compensation makes everyone better off (from 1 and 2).
4 One should do what makes people better off (premise).
5 One should shift pollution to LDCs and pay compensation (from 3 and 4).

If one assumes that the jobs and revenues provided by dirty industries are adequate compensation, then this reconstruction may capture Summers' intentions.

The uproar caused by this memo suggests that most people are not willing to accept its conclusion. Why not? Why shouldn't the World Bank encourage migration of dirty industries? One reason is that encouraging dirty industries to migrate to LDCs might lead to more total pollution. Developed countries have stronger incentives, greater administrative capacity, and more resources to enforce pollution controls than do LDCs. This is an important objection, but it does not challenge Summers' framework, and I shall say nothing more about it.

Second, even if people in both developed economies and LDCs would prefer to shift pollution to LDCs in exchange for appropriate compensation, the exchange may be *unfair*. Developed countries are exploiting the poverty of LDCs – which, in addition, they are often responsible for. Summers alludes to such objections in his last paragraph, and he offers no response. The injustice objection shows that premise four – that one ought to do what makes people better off – needs qualification. It may not be right to make people better off if doing so involves injustice. Justice matters too.

Is there no more fundamental objection? Since there is no problem with the logic of the argument, if the conclusion is mistaken there must be some mistake in its premises. We have already seen that premise four needs to be modified. What about premise two, that satisfying preferences automatically increases welfare? It is easy to question the link between preference satisfaction and welfare when the parties are ignorant or irrational, but premise two ties welfare to the preferences of rational and well-informed individuals. When mutual willingness to exchange is not based on any mistake, does it not then follow that exchanging would be mutually beneficial? What is the connection between welfare and preference? We shall turn to these questions in section three.

What about premise one, that all rational and well-informed agents would prefer to make the exchange? This premise is itself the conclusion of an argument from the fact that the (economic) costs of pollution are lower in LDCs than in developed countries. But rational and well-informed individuals do not have to accept the market's evaluation of the consequences of the pollution. Premise one turns out to be a moral premise, too. The economic costs of the harms pollution causes are lower in an LDC, because wages and productivity are lower, because people are more likely to die of other things before they can be harmed by some kinds of pollution, and because there are other pressing needs upon which individuals will spend their money first. But are economic costs and benefits – whatever they are – a reliable guide to what is truly harmful and beneficial? Given the current unequal distribution of wealth, preventing or curing a crippling injury or a case of AIDS confers much greater economic benefits in rich countries than in poor ones. But the moral significance of crippling injuries or of AIDS should not depend on whether the victim lives in a wealthy country or on the victim's own current or prospective income or wealth. One can thus reasonably raise moral objections to regarding economic costs and benefits as a guide to what *ought* to be done. Costs and prices have a contestable moral significance built into them. Summers reduces the question of whether LDCs are 'underpolluted' to the question of whether the welfare consequences of shifting more pollution to the LDCs would be favorable. 'Welfare' for Summers, as for most economists, is preference satisfaction. The 'cost' of the consequences of pollution is thus the amount by which people's preferences are less well satisfied. And Summers' measure of preference satisfaction is willingness-to-pay.[2]

Although more provocative and transparent than most normative economics, Summers' memorandum exemplifies common features of mainstream economic evaluation. Normative economists typically attempt to offer policy advice while setting aside considerations such as 'intrinsic rights to certain goods, moral reasons, social concerns'. They focus exclusively on welfare, which they associate with preference and willingness to pay. So normative economics is welfare economics. Normative economists also typically make inferences concerning welfare on the basis of data concerning willingness to pay, and these inferences are inevitably biased toward the preferences of those who are rich.

An extreme example of this is the drug eflornithine, which is a highly effective 'miracle' cure for sleeping sickness. Until 1999 the drug was produced by a US subsidiary of the Aventis Company, but when eflornithine proved ineffective against cancer (its intended target), Aventis stopped making the drug and gave the production license to the World Health Organization. Only in early 2001, when stocks of the drug were almost exhausted, was the WHO able to find drug companies to manufacture it – and then only because the companies hoped to make profits from marketing eflornithine in developed countries as a cream that removes facial hair. Because the victims of sleeping sickness are so poor, the small amount they are able to pay for eflornithine grossly understates its social value as a cure for sleeping sickness.

Let us then back up and spend some time with the philosophical foundations. Why is it that normative economics focuses exclusively on welfare and why it is committed to this particular theory of welfare?

2 Individualism, rationality, and self-interest

At the core of both positive economics and welfare economics, lie controversial commitments to individualism and to a particular view of *human nature*. Some of these commitments seem to me noble, progressive, and correct. Others are dubious and even pernicious. In particular, I would like to distinguish three varieties of individualism: ontological, explanatory, and ethical, and to distinguish between two views of human nature: human nature as rational and human nature as self-interested.

In its simplest formulation, ontological individualism maintains that only mental states and physical objects, including human beings, are real. Cultures, social institutions, and so forth are not real. They must be understood instead as reifications of features of the physical environment or of the physical and mental states of people. I believe that ontological individualism is untenable and difficult to formulate sensibly. I mention it only to distinguish it sharply from explanatory and ethical individualism.

Explanatory individualism (or what is often called 'methodological individualism') can be interpreted in many ways. Sometimes, it is interpreted as the view that explanations of social phenomena that refer to social entities are at best provisional, if not downright objectionable. But the form of commodities to fewer, more wealth to less wealth. This generalization is so important that I prefer to think of it as a second general principle of human nature to which most mainstream economists are committed.

In speaking of rationality and self-interest as general principles of human nature to which economists subscribe, I do not mean to suggest that economists regard these principles as exceptionless general laws. Just as one can in various ways qualify the claim that individuals are rational, so one can hedge the claim that they are self-interested. Economists may, for example, take self-interest to be a reasonable approximation rather than the literal truth. Economists can avoid dealing with the conflicts between self-interest and concern for one's family by 'cheating' on explanatory individualism and treating agents as households rather than as individuals. And so forth.

With the addition of self-interest, the fundamental theory now has real substance. Add diminishing marginal utility (or diminishing marginal rates of substitution), the assumption that people are well informed, and subsidiary assumptions concerning, for example, the divisibility of commodities, and economists can, for example, use their fundamental theory to explain market phenomena such as the law of demand.

3 Moral foundations: ethical individualism and welfare

To put forward a theory of normative economics requires in addition that economists say something about ethics. Here again economists are committed to a form of individualism. *Ethical individualism* is the view that social entities are of no intrinsic moral importance. There is moral reason to protect a culture, a religion, a state, a tribe, or a corporation if and only if doing so is required by moral concern for individual human beings. As I understand ethical individualism, it can accord intrinsic moral value to non-human animals, or perhaps even plants. But it denies that there is anything morally significant about the interests of social entities, unless their protection can be linked to concerns about individuals.

These days, ethical individualism is increasingly controversial, as many of those who defend multiculturalism in the United States and who oppose globalization across the world argue for the importance of protecting distinctive local cultures. But recognition of the enormous value of local cultures and of the enormous harm that results from their disruption is not inconsistent with ethical individualism. For example, Professor Bates' optimistic view (2004 and Chapter 2 of this book) that the income effect of cheap imports from developed economies will lead to increased expenditure on local culture takes no stand on whether cultures are of intrinsic value. Instead it denies that globalization threatens them.[3] Ethical individualists should value local cultures very highly, because local cultures serve individuals, and the loss of cultural *variation* in the long run may be as harmful to those who belong to hegemonic cultures as to those who belong to endangered cultures. Treating the moral value of cultures, languages, or other social practices as instrumental rather than intrinsic is fully consistent with valuing them extremely highly, but it does mean that the ethical individualist has no specifically moral regrets about the death of social practices that do not promote the rights, freedoms, and interests of individuals.

Most Western ethical theories endorse some version of ethical individualism. Utilitarianism adopts a particularly simple variant. According to the utilitarian, only the welfare of sentient beings matters morally. So social policies, processes, practices, and institutions should be appraised by their consequences for individual well-being. Utilitarians can nevertheless find room to value justice, equality and individual rights and liberties, since all these things contribute to individual well-being. Mainstream welfare economics, which was in fact influenced by utilitarianism, at first glance appears to follow utilitarianism in reducing ethical individualism – which is a plausible and humane doctrine – to the more dubious view that only individual *welfare* is of intrinsic moral importance.

It is not very informative to say that individual *welfare* is the sole thing of intrinsic moral importance until one has spelled out what welfare is, and without some means of tracing the welfare consequences of policies and of measuring welfare, this view does not help to evaluate policies. Bentham took utility to be that property of objects that causes sensations of pleasure in us (Broome, 1991a). Mill took well-being to be 'happiness', but it is far from clear what he took happiness to be (1863). Economists have not been eager to wade into these murky philosophical waters, yet without some notion of what welfare might be and some way of measuring welfare, they would have no way to evaluate policies or to offer guidance to policy-makers. In principle economists might still contribute to policy-making by pointing out consequences of alternative proposals and leaving the moral appraisal of those consequences to others. But which consequences should they examine? To inquire about the consequences of policies for welfare requires some specification of what welfare is.

Economists have opted for the view that welfare consists in the satisfaction of preferences. A is better off with X than with Y if and only if A prefers X to Y. Though there is surely some connection between welfare and preference satisfaction, it is unjustifiable to identify them. If welfare were the satisfaction of preference, then it would be not only unusual to prefer to sacrifice one's own welfare to some other end; it would be logically impossible! If welfare were the satisfaction of preference, then smoking would benefit those who prefer to smoke even if their preferences depended on their ignorance of the consequences of smoking. If welfare were the satisfaction of preference, then I would be better off if, as I prefer, there are no nuclear wars in the twenty-sixth century, even though I will by then – alas – have been dead for centuries.

Why then do mainstream economists nevertheless identify welfare and preference satisfaction? There are many explanations. One mistaken way to link welfare and preference is to equivocate on the word 'utility', which is both the name that positive economists give to an index of the extent to which preferences are satisfied and the name that the utilitarians gave to that which morality aims to maximize. If one erroneously takes the word to refer to the same thing in both contexts, then one will conclude that welfare is the satisfaction of preferences. It is also easy to equivocate on the word 'satisfaction'. A person's preference is satisfied if things are as the person prefers them to be, regardless of how well satisfied the person feels. Indeed many preferences may be satisfied without the person even knowing. Yet it is easy to slide from the view that welfare is a mental state such as a feeling of satisfaction to the view that welfare is the satisfaction of preference. A third mistaken route to the position that welfare is the satisfaction of preferences rests on the confusion of this view of welfare with the condemnation of paternalism. If whatever people prefer is automatically better for them, then the question of whether it is justifiable to coerce people for their own good can never even arise. But there are better ways to object to paternalism than to maintain falsely that people never prefer harmful alternatives. In his famous critique of paternalism in *On Liberty* (1859), John Stuart Mill criticizes the view that people should be coerced when they make choices that frustrate their own ends. He does not argue that whatever people choose is automatically what is good for them.

There are also more respectable routes to the identification of welfare and the satisfaction of preference. Given the two basic theses concerning human nature that mainstream economists accept – that individuals are rational and that they are self-interested – people will prefer X to Y if and only if they believe that they will be better off with X than with Y. If one supposes in addition – as positive economists typically do – that people's beliefs are generally correct, then people will prefer X to Y if and only if they are in fact better off with X than with Y. So welfare is the satisfaction of preferences. A 'formal' theory of the good, such as the preference-satisfaction theory also seems more modest philosophically, since it avoids any substantive claims about what things are good or bad. Finally, economists might deny that they hold a preference-satisfaction theory of welfare or indeed any other theory of welfare. Instead they assume only that preference satisfaction is a reasonable way of measuring welfare, whatever welfare might truly be. (But how could economists know whether preference satisfaction is a good measure of welfare without some view of what welfare is?)

4 Repudiating interpersonal comparisons

Mainstream normative economics is distinctive not only for its theory of welfare but also because it focuses almost exclusively on welfare. One might interpret this as a legacy of utilitarianism. But there is a crucial difference. Although well-being is the central value for utilitarians as well as welfare economics, utilitarians were very concerned with other ethical notions such as freedom, rights, and justice. They denied that these other notions provided *independent* grounds for moral judgment, but they did not deny their importance. For example, in *On Liberty* Mill formulated a utilitarian case for a general moral principle concerning individual liberty, while in Chapter 5 of *Utilitarianism*, Mill made a utilitarian case for principles of justice.

Economists have not followed suit, and the reason is, I think, that their view of welfare as the satisfaction of preferences makes it absurd to suppose that welfare economics could encompass other dimensions of moral appraisal such as freedom, rights, or justice. Given the merely ordinal representation of preferences typically adopted by economists, utilities represent only preference rankings. If one individual prefers x to y and another has the opposite preferences, then the first individual's preferences can be represented by a utility function that assigns a higher number to x than to y, and the second's preferences can be represented by a utility function that assigns a smaller number to x than to y. Since the magnitudes of the numbers are otherwise completely arbitrary, any attempt to add up the utility indices to determine whether preferences are better satisfied with x or with y shows a misunderstanding of what the indices mean. The comparison of the utility sums depends on an arbitrary assignment of utility indices and says nothing at all about which alternative satisfies preferences better. If there is nothing more to say about preferences than an ordinal utility function says, then utility differences could not be compared even for a single individual, and utilities could never be added or subtracted or compared across individuals.

If the preferences of individuals satisfy the stronger axioms of expected utility theory, then it is possible to represent them with utility functions in which utility sums and differences are not arbitrary.[4] *If* one had, in addition, some way to compare the utilities of different individuals, then the way would be cleared to formulate a utilitarian welfare economics. But what sense can one make of comparisons of the extent to which the preferences of different individuals are satisfied? Economists have stressed the problems of getting evidence concerning interpersonal comparisons of preference satisfaction, while I would stress the problems of even making *sense* of such comparisons (see Hausman, 1995). In any case, such comparisons are highly problematic, and positive economics makes no use of them. So it is easy to see why normative economists have been *extremely* hesitant to make interpersonal utility comparisons.

Denying the possibility of making interpersonal welfare comparisons – which is virtually inevitable once one identifies welfare with the satisfaction of preferences and adopts the framework for representing preferences accepted in positive economics – largely determines the character of mainstream (normative) economics. It undercuts any hope of developing a general ethical theory, like utilitarianism, that can encompass other dimensions of moral appraisal, such as freedom, rights, equality, and justice, because all of these are concerned with the differing weights of claims of different persons, which cannot be addressed within a welfarist framework unless one can make interpersonal comparisons. Few economists have the temerity to follow Bentham and to condemn all other moral considerations as 'rhetorical nonsense – nonsense upon stilts'. So some strategy is inevitable whereby economists appraise policies, outcomes, and institutions 'other things being equal' or 'along just one among several moral dimensions'.

The idea that there is thus a specifically economic dimension of evaluation determines the character of mainstream normative economics. It is this idea that makes it possible to envision a normative economic theory, as opposed to a set of normatively motivated inquiries into consequences and properties of economic policies and institutions. Welfare economics depends not only on a specific view of welfare but also on the view that inquiries into welfare can be separated from inquiries into freedom, rights, equality, and justice. In one way, this separation limits economists. They can only appraise policies along one dimension or in one regard. But it also frees them from having to be concerned with anything but welfare. Having passed the buck with respect to everything except preference satisfaction, economists have only too often felt themselves free to ignore all other moral questions and to exaggerate the significance of their own partial mode of evaluation. But even without this exaggeration, the notion that there is a separate dimension of economic evaluation is, as we shall see, questionable and misleading.

5 Pareto improvements, Pareto efficiency, and welfare theorems

Appraising policies, outcomes, and institutions in terms of welfare without the possibility of making interpersonal comparisons is like running a race with your feet tied together. Just as it is possible awkwardly to hop 100 or 200 meters, so one can judge that X is better than Y if somebody prefers X to Y and nobody prefers Y to X. In this case economists say that X is Pareto superior to Y or that X is a Pareto improvement over Y. The judgment that Pareto improvements are, other things being equal, moral improvements requires an additional weak moral judgment (which is arguably implicit in ethical individualism) that it is a good thing to make people better off. But such unanimity in preference is seldom available. In serious policy debates none of the alternatives are Pareto superior to any of the others.

In addition to the notion of Pareto superiority, economists also define the notion of a Pareto optimum or of a Pareto efficient state of affairs. X is

Pareto optimal or Pareto efficient if and only if there is no alternative that is Pareto superior to X. Notice X's being Pareto optimal does *not* mean that X is Pareto superior to the alternatives, even to non-optimal alternatives. Suppose, for purposes of illustration, that there are two people A and B and ten units of bread to distribute among them and that both A and B prefer more units to fewer, regardless of how many units they have. Then any distribution of bread to individuals that does not waste any bread is a Pareto optimum, but none of these Pareto efficient states of affairs is Pareto superior to any of the others. Furthermore, consider an inefficient state of affairs, such as one in which both A and B get four units and two units rot. Distributions whereby both get five units or one gets four and the other gets six are Pareto superior to the distribution where both get four. But a Pareto efficient state of affairs in which one gets nine units and the other gets one is not Pareto superior to the inefficient state of affairs in which both get four.

To say of a state of affairs that it is Pareto efficient is thus to express very faint moral praise. The only thing praiseworthy about a Pareto efficient state of affairs is that it is not subject to one sort of criticism: it does not pass up any opportunities to satisfy some people's preferences better without sacrificing the preference satisfaction of somebody else. The fact that a Pareto efficient state of affairs is not faulty in this way may count for very little. In the simple example above, if individuals will starve if they do not have at least two units of bread, the inefficient state of affairs where both get four units is much better than the efficient state of affairs where one gets nine units and the other gets only one.

Let me emphasize that I am here questioning the moral importance of the theoretical notion of Pareto optimality or Pareto efficiency. I am not questioning the moral importance of efficiency. Inefficiencies mean that fewer needs can be met. In harsh circumstances, inefficiencies mean more suffering. But there is a huge difference between a recognition of the importance of efficiency and an infatuation with Pareto optimality.

Mainstream economists have linked Pareto efficiency or optimality to competitive market equilibrium in two general welfare theorems. The first maintains that perfect competition guarantees Pareto efficiency. Insofar as Pareto efficiency is a good thing, so is perfect competition. The second theorem says that any distribution of income can be achieved as a perfectly competitive market outcome given the 'right' initial distribution of resources. So rather than regarding society as facing a trade-off between the efficiency provided by the market and various moral concerns about equity, one can have both. Concerns about equity can be met by fixing the initial distribution, and the market can then be relied upon to bring about an efficient outcome.

People should not be overly impressed with either of these theorems. The fact that perfect competition guarantees Pareto efficiency is of little moral importance, first because Pareto efficiency is not a big deal, morally speaking. Inefficiency means that certain kinds of attractive improvements could in principle be made. Efficiency means that those sorts of improvements are not to be had, but nothing more. A second reason why people ought not to be overly impressed with the first welfare theorem is that perfect competition is impossible. A third reason is that, as Lipsey and Lancaster established (1956), the efficiency of perfect competition does not justify attempts to eliminate particular impediments to actual competition. Unless one were to achieve perfect competition, which is impossible, eliminating market imperfections may well *diminish* rather than improve efficiency. There is no way to know, *a priori*.

Similar considerations undermine the significance of the second welfare theorem. Even if massive 'initial' redistribution were politically feasible, perfect competition remains impossible, and moving toward perfect competition by eliminating market imperfections does not necessarily improve efficiency. I don't mean to underestimate either the actual magnitude of inefficiencies in the world or the moral importance of avoiding these inefficiencies, but the two welfare theorems are of no help in identifying or eliminating real inefficiencies. Who cares whether a perfectly competitive economy, which is not possible, is Pareto efficient and whether such an impossible economy could, as a consequence of an infeasible initial distribution, also result in an equitable distribution of income?

Mainstream economists care. Whether opposed to government intervention in the economy or in favor of it, mainstream economists typically treat perfectly competitive equilibrium as a benchmark and a moral ideal. Although some economists are opposed to government intervention in the economy for non-welfarist reasons such as concerns about individual freedoms or rights, those who seek to limit the role of government usually maintain that freeing the economy from government meddling best approximates perfect competition with its Pareto efficiency. Those who, in contrast, favor government intervention in the economy do so because they believe that government can address some of the failures of actual markets, where these failures are identified against the ideal standard of perfect competition. Defenders of government interference with the market are just as impressed with the claims of perfect competition as are opponents, and they are both wrong to be so impressed.

6 Potential Pareto improvements and cost–benefit analysis

As unjustifiable as this fascination with perfect competition may be, it is easy to understand, because concern with competitive equilibrium is so central to positive economic theory and because normative economists would have so little to say if they confined themselves to endorsing specific Pareto improvements. The only other path has been to find some way of comparing policies when none is Pareto superior to the others. Kaldor

(1939) and Hicks (1939) had the following thought: Consider two economic outcomes or states of affairs X and Y. There are many different moral comparisons people might make of them. One morally significant difference between X and Y may be distributional, as in the case of the ten units of bread. Another way that economic states of affairs may differ is in the quantity of economic benefits to be distributed – that is, in their capacity to satisfy preferences. Suppose that in X, the status quo, four units of bread go to A and six units go to B. A new policy is considered that would increase bread supply and result in A getting seven units of bread and B getting five. Call the alternative Y. Y is not a Pareto improvement over X, because B gets fewer units of bread, but there is, Kaldor and Hicks argue, an unambiguous increase in economic benefits and economic efficiency. With the new policy, the capacity of the economy to satisfy preferences has increased. The 'pie' has grown larger. That increase does not show up as a Pareto improvement, because there is also change in distribution to B's disadvantage. Owing to the way the pie has been cut, B's portion diminishes. In Kaldor and Hicks' view, economists are in no position to pass moral judgments on economic distribution, but they do not have to. The increase in efficiency, the purely economic benefit, is independent of distribution. Economists should be concerned to enlarge the pie, and they should leave its division to politicians and moralists. There is a separate dimension of purely economic evaluation.

According to Kaldor and Hicks, to determine whether X is more economically efficient than Y – that is, whether it has a greater capacity to satisfy preferences than Y – one needs to determine whether X is a potential Pareto improvement over Y. X is a potential Pareto improvement over Y if there is some way of redistributing the goods available in X that makes X an actual Pareto improvement over Y. So, in the simple bread example, the distribution of seven units to A and five to B is a potential Pareto improvement over the distribution of four units to A and six to B, because it would be possible to redistribute the 12 units so as to achieve an actual Pareto improvement. (For example, both A and B could receive six units of bread.)

One can also describe a potential Pareto improvement in terms of the possibility of 'compensation': if X is a potential Pareto improvement over Y, then it is possible for the winners in a change from Y to X to compensate the losers. Whether the winners could indeed compensate the losers is then operationalized in terms of willingness to pay. If the amount that winners would be willing to pay to bring about a policy is larger than the amount that losers would need to be compensated to accept the policy, then the policy is a potential Pareto improvement over the status quo, and the policy purportedly brings about a more efficient state of affairs in which there is a 'net benefit' – a greater capacity to satisfy preferences. All things considered, the policy might be a bad thing, because of its distributional consequences. But the distributional questions are not questions with which economists have any particular expertise. Furthermore, if the problems are distributional, then so are the solutions. The judgment concerning economic efficiency stands.

There are many problems with this argument, and many of these problems are inherited by the practical implementation of this line of thought in contemporary cost–benefit analysis. The central problem is that the separation that Kaldor and Hicks envisioned between questions concerning efficiency and distribution, between the size of the pie and the way it is sliced is not in general to be had.

Kaldor and Hicks possessed, I believe, a picture like that depicted in Figure 3.1, which represents the case of the loaves of bread on the unrealistic assumption that A's and B's utilities are proportional to their bread consumption. The distribution resulting from the new policy, the point p, is not a Pareto improvement over the status quo distribution s, since B's utility is lower. But one can move along the frontier made possible by the new policy to a region of Pareto superior distributions.

This is a special case. There is no reason to rule out the situation depicted in Figure 3.2, which is borrowed from Samuelson (1950). Figure 3.2 might represent the case where redistributing bread but sticking otherwise with the status quo would increase bread output so that A could consume more than seven units, while B consumes more than five, or it might represent the case where A prefers other aspects of the status quo when the bread distribution favors him. In Figure 3.2 the new policy is a potential Pareto improvement over the old one since both A and B prefer p' to s, and the status quo is a potential Pareto improvement over the new

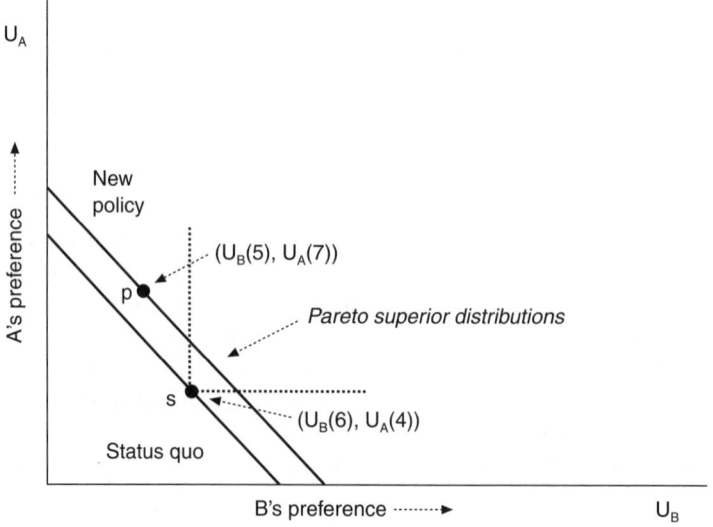

Figure 3.1

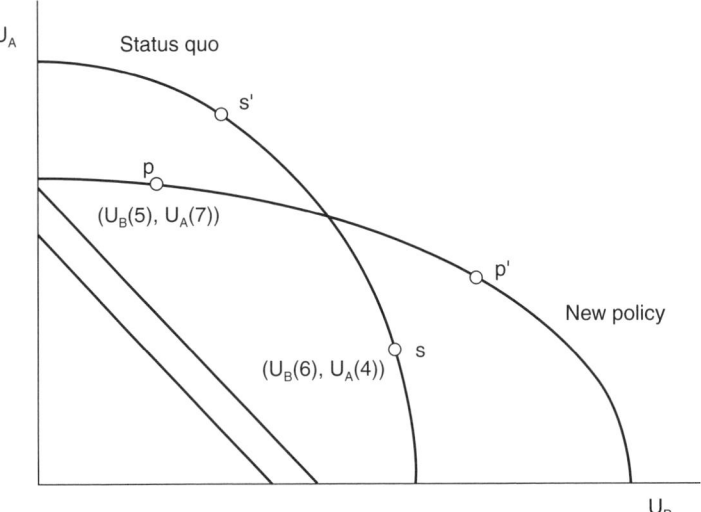

Figure 3.2

policy since both A and B prefer s' to p. Note that neither of the two figures assumes interpersonal comparability of preferences. Holding fixed the projections of the curves into the horizontal axis, it does not matter how the graphs are stretched out vertically, provided of course that the two graphs are subjected to the same transformation.

Since there is no way for the status quo to provide both a larger and a smaller 'pie' than that provided by the proposed policy change, the notion of a potential Pareto improvement does not provide a distribution-independent standard of efficiency. The fact that X is a potential Pareto improvement over Y does *not* imply that X has a greater capacity to satisfy preferences. The whole attempt to factor out a distribution-free notion of economic efficiency collapses.

This does not, in my view, mean that cost–benefit analysis is worthless or that it should be abandoned. But it does mean that it must be used with a great deal of circumspection. Indeed even actual Pareto improvements must be viewed with some caution. In Figure 3.2, p' is an actual Pareto improvement over s, but that is little reason for adopting the new policy as opposed to carrying out a redistribution that would take the economy to s'. Unless one assumes that if one pursues a consistent course of adopting policies that are potential Pareto improvements over the alternatives, then on average people will be winners as often as they are losers, one has to consider to what extent the net benefits depend on the current distribution, what their distributional consequences will be, and how distributions should be evaluated. One must abandon the hope of extracting a 'purely economic' realm of evaluation, in which moral questions about distribution can be set aside. Information concerning willingness to pay can still help to decide what to do, but it is no more than one input into the messy business of policy-making, rather than purportedly capturing a distribution-free notion of economic benefit.

Since evaluation will, typically, have to be concerned with distribution, either economists have to take into account factors other than welfare, or they have to abandon their animus toward interpersonal comparisons. They might, for example, suppose that willingness-to-pay provides an interpersonally comparable measure of welfare. So if X has net benefits as compared to Y – if X is a potential Pareto improvement over Y and Y is not a potential Pareto improvement over X – then there is more total welfare in X than in Y. On this view, cost–benefit analysis would be a means of implementing a utilitarian view of economic assessment.

But, as Figure 3.2 already shows, the path leading from data concerning willingness to pay to conclusions concerning welfare is a tangled one. The most obvious difficulty is that willingness to pay depends on an individual's preferences for money as well as on an individual's preferences for X and Y. Although the preferences of Americans differ in many ways from the preferences of Chinese, the fact that Americans are willing to pay a great deal more to diminish air pollution in their cities than are the Chinese surely has more to do with differences in incomes of Americans compared to Chinese than with differences in attitudes toward air pollution. Once economists admit the intelligibility of interpersonal comparisons, it is easy to see how the preference of A for X over Y could be much greater than the preference of B for Y over X, even though, owing to B's greater wealth, B is willing to pay more to bring about Y rather than X than A is willing to pay to bring about X as opposed to Y. Any inferences concerning welfare will require that economists address the effects of the distribution of income on willingness to pay.

Additional serious difficulties that I do not have time to discuss with any care include the problems due to uncertainty and due to the fact that preferences and willingness to pay typically depend on beliefs. When people have mistaken beliefs about the constitution of the exhaust from the factory down the road, their willingness to pay to avoid breathing it will be an unreliable indicator of their true preferences, let alone the welfare consequences of the exhaust (Hausman and McPherson, 1994; Broome, 1991b). Uncertainty further complicates matters, since people typically do not know the consequences of alternatives and hence which alternative they would prefer if they did know the consequences. The problems of uncertainty are usually finessed by supposing that individuals possess subjective probability distributions over all the possible outcomes, but to suppose this involves extreme idealization; and there is little justification for respecting preferences based on these largely fictitious probability distributions.

It is still possible to make some reasonable guesses concerning the welfare consequences of alternative policies, and I believe that economists have an important role to play. But it is easy now to see both how much harm economists can do and the challenges that must be met in order for them to do good. In particular, economists need to surrender the view that they can focus on welfare alone, that preferences are always a reliable guide to welfare, and that uncertainty can always be tamed by reliance on subjective probabilities.

7 Conclusions

In making cautious use of the findings of a cost–benefit analysis, policy-makers need to ask how dependent the net benefits are on the existing distribution of income and wealth and whether greater benefits might be obtained through redistribution. Recall Larry Summers' memorandum. It is plausible that redistributing income from rich nations to poor nations would increase overall well-being much more than redistributing pollution. And once one begins thinking of 'overall' well-being, one has left behind cost–benefit analysis and the futile hope that 'economic' questions can be sharply separated from distributional questions. The notion that welfare economists can offer a precise 'economic' analysis to which vague moral concerns about justice or rights can be counterposed must be vigorously resisted. The evaluation given by the market or simulated by welfare economists depends on a highly contestable theory of welfare and is no more solid or objective than other sorts of moral appraisals.[5]

The other chapters in this book show that these conclusions – that economic appraisal cannot be separated from distributional issues and that welfare is not the only important value – are well understood by many economists. For example, Nattrass and Seekings (2004) emphasize the costs of the South African 'high-productivity now' strategy to unskilled workers, especially in a context in which the state provides so little assistance to those who are unemployed. The question is not whether this strategy leads to a larger pie. The issue is rather the suffering of those who are indigent. Indeed, in this regard, a philosopher such as Alexander Rosenberg (2004) shows a greater fixation on overall welfare and a greater attachment to abstract economic argumentation in his case for respecting patent rights, regardless of the immediate human costs, because of the speculative future benefits of innovation.

In the past, economic development has not only increased the welfare of most individuals, it has also expanded their freedom and opportunities. By weakening the constraints of poverty and facilitating education, it creates a space in which justice and respect for human rights are increasingly feasible. But none of these goods is automatic, and not all development serves such moral interests. Furthermore, as many of the contributions to this book make clear, not all policies designed to foster development in fact do so. There are no short cuts to policy appraisal, and appraisals that ignore the full range of moral considerations bearing on economic policy are dangerous and misleading.

Notes

1 This section abbreviates and adapts material from Chapters 2 and 14 of Hausman and McPherson (1996).
2 Summers' other argument does not have this flaw. In some cases a given exposure to a pollutant will in fact diminish the health and welfare of people in LDCs less than it will diminish the health and welfare of people in rich countries. If, to use Summers' own example, a pollutant increases the risk of prostrate cancer – which is a disease mainly of elderly men – then the pollutant will not increase the risk of suffering or death as much if a few men live long enough to contract the disease. Furthermore, for purely medical reasons, a given dose of a particular pollutant may have fewer negative health consequences if the total amount of pollution is small, than if it is large. Although these differential effects might not exist if there were not other inequalities between developing nations and LDCs, claiming that such pollution has a lower cost in LDCs does not involve valuing the lives of those who live in LDCs less. The weight of these arguments can be questioned, however, since the consequences of increased pollution may lie many years in the future, when the difference in longevity and levels of background pollution on which the differences in effect depend may have disappeared. Furthermore, the interaction between pollution effects and the generally worse health status of people in LDCs might render some of the effects of pollutants more rather than less serious. The numbers of people affected by pollution must also be considered. Adding up all these factors; there seems to be no justified presumption that transfers of pollution toward poor countries is morally desirable. It is thus questionable whether thoughtful people should or would be willing to transfer pollution from developed to developing countries. One further problem should also be mentioned. The idea of compensating a country is a cheat: to claim that everyone would be willing to transfer pollution illegitimately treats countries as if they were individuals. Even in its own terms the argument does not go through, because the compensation may fail to reach individuals who are harmed by pollution.
3 I am doubtful about Bates' argument, because it provides no evidence that increased income would be spent on traditional cultural products, and because of less income by domestic producers there may well be an influx of cheaper imported goods.
4 More precisely these 'cardinal' utility functions are provably unique to a positive affine transformation. This means that if one cardinally significant utility function, U, represents my preferences, rather than another cardinally significant utility function, U', this function will represent my preferences if and only if $U' = aU + b$ where a is any positive real number and b is any real number.
5 Provided that one takes account of distributional presuppositions and consequences and recognizes that cost–benefit analysis is a source of data rather than answers, cost–benefit analysis can provide useful inputs into economic decision making. Of course it is subject to abuse and misinterpretation, and the techniques employed to correct for distributional effects and to input willingness to pay information from market data are certainly imperfect. But, provided that we don't forget that there are other things that matter besides welfare (let alone willingness to pay), what do we have that is less biased, more accurate or that provides a better insight into what will serve people's material interests?

References

Bates, R. (2005). Globalization: Less than meets the ear?, in M. Ayogu and D. Ross (eds), *Development Dilemmas: The Methods and Political Ethics of Growth Policy*, London: Routledge, pp. 30–39.

Broome, J. (1991a). Utility, *Economics and Philosophy*, 7: 1–12.

Broome, J. (1991b). *Weighing Goods: Equality, Uncertainty, and Time*, Oxford: Blackwell.

Hausman, D. (1992). *The Inexact and Separate Science of Economics*, Cambridge: Cambridge University Press.

Hausman, D. (1995). The impossibility of interpersonal utility comparisons, *Mind*, 104: 473–490.

Hausman, D. and M. McPherson (1994). Preference, belief and welfare, *American Economic Review, Papers and Proceedings*. 84(2): 396–400.

Hausman, D. and M. McPherson (1996). *Economic Analysis and Moral Philosophy*, Cambridge: Cambridge University Press

Hicks, J. (1939). The foundations of welfare economics, *Economic Journal*, 49: 696–712.

Kaldor, N. (1939). Welfare propositions of economics and interpersonal comparisons of utility, *Economic Journal*, 49: 549–552.

Lipsey, R. and K. Lancaster (1956). The general theory of the second best, *Review of Economic Studies*, 24: 11–31.

Mill, J.S. (1859). *On Liberty*. Currin V. Shields (ed. 1985), New York: Macmillan.

Mill, J.S. (1863). *Utilitarianism*. Reprinted in Marshall Cohen (ed.) (1961), *The Philosophy of John Stuart Mill*, New York: Modern Library, pp. 321–398.

Nattrass, N. and J. Seekings (2005). The 'new (global) economy' and inequality in South Africa, in M. Ayogu and D. Ross (eds), *Development Dilemmas: The Methods and Political Ethics of Growth Policy*, London: Routledge, pp. 170–189.

Rosenberg, A. (2004). Good ideas and human welfare: the political philosophy and economy of intellectual property, in M. Ayogu and D. Ross (eds), *Development Dilemmas: The Methods and Political Ethics of Growth Policy*, London: Routledge, pp. 125–143.

Samuelson, P. (1950). Evaluation of real national income, *Oxford Economic Papers New Series*, 2: 1–29.

4 Development theory and the philosophies of science[1]

Harold Kincaid

Development economics provides fertile ground for philosophers of science and of the social sciences. It does so in large part because those who study economic development disagree deeply about what their enterprise should look like. But this disagreement means that development economics may have something to learn from the philosophy of science. Any time science disagrees about fundamentals, philosophical issues are frequently just below the surface. So we should not be surprised to find various approaches in development economics the slave of the ideas, to paraphrase Keynes, of some dead philosophy of science.

This chapter thus discusses controversies in development economics and controversies in the philosophy of science with the aim of shedding some light on both. I am of course more confident in what I say about the latter. Correspondingly, my aim is to make a case that the philosophy of science issues are worth paying attention to.

The controversies in development economics that I discuss include the adequacy of neoclassical growth theories and of cross-country regression results, the place of 'noneconomic' factors in explaining underdevelopment, and the possibility of a development economics as a separate subdiscipline. The controversy in the philosophy of science is between two visions of what science, and in particular, economic science, is and/ought to be like. One vision sees science as explaining via universal regularities and confirming by means of universal inference rules or methods. The other focuses on explaining by the citing of causes or processes and confirming by means of domain-specific knowledge and contextually relevant arguments. It is the latter that I favor and the chapter is largely devoted to tracing out its consequences for development economics.

The chapter is organized as follows. Section one outlines the two different approaches to science. Section two discusses neoclassical growth theory, new growth theory, and cross-country regression approaches, arguing that they are committed in various ways to the philosophy of science that I reject, with unfortunate consequences. Section three discusses other approaches in development economics – supply and demand and game theory reasoning with particular applications to rural development economics – that are consistent with the philosophy of science I advocate.

1 Two visions of science

I want to sketch two broad, opposed pictures of the scientific enterprise. These visions are not the only ways of viewing science and nothing precludes these views from being more enlightening for some sciences than others. The various tenets that compose these views are also not inevitably connected – some might be plausible and others not. However, there is a natural affinity among the ideas composing each vision and as I shall show below, these two visions are often at play in development economics.

Any account of science has to say something about the *products* of scientific inquiry and the *process* by which those products are produced. The two views I am interested in differ significantly on these parameters. The first view I shall dub Humean because of its family resemblance to Humean empiricist doctrines. It holds that:

> The products of science are laws in the sense of universal regularities between actual events. The process of science is guided by universal rules of inference.

The second view I shall label post-positivist. Its take on the two issues above is:

> The products of science identify causes, processes and forces; universal regularities of actual events are seldom available and in any case nonexplanatory unless they identify causes. The processes of science are guided by contingent, empirical and domain specific considerations rather than universal formal rules.

From these different basic standards various other commitments naturally follow on the role of models, the relation between various sciences, particularly economics, vis-à-vis the other social sciences, and other issues. So, for the Humean, having a distinct science or discipline requires that there be clearly separable events of the relevant kind, for science is about finding universal regularities between them. This then results in the Millian view (see Hausman, 1993) that there is a distinct realm of purely economic causes. Post-positivist accounts are not committed to this separateness thesis because they are not committed to universal regularities; causes can be picked out in varying levels of detail in different ways and in different languages. This allows us to talk of economic causes without thinking that the economic is to the social as the terrestrial is to the lunar, i.e., ontologically and causally largely separate.

Another dichotomy that naturally arises concerns models. For the

Humean, good models are those that capture in some sense universal regularities. That makes it easy to see a set of equations as necessary and sufficient for a model. Equations are universal regularities, and if that is all that is required – if no causal interpretation is required – then models are easily equated with sets of equations.

Furthermore, given that models are generally idealizations or abstractions, that then requires some way to separate the good from the bad. In the philosophical literature this has led to a contorted literature trying to make sense of a regularity true *ceteris paribus* (Earman and Roberts, 1999).[2] In the social science literature, as we shall see, this problem has led either to appealing to insight provided by the model or to purely formal tests of goodness of fit.

For the post-positivist view as I define it, models are not about universal regularities but about picking out causes. A good model gets at the causes; 'insight' is not enough, *purely* formal tests of causality will not suffice – no causal knowledge into a model means none out (see Cartwright, 1989).

As should be obvious, my sympathies are with the post-positivist. But I think it a broadly empirical question which view best fits scientific practice in a particular case and what conclusions we should draw from fit or lack thereof. Philosophy of science and science are continuous, and neither can be assessed in complete isolation from prior judgments about the success of the other. The next section instantiates that process and in doing so will tie down more firmly these abstract ideas. My claim is that an important trend in development economics embodies the Humean vision of science, to its detriment.

2 Neoclassical growth theory, old and new

A dominant approach to development in the neoclassical tradition is that stemming from Solow's work (1956), now labeled old growth theory. I discuss here three contemporary accounts in this tradition.

The first model is called an 'augmented Solow model' (Mankiw, 1995). The Solow (1956) model dates from the mid-1950s and has dominated neoclassical thinking about growth and development. Output is determined by an aggregate production function that makes output a function of the supply of capital and labor, where the size of the latter is determined by an exogenously given level of technology. The size of the capital stock is determined by the savings, population growth, depreciation, and technological growth rates, all of which are taken as exogenous.

There are two crucial implications of this model for development. First, increases in savings and capital investments are central for growth, and second, economies will converge toward a steady state where growth is constant. The level of growth in the steady state depends only on the exogenously given technological change.

The augmented Solow model arises because the original Solow model had some unwelcome consequences. Given the observed differences in capital investment between rich and poor countries, the model predicts incomes in those countries that differ by a multiple of two. In fact the actual differences are in the order of ten. Moreover, the model predicts that additional capital investments in the poor countries should have a much higher rate of return and thus that we should see considerably more movement of capital from rich to poor nations than we do.

The augmented Solow model results from seeing that the unwanted predictions depend crucially on the relative share of capital. A higher share of capital implies greater effects on income of savings and that return to capital varies less with income. But if we add to the Solow model another capital variable – for human capital – we get a change of the relative share of capital (physical and human) and thus the troubling predictions go away. Since human capital theory was a major innovation in the period after Solow's account was proposed, this is a natural emendation.

Contrary to the augmented Solow model of Mankiw, new growth theory makes technological change endogenous. In many versions it also departs from the general competitive equilibrium assumptions in that economies of scale and spillover affects are allowed, factors traditional development economics (e.g., pre-Solow) thought unimportant. Romer's (1990, 1994) models, on which I focus here, have these features.

Like the augmented Solow model, new growth theory includes both physical and human capital as factors of production. Technological change becomes explained in that there is a knowledge-producing sector that takes physical and human capital and existing knowledge as inputs and produces technological designs as output. This sector also introduces economies of scale and drops perfect competition in that part of the knowledge produced is proprietary and produced by monopolies and that part of the knowledge produced becomes a public good. So we have the promise of explaining technological progress and doing so with a more realistic model that breaks with some general equilibrium theory simplifications found in the augmented Solow model.

Romer's model is rounded out with rather several rather less realistic components. An intermediate sector takes designs and foregone output of consumer goods to produce durable (capital) goods. The consumer goods sector consists of one firm that produces all output, owns no assets, and makes zero profits. Consumers own the durable goods firms and receive net proceeds; consumers are Ramsay style infinitely lived individuals. Because the production functions in the consumer goods and durable goods section are identical, consumers can substitute a fixed number of consumer goods for production of capital goods; they do so in a way that maximizes over the infinite future. The growth rate is thus determined in this way given the initial stock of capital, knowledge, and labor.

A third approach to explaining growth and development is both a model and means to testing models. It is also consistent in broad approach with the new growth and augmented Solow models, as we will see below. The work I have in mind focuses on cross-country regressions. Using data sets on a hundred countries over 40 years, growth rates are regressed on variables that are thought to be their causes. Barro (2001) is perhaps the best known advocate of this approach. He finds that male schooling (but not female), investment rate, extent of rule of law, and favorable terms of trade are positive determinants (his term) of growth. Run away inflation (above 20 percent) and unproductive (his term) government spending are associated with lower growth rates.

These three approaches fairly clearly rely on the Humean picture of science that I described above. The Humean view took a distinctive position on the nature and place of laws, inference, models, social factors, and the economic vis-à-vis the social. That position is reflected consistently in the three neoclassical approaches to development.

2.1 Science produces laws that are universal regularities

This Humean view shows up in several guises. Augmented Solow growth, new growth, and cross-country regression approaches describe a single production function that holds for all economies. While these theories describe different variables, the variables present are everywhere the same and have the same effects. Individual countries may be at different points relative to the production frontier, but they are all instantiating the same regularity. For augmented growth theory, all economies are even at the same level of technology.

For the cross-country regression reproach, the regularities are not purely economic ones – to this extent there is not as strong an assumption of universal regularities. Yet in another sense, the assumption is even deeper. The effects of the non-economic factors are everywhere the same, given the same levels of the other variables. The rule of law, for example, denotes the same causal mechanism in every context (though Humeans cannot express this presupposition since they reject causal notions). Furthermore to take a string of variables itself as explanatory – rather than just as a piece of evidence about what might be explanatory – is a paradigm of the Humean thought that science explains by producing laws that are real world regularities.

Of course, advocates of the above models are not strictly Humean in that they switch back and forth between talking about associations (the only proper notion on the Humean view) and causes. But their notion of cause usually seems to be that of a universal regularity – they switch interchangeably between 'cause', 'is a function of', and 'is associated with'. This ambivalence is a natural outcome of wanting to talk about causes, yet to do so only in the framework of laws as universal regularities.

The universality idea also shows up in the very common urge to make development the result of *one* factor, a particularly strong form of universalism. So, for example, Lucas claims that investments in human capital are the most important (Lucas, 1988).

2.2 Scientific inference requires universal, formal rules of inference

This assumption shows up in the standards assumed both for good evidence and good explanation. The overwhelmingly dominant standard for assessing a theory reads 'not statistically significant, not believable; statistically significant, believable'. Over and over this criterion is invoked when evidence is presented for these theories (Mankiw, 1995; Barro, 2001). Even when there are doubts about the statistical significance criterion, the proposed fix instantiates the universalist ideals. So critics of the three approaches raise doubts based on the fragility of significance tests, depending on which variables are included in the regressions (Kenney and Williams, 2000). The solution they propose is just a somewhat more complicated rule, basically statistical significance across multiple specifications. Not surprisingly, defenders of these approaches to growth can simply adopt the more complicated rule (as does Sala-I-Martin, 1997).

In evaluating explanations, the universalist ideal shows up in the use of explained variance (R^2). R^2 measures in intuitive terms how close the data are to the regression line, with the slope of the line determining the strength of relationship expressed in the regression coefficients. All three growth models are defended on the grounds that they have high or higher explained variances than other accounts (Mankiw, 1995; Romer, 1994; Barro, 2001). This is adjudicating models by a purely formal criterion, i.e., by one that relies on logical, not substantive, theoretical considerations.

To be sure, the statistical significance and R^2 rules are widespread in economics and the social sciences more generally. No doubt some defenders of the alternative approaches to development that I favor invoke these rules as well. But these rules have a natural affinity with the other ideas of the Humean vision shared by these three approaches, and, I will argue shortly, are a poor fit with the post-positivist vision embodied in other approaches to development.

2.3 A science of economics requires a distinct realm of economic events

For the old and new growth theories, this assumption is obvious. The relevant variables are seemingly only economic ones. I say 'seemingly' because non-neoclassical economists such as Marx or Robinson might well describe models where the variables are also capital, labor, level of technology, etc. However, these economic variables are conceived in terms of classes and social relationships. For the neoclassical models discussed here, no such reading is intended; talk of capital in general is an analogy from and should ultimately be based on a general equilibrium model where the basic entities are specific physical capital goods and skills of specific individuals.

The cross-country regression approach would seem to be different in that it explicitly invokes non-economic variables. Yet the appearance is deceptive. The regressions only make sense if the economic and social variables can vary independently, and they can do that only if they are separate factors. That social variables are included does not deny the fundamental presupposition that the economic and the social are distinct. At most it makes it possible to reject one very stringent interpretation of the separateness requirement, viz. that the economic factors are not only separate but the most important (and then only if you buy the questionable assumption that regression coefficients measure relative causal influence).

2.4 A set of equations is necessary and sufficient to have a model or theory; models are evaluated by the insight they provide

If science produces universal regularities, mathematical equations are a natural and paradigm way to express such regularities. Every equation expresses a regularity; if you cannot write down your model in equations, you do not have the required regularities.

It is fairly non-controversial that neoclassical economists in general find equations necessary. It might seem that they are not sufficient, for there are other reasonable requirements they ought to meet, e.g., compatibility with general equilibrium analysis. Krugman, for example, claims that traditional development economics was not taken seriously because it had no models (1996). Yet that is patently false, since Kaldor among others modeled his ideas explicitly in sets of equations (1957). Arguably they were not taken seriously because they did not have general equilibrium foundations.

However, the notion of general equilibrium foundations has been very plastic and much more of a rhetorical flourish than a real constraint in neoclassical accounts of development. In practice, a set of equations has sufficed, with the tie to general equilibrium remaining metaphorical. So the cross-country regression equations have no explicit general equilibrium interpretation and even include non-economic variables. Old and new growth theory invokes representative individuals and aggregate production functions. These are treated as if they were the same as the components of a general equilibrium model – as rational maximizing of individual consumer utility and individual firm production functions. But they are not that at all. In the end the fit with general equilibrium theory does little work so long as one can get a set of equations.

The new and old growth models are judged in part by their ability to fit various facts, frequently cross-country regressions. However, the models are generally at a high level of abstraction from measurable variables and moreover rest on numerous simplifications that have no prospect of even being approximately correct. So we would not expect fit anyway, and the appeal to facts is then replaced by their ability to provide 'insight' or 'understanding'. So witness Krugman (1996: 15) on new growth theory: 'to do development theory, one must have the courage to be silly, writing down models that are implausible in the details in order to arrive at higher-level insights'. Or Mankiw (1995: 282): 'The issue at hand is not whether the neoclassical model is exactly true. The issue is whether the model can even come close to making sense of international experience.'

As should be obvious by now, I find these general philosophical assumptions suspect. Thus I should be able to point to specific resulting inadequacies in these growth theories. I can.

The statistical significance rule results from the desire for something that does not exist, viz. a mechanical decision rule to decide when the data support a hypothesis. The flaws in hypothesis testing have been detailed again and again (Cohen, 1994), so I will only briefly summarize them. The standard Neyman–Pearson approach takes probability to be about long-run frequencies only; probabilities are undefined for single cases. Significance tests require taking a random sample to infer about a population. Significance tests tell us the probability of seeing the observed correlation in the sample when in fact there is no correlation in the population. Probability here means frequency in indefinitely many repetitions – it entails nothing about the probability that this particular sample is due to chance. I only learn about the long-run characteristics of multiple applications of my testing procedure.

However, consumers of statistics want to know something other than what would happen on average in indefinite repetitions – they want to know whether this particular set of data support one hypothesis or another. So not surprisingly, in practice users of significance tests try to turn them into what they are not, i.e., a measure of support. Even if we took significance tests to tell us about single cases, the information they provide is insufficient to make any judgment about how plausible a hypothesis is given the data. That judgment is one about the probability of the hypothesis, given the evidence we have (p(H/E)). As Bayes' theorem shows,[3] that cannot be calculated from the probability of the evidence, assuming the null hypothesis (p(E/not H)) alone, which is what a significance test would tell us (i.e., the probability of seeing this sample when the hypotheses that it represents the population correlation is false). It is a common and probably hardwired (Kahneman and Tversky, 2000) fallacy to confuse the probability of H, given E, with its inverse, the probability of E, given H.

These problems are multiplied when it comes to econometrics in the work discussed above, because the traditional Neyman–Pearson justification for significance tests requires random samples. But the cross-country regressions are not based on a random sample of anything (either a real population or a hypothetical population produced by random assignment to treatment or control). It is an interesting but largely untold story how econometrics with such incoherent intellectual foundations became dominant.[4]

There are some attempts to develop more sophisticated analysis in the growth literature. Yet they are nonetheless a hodgepodge of frequentist and non-frequentist rationales still longing for the mechanical procedure that will tell you if the hypothesis is supported by the data. These attempts are variant's of Leamer's (1985) idea of testing for fragility of regressions – seeing what happens to significance when variables are dropped and added to the regression equation. Nonetheless, statistical significance is still the decision criterion and thus these approaches inherit the same liabilities as simple significance testing does. Moreover, from a significance testing perspective they bring enormous problems as well, for repeated significance tests confound their interpretation in frequentist terms. In analyzing clinical trials, for example, multiple significance tests are standardly allowed only by setting the threshold for rejection extremely low, i.e., at p values in the order of 0.0001 (O'Brien and Fleming, 1979). This is thought necessary to prevent spurious results – if you repeat a significance test 20 times, you will find one significant result at $p < 0.05$ even when there is no real relation. So when Sala-I-Martin (1997) runs two million regressions to determine the causes of growth and takes significance tests as a decision criterion, we have to wonder what to make of such results.

The other Humean standard used in cross-country regressions and in defending old and new growth models is R2, explained variance. This is a quite misleading measure of explanatory power. In particular, high R2 values are compatible with factors that are only causally unimportant and low values are compatible with factors that are causally quite significant. Only if you eschew causal notions and take explanation to involve nothing but regularities will this result not bother you.

This difficulty also suggests, I think, that the emphasis on universal regularities is misguided. As anyone aware of the philosophical debates over explanation knows, there are many examples demonstrating that universal regularities need not be explanatory (Salmon and Kitcher, 1989). This is fortunate, since there is also good evidence that they are hard to come by (Cartwright, 1983). Much science consists in identifying causal processes and patterns that interact in complex ways with each other and with initial conditions. As a result, exceptionless statements about what happens in all circumstances – universal regularities – are rare. Moreover, we often know that we leave out causes in explanations and thus that we should not expect to see the generalizations of our models precisely instantiated.

Thus the new and old growth approaches and the cross-country regressions are both too demanding and not demanding enough. Even apart from the statistical significance issues above, a well-established correlation between a string of variables can leave the phenomena completely unexplained. That is arguably the case with the Barro style 'accounts' of growth. Taken non-causally, they leave growth unexplained and tell us only that some things are related.

Yet there is no attempt to show that the regressions offer support for a causal model, and for good reason.[5] Growth, the so-called dependent variable, can be a cause of the many factors treated as independent variables. The independent variables obviously can causally interact. (This of course raises yet another set of doubts about the statistics beyond the problems raised above.) When mutual causation is allowed, then the number of possible causal models for correlational data on 12 causal factors (Barro's common number) is enormous. The cross-country evidence does little to narrow that number down. Added to this problem is the fact that the national data in many countries is enormously problematic (see Dezhbakhsh, Chapter 5); the regression results are likely to be substantially influenced by these measurement errors.

The neoclassical growth approaches described above are also too demanding in asking for laws. Given the aggregative nature of the production function and its admitted dependence on social and political factors, there is little reason to think that all countries are somewhere on the same production frontier. Even if we think that there are fixed universal laws describing the *individual* behavior of consumers and producers, we would not expect every aggregation of those activities to follow the same law. Yet that is what assuming the same aggregate production function requires.

The way that growth theories and cross-country regression accounts define and assess models is also deeply flawed in my view. The growth models build in an enormous number of simplifying and falsifying assumptions. Among them are:

- *Equilibrium assumptions*: Both the old and new growth theories assume that all markets clear. This rules out by fiat the Keynesian and sectoral distortion concerns of traditional development economics.
- *Closed economy assumptions*: All the models are closed economies, again ruling out issues that traditional development economics thought central.
- *Representative and perfectly rational individuals*: Sectors are treated as if they were individuals optimizing with perfect foresight. Missing markets, asymmetric information, transaction costs, etc. are thus ruled out.
- *Assumptions about capital*: Despite the Cambridge controversy's acknowledged outcome that marginal product need not have an inverse and monotonic relation to the quantity of capital (Samuelson, 1966), these models presuppose just that. They also treat capital as perfectly fungible and measurable independently of the rate of interest, another parable called into question by the Cambridge critique.

- *Knowledge and technology assumptions*: Neoclassical growth models either assume that the best current technology is available to all or that at least all non-proprietary technology is. This removes by assumption the traditional developmentalist concern that the level of infrastructure and development make adopting such technologies unfeasible.
- *Independence of the economic*: Both old and new growth theory assume that social and institutional variables are either constant or irrelevant to growth.

This list of idealizations could be expanded, but the above suffice to make the point – the neoclassical growth models rely on false assumptions that in no way can be seen as rough approximations.

As we saw above, the standard defense of this procedure is that the models are valid despite their counterfactual nature because they provide 'insight' or 'understanding'. That might be plausible if it was shown by standard methods that the models were getting at real causal processes despite their simplifications – e.g., by showing that as the models are made more realistic, their predictions become more accurate or that the predictions of the models are not sensitive to the false assumptions made. However, that is not the route taken, which is not surprising given the Humean bias in favor of laws over causes. So we are left with an appeal to insight without any objective grounding for the models taken as anything other than as about logical relations in hypothetical possible worlds where the false assumptions hold. Those back in the real world of poverty and policy choices are understandably skeptical that much has been learnt.

The separateness assumptions built into these models are harder to evaluate in that there is relatively little clear philosophical investigation into what separateness entails. One traditional view is that economics studies a set of causes distinct from those studied by the other social sciences and that those economic causes are most important for the production of material wealth. Yet this view is of dubious coherence once pressed. Individual agents and firms are always simultaneously involved in economic, sociological and cultural processes in such a way that thinking of them as distinct causes – as opposed to distinct vocabularies for picking out patterns in human behavior – makes little sense. Even if it did make sense, specifying in what sense one cause is more important in this context is not at all obvious.

However, if we eschew causal notions in Humean fashion, one reasonably clear claim involved in growth and cross-country models that may not face the above problems is:

> The relevant economic facts suffice to determine the facts about growth when markets function unimpeded by distortions,[6] where the 'relevant economic variables' are initial factor endowments, utility and production functions, etc.

This does not commit us to a separate realm of economic causes, only to the ability to pick out economic events.

The problem is that even this more defensible separateness thesis is implausible on empirical grounds. I take that to be the upshot of the explosion of work in the 'new institutionalist' vein and developments in game theory more generally. Asymmetric information, missing markets, etc. matter and ensure that the economic facts narrowly defined do not fix the facts about growth. Institutional differences matter in a deep way to development.

3 Post-positivist philosophy and development economics

These comments bring me to my more constructive claims. Recall the alternative philosophy of science I advocate: science produces causal explanations, frequently without universal generalizations; models are successful to the extent that they pick out causes despite their simplifications; assessing the explanatory power of a model or the extent to which data supports a hypotheses requires a substantive scientific argument based on background knowledge and is not decidable by formal inference rules alone; and economic events and causes are not a separate sphere independent of the social in general.

I believe there are recent trends in development economics and development social science that to varying extents embody these ideals and constitute a promising alternative to the aggregate neoclassical growth theories. I have in mind (1) a variety of empirical case study work, often historical in approach and relatively atheoretical, and (2) less empirical and more theoretical work loosely associated with the new institutional economics, political economy, and sociology. I make no claim that this batch of work is entirely self consistent, uniformly on the right track, and entirely uninfluenced by the Humean alternative. The new institutional economics has its origins in the neoclassical tradition and sometimes reflects its birth pangs. In particular, the simplifying assumptions of optimizing and equilibrium do not get substantiated by detailed evidence showing that the real causal process has been described (Bardhan, 2001); and the integration of the economic and the social invokes an anemic sense of the latter (Peters, 1993). That said, there are some important and plausible fundamental assumptions common to this work.

Those assumptions include:

1 Universality and explanation come not from producing universal regularities but from employing a common explanatory strategy or schema based on common mechanisms or processes.
2 Applying those strategies is a case-by-case process that produces contextually sensitive accounts (and policy recommendations).

3 Models based on these strategies are designed to get at real causal processes explaining development.
4 Evidence for the veracity of these models must come from a variety of sources, including surveys, field work, and historical studies, and must constitute good reason to believe we have an approximate knowledge of locally acting causes; cross-country aggregate regressions are usually too crude a tool to provide the needed evidence.
5 The processes causing development are simultaneously both economic and social. How exactly this assertion is interpreted is open for debate, but common to any interpretation will be a denial of the Humean claim that the facts about growth (not to mention development in the broader sense) are fixed by the narrow economic facts.

It is worth noting three things about this work: (1) It is at odds with Hausman's claim (Chapter 3) that general equilibrium theory underlies assessments in development economics. The body of studies I am pointing to is quite explicit in rejecting the assumptions of general equilibrium theory. (2) This work is also quite at odds with the assumptions of the Washington Consensus, something Stiglitz argues in Chapter 1 and many other places. (3) The contextual and institutional knowledge that these approaches presuppose certainly leaves a space for development economics as an independent discipline, contra the neoclassical growth theories.

Let me illustrate this alternative approach by looking at work on agrarian financial markets in the developing countries. Much of agrarian lending and borrowing is done in the informal sector where interest rates are very high. It has often been suggested that the lack of access to formal financial infrastructure (something simply assumed away by neoclassical growth models) is a barrier to growth and many government programs have attempted to change the situation in the hope of encouraging growth. To be explained then is the presence of a dual financial structure – institutional bank loans and informal individual money lending with different interest rates and the successes and failures of government programs in trying to provide greater access to financing at lower interest rates to poor farmers.

The work detailed next invokes two broad kinds of argument patterns[7] – what elsewhere (Kincaid, 1996) I have called a supply-and-demand argument pattern and what I shall call a best-response-to-market-failure approach. The supply-and-demand pattern is familiar if under-appreciated because of overemphasis on general equilibrium theory in accounts of what economics is about by both economists and philosophers. The supply-and-demand pattern works as follows:

1 The relevant commodity, market and price measure is identified.
2 The behavior of the market is explained by determining the rough slope of the demand and supply curves and by identifying changes along and shifts in the curves.

3   The basic factors are identified that cause shifts in the supply and demand curve.

This argument pattern picks out basic supply and demand forces; it does so without relying on the assumptions of perfect competition of general equilibrium theory. It is a kind of causal explanation offered repeatedly in applied economics.

The best-response-to-market-failure argument pattern works as follows. Phenomena that deviate from what would be expected in a perfectly competitive market at equilibrium are identified. Those phenomena are then shown in a model to be the rational response of individuals to specific types of market failures – asymmetric information, incomplete contracts, transaction costs, etc. Then it is argued that postulated market failure and ensuing behavior is in fact instantiated in the case at hand. These arguments and the supply-and-demand form can complement each other, since the supply-and-demand pattern does not require perfect competition.

These argument patterns are used to explain the nature of rural credit markets. A variety of studies have found that rural credit markets typically display the following characteristics:

1   They are segmented into informal and formal sectors with differing interest rates.
2   Most institutional loans go to wealthier farms and informal loans to poorer and often landless farmers.
3   Informal loans are seldom secured by collateral but frequently involve linking contracts, e.g., commodity contracts requiring the borrower to sell his or her crop to the loaner.
4   Informal loan markets are generally local in nature.
5   Government loan programs through formal institutions do not lower the interest rate charged for informal loans or much increase access to credit for poorer farmers; some government loan programs involving cooperatives are successful in these goals.

The explanation of these phenomena involves applying the supply-and-demand and best-response mechanisms. Formal institutions lack information on the riskiness of prospective borrowers. Thus collateral is required on all loans (a best response to market failure). Increased funds for formal institutions thus go to wealthier farmers (who also have greater political influence in the formal sector bureaucracy). Thus an increase in loanable funds does not drive down the interest rate in the informal sector (a supply-and-demand argument).

Informal loans are generally local and involve interlinkages with contracts in other markets, for several reasons. Only local lenders – those with strong social ties to the potential borrowers – can acquire sufficient information about the credit worthiness of borrowers. Interlinkages minimize enforcement problems (best response to perfect market failure). Interest rates are higher than in the formal sector because of the costs of screening and monitoring, which the formal sector finds impossible (best-response argument) and because screening and monitoring create relation-specific capital for the borrower (supply-and-demand argument).

Some government lending programs involving loans to cooperatives are successful because they solve the information and monitoring problems. By loaning to small groups of similar individuals (thus with similar risk characteristics) with collective default provisions, monitoring and incentive problems that face other loan programs are eliminated (best response argument).

The evidence for these causal explanations is diverse. Udry (1993) conducted a household survey in northern Nigeria and found that nearly all loans are informal between individuals well known to each other, consistent with the postulated differences in information. Aleem (1993) conducted a microsurvey of supply and demand for credit in a market town in Pakistan. Average and marginal costs for screening and monitoring for informal lenders was measured as was the default rate in the informal and formal sectors. The extent to which borrowers switched lenders or borrowed from multiple lenders (a measure of relation-specific capital) was recorded. All this data was consistent with the postulated mechanisms.

Studies of the BAAC government loan program in Thailand (Siamwalla *et al.*, 1993) also support the causal stories above. BAAC loans are formal sector loans to groups of eight to 15 individuals with joint liability. The default rate on these loans is far below that for other government lending programs aimed at poorer rural farmers. Measures of transaction costs for borrowers find they come to 9 percent of the loan, suggesting that in these loans the group is taking over the costs normally incurred by informal lenders. The low default rate suggests that the incentive system set up by the small group lending (only lend to other individuals with similar credit worthiness, monitor their compliance) is successful in overcoming the normal market failures that confront the formal sector.

Note that there is little appeal here to formal tests of models or defense of models by claims to insight. Some significance testing does occur, but it plays a minor role and only occurs when there are actually random samples. Formal models are indeed developed, but the evidence is not thought to come from the modeling exercise itself but from concrete evidence that the mechanisms in the models are instantiated.

Note also that these explanations clearly do not require any separateness assumption about the economic and social. Social and economic factors are aspects of one process. So kinship relations are part of the economic process involved in solving information and monitoring problems. 'Class relationships' can arguably be essentially involved in that patterns of land ownership play an essential role.

There are many other such studies of factors in development embodying this alternative to the Humean vision for development economics. The argument of Nattrass and Seekings (Chapter 9) is a case in point. They suggest that institutional structure is crucial, and their analysis is driven by the kinds of informational asymmetries and game theoretic considerations (concerning, in their case, costs of signaling credibility) typical of the work informed by the post-positivist vision.

My claim is not that all these studies are flawless. However, I think there is no doubt that at their best they embody a very different vision of how development economics should proceed.

4 Conclusion

Keynes was right that ideas matter and that they often do so in subtle and unrecognized ways. Research paradigms can have a life of their own, influencing the choice of problems pursued, the vocabulary and categories employed, and the standards for evidence and explanation. I have sketched the ideas behind the neoclassical growth tradition and argued that they presuppose a quite specific picture of science that is of questionable value. That philosophy of science influences important parts of economics – neoclassical growth theory – and it probably has far wider influence still on the study of development: the one-shoe-fits-all approach of the Washington Consensus arguably relies on similar presuppositions. Instead of searching for universal laws of growth evaluated by formal procedures, development economics and development social science (for the two are no longer independent on the views I am championing) may profit by explaining development as the outcome of diverse complexes of common causal processes and defending those explanations with arguments from diverse kinds of empirical evidence.

Notes

1 Thanks to Don Ross for helpful comments on an earlier draft of this chapter.
2 Earman and Roberts take me to have contributed to this questionable project. That is a misunderstanding: the view expressed in Kincaid (1996) and further developed in (Kincaid, forthcoming) is that models must be judged by whether they manage to get at partial causal factors despite their simplifications. *Ceteris paribus* claims are confirmed to the extent that they do. Nothing in this necessarily involves providing truth claims for *ceteris paribus* laws.
3 Bayes' theorem is: $p(H/E) = p(H) \times p(E/H)/p(H) \times p(E/H) + p(\text{not } H) \times p(E/\text{not } H)$, where H is the hypothesis and E the evidence. Calculating $p(H/E)$ – the probability of the hypothesis given the evidence – can only be done with all the information given on the right-hand side of the equation, as is well known in the interpretation of tests in medicine and elsewhere (see Motulsky, 1995). This is true regardless of what we think of Bayesian theories of confirmation in general: Bayes' theorem is, after all . . . a theorem.
4 Standard works (Morgan, 1989; Duo, 1993) note that the new econometrics of the 1950s did not fit easily with the frequentist accounts of hypothesis testing, but do not explain how the consensus that hypothesis testing is nonetheless

legitimate was formed nonetheless. Most standard works in econometrics make no pretense of explaining the probability foundations of econometric inference by reference to a real chance set up and instead just assume from the beginning that there exist some joint probability functions.

5 One sign that causal models are not being seriously tested is that variables such as inequality, which some have argued influence growth, are not even included. It is hard not to see ideology at work when 'unproductive' government spending is included in the regressions and inequality is not.

6 'Determines' does not have to be taken as causal – variables in equations determine other variables for example – but the notion of 'distortion' may be.

7 The notion of an argument pattern is taken from Kitcher (1993).

References

Aleem, I. (1993). Imperfect information, screening and the costs of informal lending: a study of rural credit market in Pakistan, in K. Hoff, A. Braverman, and J. Stiglitz (eds), *The Economics of Rural Organization*, Oxford: Oxford University Press.

Bardhan, P. (2001) Distributive conflicts, collective action and institutional economics, in G. Meier and J. Stiglitz (eds), *Frontiers of Development Economics*, Oxford: Oxford University Press.

Barro, R. (2001). *Determinants of Economic Growth*, Cambridge: MIT Press.

Cartwright, N. (1983). *How the Laws of Physics Lie*, New York: Oxford University Press.

Cartwright, N. (1989). *Nature's Capacities and their Measurement*, Oxford: Oxford University Press.

Cohen, P. (1994). The earth is round ($p < 0.05$), *American Psychologist*, 49: 997–1003.

Duo, Q. (1993). *The Formation of Econometrics*, Oxford: Clarendon Press.

Earman, J. and J. Roberts (1999). Ceteris paribus, there is no problem of provisos, *Synthese*, 118: 439–478.

Hausman, D. (1993). *The Inexact and Separate Science of Economics*, Cambridge: Cambridge University Press.

Kahneman, D. and A. Tversky (2000). *Choice, Values, and Frames*, Cambridge: Cambridge University Press.

Kaldor, N. (1957). A model of economic growth, *The Economic Journal*, 82: 1237–1255.

Kenny, C. and D. Williams (2000). What do we know about economic growth? Or, why don't we know very much? *World Development*, 29: 1–22.

Kincaid, H. (1996). *The Philosophical Foundations of the Social Sciences: Analyzing Controversies in Social Research*, Cambridge: Cambridge University Press.

Kincaid, H. (forthcoming). Are there laws in the social sciences? Yes, in C. Hitchcock (ed.), *Contemporary Debates in the Philosophy of Science*, London: Blackwell.

Kitcher, P. (1993). *The Advancement of Science*, Oxford: Oxford University Press.

Krugman, P. (1996). *Development, Geography, and Economic Theory*, Cambridge: MIT Press.

Leamer, R. (1985). Sensitivity analyses would help, *American Economic Review*, 75: 308–313

Lucas, R. (1988). On the mechanics of economic development, *Journal of Monetary Economics*, 22: 3–42.

Mankiw, N. (1995). The growth of nations, *Brookings Papers on Economic Activity*, 25: 275–310.

Morgan, M. (1989). *The History of Econometric Ideas*, Cambridge: Cambridge University Press.

Motulsky, H. (1995). *Intuitive Biostatistics*, Oxford: Oxford University Press.

O'Brien, P. and T. Fleming (1979). A multiple testing procedure for clinical trials, *Biometrics*, 35: 549–556.

Peters, P. (1993). Is 'rational choice' the best choice for Robert Bates? An anthropologist's reading of Bates's work, *World Development*, 21: 1063–1076.

Romer, P. (1990). Endogenous technological change, *Journal of Political Economy*, 98: S71–S102.

Romer, P. (1994). The origins of endogenous growth, *Journal of Economic Perspectives*, 8: 3–22.

Sala-I-Martin, X. (1997). I just ran two million regressions, *American Economic Review*, 87: 178–183.

Salmon, W. and P. Kitcher (1989). *Scientific Explanation*, Minneapolis: University of Minnesota Press.

Samuelson, P. (1966). A summing up, *Quarterly Journal of Economics*, 568–583.

Siamwalla, A., C. Pinchong, P. Satsanguan, P. Nettayarak, W. Minggmaneenakin and Y. Tubpan (1993). The Thai rural credit system and elements of a theory, in K. Hoff, A. Braverman, and J. Stiglitz (eds), *The Economics of Rural Organization*. Oxford: Oxford University Press.

Solow, R. (1956). A contribution to the theory of economic growth, *Quarterly Journal of Economics*, 70: 65–94.

Udry, C. (1993). Credit markets in northern Nigeria: credit as insurance in a rural economy, in K. Hoff, A. Braverman, and J. Stiglitz (eds), *The Economics of Rural Organization*, Oxford: Oxford University Press.

5 The political economy of statistical evidence

Economic data problems in developing countries and their impact on empirical research*

Hashem Dezhbakhsh

1 Introduction

A distinctive characteristic of the 'new economy' is its historically unparalleled reliance on information, and especially on numbers and data. The quantification of human civilization and the advent of computers have diminished the cost of generating and handling large volumes of data, leading to a 'numbers explosion' during the second half of the twentieth century. While quantities have been expanding dramatically, their quality has advanced only modestly. Mismeasurement of economic variables, missing observations, and administrative intervention to *re-form* the data for political purposes all detract from the reliability of economic data. Bad numbers, in turn, may have devastating repercussions in scientific inquiries, governmental policies and actions, and policy evaluation.

Data problems loom much larger in the developing countries, where resources devoted to data collection are scarce, where information infrastructure is weak or non-existent, and where politics may play a large role in shaping the data. In this chapter, I address these issues as they relate to economic research and policy formulation and evaluation in the developing countries. I enumerate the most common data shortfalls and identify the factors that contribute to them. I then discuss the statistical consequences of flawed data and specific remedies that researchers and authorities seeking to reform the data collection process can use. An important question here is 'how can the problem be diminished before we can even contemplate its eradication'? Authorities need to allocate more resources to improve the quality and quantity of data by reforming the data collection process.

In absence of high-quality data, researchers must rely on econometric methods that are appropriate for weak data to safeguard their findings. Unfortunately, this does not seem to be the prevailing practice. I conducted a survey of leading economic journals in the areas of development and international economics to examine the current practice of analyzing bad data. The results are alarming, as only a fraction of the surveyed empirical studies seem to deal effectively with data problems. The lack of attentiveness to data problems at the highest level of research warrants attention, given that empirical findings help shape public and business policy. I will also explore policy consequences of using bad data without econometric correctives.

This study is intended to bring the severity of developing countries data problems to the attention of practitioners and generate discussions that will hopefully lead to a more balanced and reasoned use of econometric methods for bad data. Such a balance will have a positive impact on the quality of empirical economic research, thereby contributing to better economic policy and more reliable policy evaluations in developing countries. Given the obstacles that the developing countries face in financing their economic growth (Stiglitz, 2005), unreliable data and invalid program and policy evaluation can only compound the existing risk, making investment in these countries less attractive both for foreigners and domestic investors.

The chapter is organized as follows. Section two specifies the various shortcomings of economic data in the developing countries. Section three describes how each shortcoming can affect statistical inference. Section four details the steps that can be taken to mitigate data problems. Section five presents the results of a survey conducted to examine the current practice of analyzing contaminated data. This section also explores how inadequate treatment of bad data may misguide policy. Section six offers a summary and some concluding remarks.

2 Economic data and data problems in developing countries

There are two kinds of economic data, experimental and non-experimental. Experimental data are usually obtained from controlled experiments; non-experimental data are generated by society and collected passively. Since most data problems originate from non-experimental data, I focus exclusively on this type of data. Much of the non-experimental data are collected for administrative purposes, and initially from tax and customs collection records. This has given rise to the term 'found data', which reflects the researchers' lack of influence on data collection and overall data quality.[1]

Economic data can also be characterized by form – time series, cross section, or panel – or the level of aggregation – macro or micro. Surveys conducted by various government agencies, international organizations, or private parties provide large amounts of microdata. Economic data are susceptible to various problems, depending on their type, collection method, and collecting agent.

Data problems have been known for decades. Morgenstern (1963), for example, warns the profession about the inaccuracy of economic data and the perils of using these data without any consideration of their error and its possible influence on the analysis. He urges the economic profession not to operate under the pretense that economic data enjoy a high level of precision. Leontief (1971) criticizes the common practice of 'stretching to the limit the meager supply of facts', arguing that the glaring weakness of the data cannot be compensated for by econometric sophistication alone. He calls for a sharp increase in resources allocated to data collection and maintenance, admitting, however, that such calls never seem urgent enough to have an impact. Griliches (1986) acknowledges that there are still many conceptual and practical problems in using economic data, despite considerable progress in data quality and quantity and the econometrics of deficient data.

Most data problems in economics can be classified as measurement error, missing observations, or aberrant data. Measurement error can affect both microdata and macrodata. In general, mismeasurement can be due to inaccurate survey response related to falsification or misunderstanding, administrative data-tampering, reporting of provisional macroeconomic data, or errors of transcription, recording, or transmission. Mismeasured durations, for example, are common traits of many survey responses. Hausman (2001) notes that more than one-third of workers overstate the duration of their unemployment in the Current Population Survey, and the error is larger for longer spells. Another common measurement error originates in provisional macrodata – the early reports on economic variables like GDP that later go through several rounds of revision. The error is argued to be due to either the inadequacy of the information used to construct the early estimates or the non-representativeness of samples on which these estimates are predicated (see, e.g., Mankiw and Shapiro, 1986). World Development Report also regularly warns against using data of different vintages published in various editions of World Bank publications (see, e.g., World Bank, 1997).

Macroeconomic time series may be missing observations due to war, civil crises, or other exigencies. Long historical data may also lack regularly collected observations of the distant past. Missing or incomplete data is a problem that affects both microdata and macrodata. Observations can also be excluded from the sample for a variety of reasons. In survey-based microdata, for example, respondents may miss (or avoid) some items or give incorrect answers, or an interviewer may miss recording a response. Moreover, sampled subjects may choose not to respond to the survey at all, or they may be excluded by interviewers, causing coverage error. The problem is far more serious if the unavailability of observations is due to sample- or self-selection. This is called 'behavioral missing', because the exclusion of subjects or their failure to respond to some survey items is induced by some of their common characteristics.

Aberrant observations and outliers generated by peculiar data or gross mistakes are the source of yet another data problem. Unusual political, economic, or natural events – such as floods, earthquakes, hurricanes, or other natural calamities – cause transient changes that lead to observations that are several orders of magnitude different than the norm. Similarly, sudden political or economic changes can severely disturb markets for a short period of time, leading to a few unusual data points. Moreover, mistakes can be made in recording or transcribing the data – a misplaced decimal point or an extra zero can change the magnitude of an observation enormously. Unusual data points may go unnoticed by researchers, given the extensive use of computers in copying data.

The magnitude of data problems varies across countries, depending on political, institutional, and economic factors. The problem is particularly serious in developing countries, where data collection efforts suffer from a multitude of shortfalls including sparse resources, inadequate institutional infrastructure, and inappropriate political intervention aimed at *reforming* the data.

Political considerations, for example, may influence economic data. Drawing on existing evidence, Griliches (1986) argues that the national income statistics for some of the developing countries are 'more political than economic documents'. Governments may falsify statistics to improve their image or gain strategic advantage when negotiating with other countries. To avoid admitting the lack of data, officials may also create data without much empirical basis. The attempts by government officials to create or alter data detract from the reliability of economic data and distort the factual basis of statistical evidence.

Atkinson and Brandolini (2001) raise concerns about the quality and consistency of 'secondary' data sets complied by various authors. These data sets that are used increasingly in empirical economic research consist of a series covering a large number of variables and countries (e.g., Summers and Heston, 1991; Easterly and Rebelo, 1993; Barro and Lee, 1996, and the income distribution data sets assembled by the World Bank (n.d.) and the United Nations). For illustration, Atkinson and Brandolini (2001) document problems in income distribution data, using examples from OECD countries. The criticism applies equally, and perhaps to a greater extent, to the 'secondary' data for developing countries. One of the most widely used secondary data sets is the Penn World Table (2002) that displays national expenditure series, relative prices within and between countries, demographic data, and capital stock estimates. The expenditure entries in the table are denominated in common prices and a common currency to facilitate international comparisons. Summers and Heston (1991) report estimates of the quality of data for 138 countries in the Penn World Table (Mark 5). The quality grades range from A to D with some pluses and minuses. The scores for most developing countries are in the C and D range.

Microdata, and particularly survey-based series, are becoming more

Figure 5.1 Lorenz curve.

available in developing countries. National agencies in many developing countries, for example, have recently expanded their data collecting activity. Many of these agencies, however, have the responsibility of monitoring and evaluating development programs rather than collecting official statistics, so their staff does not have adequate training in survey methods (Casley and Lury, 1987). The quality of much of these data are, consequently, suspect.[2]

International agencies also initiate and/or supervise microdata collection. Among the programs launched for this purpose are the Household Survey Capability and World Fertility Survey Programs sponsored by the UN, anthropometric surveys of young children instituted by the WHO and UNICEF to determine nutritional status, and the Living Standard Measurement Study of the World Bank to improve the type and quality of household data in twenty developing countries. Much of the developing countries' microdata, nonetheless, are still replete with measurement errors, missing observations, and selectivity bias (see, e.g., Casley and Lury, 1987; Tybout, 1990).

Authors have also documented serious inaccuracies in international trade data. Several decades ago, Morgenstern (1963) reported significant disparities in the trade statistics of exporting and importing countries. The error as a percentage of world export ranged from 12.3 percent in 1938, the first sampled year, to 2.4 percent in 1953 and then up to 5.1 percent in 1960, the last sampled year. These estimates are derived from aggregate trade volumes, and errors for most individual countries are much larger.

Not much has changed since then, as the error in trade statistics still looms large. For example, Rozanski and Yeats' (1994) finding about the internal consistency of trade data is, in their own terms, 'disquieting'. They examined the consistency of (i) trade data under different UN classification schemes, (ii) trade statistics compiled by one reporting agency (UN) with those reported by another agency (IMF), (iii) total trade with the sum of trade with individual partner countries, and (iv) total trade with the sum of less aggregated trade components. They find significant discrepancies in all four categories. For developing countries, some of the classification-based discrepancies averaged over 60 percent in the early 1980s, and the discrepancies in trade values reported by different agencies exceed 100 percent in many cases. The inconsistencies between total trade and the sum of its components also worsened during the late 1980s and early 1990s.

Since many developing countries do not report trade statistics to the United Nations, partner–country data are widely used to fill the gap. Yeats (1995) reports that these data are unreliable even for estimating trade in broad aggregates such as foodstuffs, fuels, and manufactures. Yeats' analysis that covers thirty developing countries also shows that partner–country data are equally inaccurate for estimating the direction of trade.

The developing countries data problems are rarely brought to the attention of the global public. These include cases involving the under-reporting of epidemic diseases. Recently, for example, attempts to conceal the gravity of the AIDS epidemic in Africa have made it to the popular press. Most data shortcomings, however, still remain in the academic domain, never gaining the urgency needed for change.

3 Statistical inference with problematic data

Since regression methods play a central role in economic research, I use them to illustrate the consequences of using bad data. Data problems include measurement error, missing data, and outliers, which are all too frequently encountered in practice.

3.1 Measurement error

Mismeasured or misrepresented data leads to invalid inference when no corrective measure is adopted to deal with the problem. In a regression context, for example, the errors contaminate the dependent variables and/or the explanatory variables. For illustration, consider the standard linear model

$$y_i = X_i\beta + \epsilon_i, \tag{5.1}$$

where X_i denotes a set of explanatory variables, β is a k-element coefficient vector, and ϵ's are regression errors (disturbances).[3] Assume the dependent variable is measured with error; so, $y_i^* = y_i + u_i$, where y_i^* is the error-infested variable, y_i is the unobserved (unreported) error-free variable, and u_i is the measurement error. Here the least squares estimate of β is still consistent and the standard restriction tests about β are valid, provided that the measurement error u_i has zero mean and is not correlated with X_i. The measurement error, however, reduces the estimation accuracy, as the estimable equation, $y_i^* = X_i\beta + \epsilon_i + u_i$, has a compound error term. If the measurement errors are heteroskedastic or serially correlated, an appropriate generalized least squares method, or at least robust asymptotic standard errors, should be used.

The problem is more serious when one or more of the explanatory variables are measured with error. For example, let $X_i^* = X_i + V_i$, where X_i^* is a vector of error-infested variables, X_i denotes the corresponding unobserved and error-free variables, and V_i denotes a vector of measurement errors. Note that some elements of V_i may be zero as some of the explanatory variables may be measured without error. The least squares estimator of β in this case may be expressed as

$$\hat{\beta}' = \beta + (X^{*'}X^*)^{-1}X^{*'}(-V\beta + E), \tag{5.2}$$

where X^* is a matrix of observations on all explanatory variables, V is the corresponding matrix of measurement errors, and E contains the regression errors, ϵ's. The second term on the right-hand side of equation (5.2) captures the estimation bias that can be evaluated by taking the probability limit (plim) of both sides of this equation. This yields

$$\text{bias} = Q^{-1}\left(-\text{plim}\left(\frac{X^{*'}V}{N}\right)\beta + \text{plim}\left(\frac{X^{*'}E}{N}\right)\right), \tag{5.3}$$

where N is the number of observations and Q is the limiting cross-moment matrix of the observed explanatory variables.

Note that even when measurement errors have zero mean and are independent of the regression errors, the bias will not vanish, as the bracketed term is usually non-zero. This implies that the least-squares estimate of the coefficient(s) of the mismeasured explanatory variables are inconsistent and any restriction tests based on these estimates are invalid. More importantly, the estimates of the other coefficients in β are also inconsistent in the usual case where some of the explanatory variables are correlated. The transmission of the bias from the estimated coefficient(s) of the erroneous variable(s) to the rest of the estimated coefficients adds to the severity of the problem.

The estimation bias can be theoretically evaluated only in special cases where the measurement errors are assumed to follow a set of assumptions like identical distribution, zero mean, serial independence, and independence from other model variables. This restrictive structure can still characterize errors observed in a variety of microdata sets (Griliches, 1986). Although the direction of the bias cannot be ascertained without these assumptions, the inconsistency of the coefficient estimates can still be demonstrated.

When the dependent and some of the explanatory variables are mismeasured, the bias becomes similar to the case of mismeasured explanatory variables, only with added inaccuracy due to the compounding of errors. Measurement error has a biasing effect also on nonlinear, probit, logit, duration, and hazard models (see, e.g., Hausman, 2001).

3.2 Missing data and outliers

Measurement error seems to be the econometricians' 'favorite' data ailment, but there are other commonly encountered data problems that deserve attention. Missing or incomplete data, for example, is a problem that affects both micro- and macrodata. The problem is far more serious if the unavailability of observations is due to sample-selection or self-selection. Parameter estimates obtained from such samples are generally biased and restriction tests are invalid.

In cases where selection bias is absent, missing some observations on one or more variables only leads to a lower estimation accuracy.[4] The loss of information in such cases obviously leads to loss of efficiency. In these less harmful cases, observations do not need to be randomly missing. In other words, it is not necessary for the missing observations to have the same distribution as the available observations to avoid biased estimation. As long as there is no self-selection, the damage is limited to a loss in precision, even if missing observations all have higher values, for example, than the available observations.

The presence of outliers also introduces problems that are quite common but often ignored. Unlike mismeasured variables, the outliers generated by unusual events are not necessarily erroneous because these observations may be correctly measured and recorded. The statistical framework used to examine and treat such outliers is, therefore, different than the one used to examine the classical measurement error problem. The same holds true for outliers caused by gross recording or keypunch errors. These are occasional blunders that are too sporadic to be treated as standard measurement errors, which are usually systematic and persistent.

The least-squares regression is particularly susceptible to outliers. Even a few outliers can change the coefficient estimates significantly. Textbook examples demonstrate how the addition of one outlier can make a positive slope estimate negative (see, e.g., Rousseeuw and Leroy, 1987). Unfortunately, outliers, and particularly those in explanatory variables, are not easy to detect with residual diagnosis. In such cases, outliers may form leverage points that have a large influence on the parameters' estimates. Leverage points are usually masked when one tries to identify them by inspecting the regression residual. Such inspection often results in misclassifying good data points as outliers. I will discuss robust methods that are developed to deal with outliers in section four.

4 Remedies: better data, better methods, and better applications

The discussion in the previous section indicated that problem data can lead to invalid statistical inference. Practitioners, however, often ignore data problems. Bad data can misguide research and any policy that is predicated on empirical findings. The problem is too complex for a quick fix. The involved parties, however, can implement strategies aimed at mitigating the problem and diminish its undesired repercussions. Simply put, the trinity of better data, better methods, and better applications should constitute the core of a solution. Improving data quality and availability is the task of government agencies and international organizations that collect and maintain data. Making the best use of the available data, on the other hand, is a responsibility of the economists. In particular, econometricians should develop better methods and practitioners should implement the best available methods to deal with data shortcomings. Econometric software developers can also play a critical role in making advanced technologies easily accessible to researchers.

4.1 Econometric remedies

An extreme view in econometrics maintains that there are no data problems, since for any set of data there is a right model; the problem is to find it.[5] Although the mainstream sentiments in econometrics are far from this view, considerable effort has gone into developing statistical methods that are specifically designed to analyze flawed data. In fact, the econometricians have even led the statisticians in developing methods that correct for measurement errors or selectivity problems.

Econometricians have studied measurement error for decades, developing solutions that are based primarily on instrumental variables. In the most basic case, where the errors in explanatory variable(s) are independent (serially and also from other model variables) and identically distributed with zero mean, an instrument that is independent of the regression errors but correlated with the explanatory variable(s) will produce consistent estimation and valid restriction tests. The instrumental variable (IV) estimator in this case is

$$\beta'_{IV} = (Z'X^*)^{-1}(Z'Y), \tag{5.4}$$

where X^* and Y are defined in section three and Z is the matrix of instruments. High correlation between the instruments and the explanatory variables enhances estimation accuracy by producing smaller standard errors.[6]

Selection of instruments turns out to be an arduous job in practice. Various methods have been offered to choose instruments and to examine their adequacy in the basic model as well as models with more elaborate measurement error schemes (see, e.g., Griliches and Hausman, 1986; Lewbel, 1997; Wooldridge, 2000; Hausman, 2001; Hahn and Hausman, 2002). Potential instruments include group averages of contaminated observations, lagged values of the model variables, linear functions of several instruments and model variables, and the rank vector(s) corresponding to observations on the explanatory variable(s).[7] Ranks are reasonable instruments, particularly when measurement errors leave the *relative* magnitude of most observations unchanged.

Methods that deal with measurement errors in more complicated econometric models are also available. These include panel data models (Griliches and Hausman, 1986), non-linear models (Hausman and Newey, 1991, and Hausman *et al.*, 1995), binary choice models (Hausman *et al.*, 1998), and discrete choice, duration, and hazard models (Abrevaya and Hausman, 1999).

There are also methods to deal with missing data points. In cases where time-series observations are missing, simple techniques like replacing a missing value with an adjacent observation as well as more sophisticated techniques like interpolation, forecasting based on related series, and state–space modeling and Kalman filters are recommended (see, e.g., Chow and Lin, 1971; Harvey and Pierse, 1984; Harvey *et al.*, 1998; Ryan and Giles, 1998).

When cross-section or panel data have missing observations, other variables (in or outside the model) can be used to predict the missing values and enhance estimation accuracy. Alternatively, the model can be fitted to the observed variance–covariance matrices that summarize the available data (see, e.g., Gourieroux and Monfort, 1981; Bound *et al.*, 1986; Griliches, 1986). In cases where selectivity is present, which include the standard sample- and self-selection cases as well as survivorship cases in financial data analysis and attrition cases in clinical research, selectivity correction needs to be made to avoid biased estimation (see, e.g., Heckman, 1990).

There are statistical methods that deal with outliers in regression analysis. Two interrelated approaches are available for this purpose. First, one can rely on the existing outlier detection techniques to identify and remove outliers, particularly in situations where leverage points – points that have unusually large influence on estimation outcome – are present. Simple data plots may be useful in identifying outliers, but mainly in bivariate regression. Even then, residual plots can be misleading, because leverage points are often masked as the least-squares regression line gravitates toward these points, making the corresponding residuals small. This point does not seem to be well known by data specialists who recommend casual inspection of residuals plots as a way of retaining contact with the data, or practitioners who follow such advice (see, e.g., Casley and Lury, 1987).

The situation is more complicated in multivariate regression, and particularly when there are multiple outliers. In such cases, a subset of observations are outlying in the multidimensional scatter of points generated by explanatory observations. Statistical procedures have been developed, however, that use repeated sorting of observations and robust estimates of location and scale to identify such points. While the older outlier detection methods are powerful in cases with a single outlier, the new methods can detect multiple outliers (see, e.g., Cook, 1977; Rousseeuw and van Zomeren, 1990; Hadi, 1992).

The second approach for treating outliers involves using robust methods to perform data analysis, especially in cases where the regression design is simple. Robust estimators are designed to estimate the parameters of a probability model by emphasizing the bulk of the data and reducing the influence of gross errors that may show up as outliers. Under ideal data conditions, robust estimators preserve many of the desirable statistical properties of their classical counterparts.[8]

Yet, robust estimators outperform classical estimators in the presence of gross measurement error in the data or when basic assumptions like normality are violated – a situation that may rise when regression errors are compounded with measurement errors in the dependent variable. Nonetheless, robust methods are rarely used in economics. Indeed, the commonly used linear regression analysis in economics is almost exclusively based on the classical least-squares method. This practice prevails despite ample evidence suggesting that the least-squares estimators are highly fragile, so even a small departure from the assumed ideal conditions has a serious effect on their performance.

The robust alternatives to the least-squares estimators in the linear model are the L-, M-, and R-estimators specifically chosen because their large sample distribution in the present context is known. The L-estimator is based on linear combinations of ordered statistics. The least absolute deviation estimator is an example of an L-estimator. The M-estimator is obtained by optimizing based on pseudo-likelihood functions of the sample. The R-estimator is based on linear rank procedures that minimize functions of residual ranks, rather than residuals, to derive parameter estimates.[9] These methods can provide useful alternatives to the least-squares method of regression analysis in cases where outliers, sporadic errors, local contamination of data, or non-normality of errors are suspected.

Econometrics has made considerable progress in the area of measurement error. The issue is now considered important enough that many textbooks devote a whole chapter to it. Nonetheless, there is still a long way to go. For example, the scope of the error-in-variable model has extended far beyond the linear regression model. But we have not moved far enough from the convenient assumptions of the ideal measurement error. Absent, for example, are remedies useful for a wide range of commonly encountered measurement error schemes – e.g., errors with an unknown serial correlation pattern and non-orthogonal to the model variables.[10] The robust regression methods also are still in their early development stage when compared to least squares.

Invention of new techniques is necessary but not sufficient to help overcome statistical problems induced by flawed data. The diffusion of these techniques is equally important. But new methods can disseminate only if they are incorporated in statistical software packages. In this area, software developers can help by making new methods accessible, functional, and user friendly.

4.2 Institutional remedies

Despite the remarkable econometric progress in mitigating the ill-effects of bad data, data problems still exist that cannot be treated, or even formulated, absent an exhaustive statistical theory. We might, indeed, be at a point of diminishing marginal returns on minor technical enhancements. An alternative and promising strategy is to enhance the quality and availability of data, particularly in developing countries where there is ample room for improvement. Governmental agencies as well as international institutions that collect and maintain data must play a leading role in reforming data collection.

Conducting more surveys and improving survey techniques are important for microdata. There are calls to investigate the activities of masses of population rather than refine macro indices (Casley and Lury, 1987). In the USA and other industrialized countries, periodic collection of large labor force data has become routine. Given the widespread use of these longitudinal data sets and the econometric advances in this area, it is wise to direct more resources toward collecting such data in developing countries. In fact, there are real benefits to be gained from incorporating panel elements into household surveys, despite the possibility of measurement error (Ashenfelter *et al.*, 1997). The task, however, is complicated because many developing countries are in the state of rapid economic, demographic, and cultural transition. Those who design surveys need to be mindful of the transition dynamics.

Collecting more data is not the only solution to the data problems in developing countries. Indeed, as Casley and Lury (1987) argue, there has been an explosion of data collected by agencies not officially in charge of data collection. Such data are often collected to monitor and evaluate specific agricultural and development programs. The staff who design or implement surveys often do not have adequate training or experience in modern survey methods. For a transition from judgment surveys to probability-based survey sampling, a professionally trained staff is imperative.

These initiatives should not be limited to collecting data. Transforming data into useful information presented in easily accessible medias are equally important. There is evidence that in some developing countries collected raw data are permanently buried in the bureaucrats' desk drawers (Mule, 1993). Moreover, data collection efforts by a multitude of sources including governmental agencies, universities, research institutes, and individuals may strain the already scarce data collection resources. There are synergies and complementarities that can be exploited through better communication and coordination among the concerned parties.

Aggregate time-series data also need improvement. Data-tampering and other administrative interferences will only harm empirical research and any policy predicated on such research. The involved agencies should also work toward reducing the lag in reporting aggregate economic data to ensure the timeliness of empirical findings.

Many researchers obtain their data from international organizations who compile much of the developing countries data.[11] Given the discrepancies between data reported by various sources, the reporting organizations need to better coordinate data compilation and recording efforts. It will be useful, moreover, if these organizations regularly evaluate the data, and accordingly assign data quality grades. Currently, the UN classifies the trade data for various countries into D Series and non-D Series based on the quality of the reported data. The former series covering about 100 countries are supposedly of a higher quality. Such classification, however, does not have enough gradation to be useful. The detailed grading scheme that Summers and Heston (1991) report for The Penn World Table of national accounts series is far more informative.

Detailed grades assigned to data serve two purposes. First, they can help improve research outcomes, as they convey an explicit message that has a pressuring effect on authors. They may also induce the reviewers – in journals or sponsoring agencies – to demand proper treatment of low-quality data. Second, the grading can provide incentives for countries to improve their data quality and ranking, at least for national image and public relations.

Collecting data is a resource-intensive undertaking, and so is reforming data collection and compilation. The above remedies, therefore, are quite costly. But just like any other allocative decision, the costs must be evaluated against alternative scenarios. Data deficiencies can lead to invalid statistical inference and flawed empirical work that, in turn, misguides public and business policy. The costs of bad policy can far exceed the cost requirements of better data. Data collection costs should be viewed as investment expenses because any data collected currently will benefit generations of researchers.

5 Current practices and their implications for policy

Four decades ago, Oskar Morgenstern wrote

> We observe that *at least all sources of error that occur in the natural sciences also occur in the social sciences*: or, in other words, the statistical problems of the social sciences cannot possibly be less serious than those of the natural sciences. ... Consequently, the treatment of errors of observation in the social sciences has to be at least as severe as those used in the natural sciences. In fact, however, there is much less occupation with errors than in the other fields.
>
> (Morgenstern, 1963: 7)

The lack of attentiveness to data errors that Morgenstern alludes to appears to be still pervasive and deeply rooted, particularly in empirical studies on the developing countries. For instance, the only econometric textbook written specifically for data analysis for developing countries does not have any discussion of measurement error (Mukherjee *et al.*, 1998). In fact, the words 'measurement error' do not even appear in the book's subject index.[12] This omission perhaps exemplifies the attitude of practitioners who work with developing countries' data.

5.1 Journal survey

To examine how detached is the empirical research on the developing countries from data realities, I conducted a survey of the three top journals in development and international trade. The survey identifies cases where authors take steps to deal with the common data shortcomings discussed earlier. The sampled journals were *Journal of Development Economics*, *Journal of International Economics*, and *Economic Development and Cultural Change*. The first two are the leading journals in development and international trade, respectively. The third journal is the highest ranked development journal according to *Journal Citation Report – Social Science Edition*, 1999. I chose this journal to include more studies on developing countries. All three journals publish a large number of empirical studies. The sampling period is 1996 through 1999.[13] The time requirement of reviewing every page of every sampled issue prohibits using more journals or a longer time span.

The survey results are reported in Table 5.1. The first column gives the journal names and publication dates. The second column reports the number of articles published in each journal during the entire sampling period as well as the number of articles in all three journals during each sampled year. In this column, the counts include both empirical and theoretical articles – narrative as well as formal theory. These numbers also include short articles and notes. (The counts for short articles and notes are reported separately in parentheses). The third column presents the number of empirical articles in each case, defined as any article containing data analysis.[14] The fourth column reports the number of empirical articles that acknowledge data shortcomings and take corrective action. The corresponding percentages are reported in brackets. In identifying these articles I have been rather admissive; any article dealing with one type of data problem was included even if it did not correct for other existing problems. About one-third of the reported corrections relate to the selectivity problem.

Table 5.1 Survey results: articles that deal with data problems

Journal	Number of articles including (short papers or notes)	Number of empirical articles [as percentage of all articles]	Number of empirical articles that deal with data problems [as percentage of all empirical articles]
Journal of International Economics	187 (1)	76 [40.6]	8 [10.5]
Journal of Development Economics	259 (27)	146 [56.4]	16 [10.9]
Economic Development and Cultural Change	137 (3)	118 [86.1]	10 [8.5]
Total:	583 (31)	340 [58.3]	34 [10.0]
Breakdown by year			
1996	137 (4)	81 [59.1]	7 [8.6]
1997	146 (8)	77 [52.7]	5 [6.5]
1998	140 (8)	91 [65.0]	9 [9.9]
1999	160 (11)	91 [56.9]	13 [14.3]

Notes
The counts in the second column include both empirical and theoretical articles. These numbers include, in parentheses, the number of short papers or notes. The third column presents the number of empirical articles, defined as any article containing data analysis. The fourth column reports the number of empirical articles that acknowledge data shortcomings and take corrective action. The corresponding percentages are reported in brackets.

It is observed that only a small fraction of the sampled articles address data deficiencies.[15] The two leading journals have a slightly larger share of these articles, and a small upward trend is detected in the percentage of articles that treat data problems. The differences, however, are too small to warrant any definitive inference. While conducting the survey I noticed that many authors, indeed, admit that their data have serious weaknesses but neglect to deal with them. Appearing unaware of econometric remedies, some authors declare in an exonerative passive language that 'better data must be collected'. The pervasiveness of the problem and the serious consequences that it may have warrants attention by journal editors and reviewers.

Unsound empirical practices are usually disseminated from journal articles to policy-oriented research conducted at various national and international agencies. One may wonder if neglecting data problems is equally common in the resulting policy reports and working documents. Generally speaking, the leading journals usually have the highest quality standards. It is, therefore, unlikely that data issues receive a more prominent treatment in other outlets. My search of the World Bank's electronic working papers, moreover, turned out very few studies that deal with data issues. I have referenced these studies at various places in the paper. Unlike the journal survey, this heuristic search was conducted electronically, using various combinations of key words – e.g., data problems, data shortcomings, data quality, missing observations, measurement error, outliers, etc.

5.2 Can flawed data and econometrics misguide policy? Some exploratory evidence

Data flaws can undoubtedly affect empirical results. Skeptics may wonder, however, whether guarding against the foibles of data, by using econometric methods that are less affected by data flaws, has any material impact on empirical findings and, consequently, on policy. For one thing, even if the choice of method did not considerably alter empirical results, the researcher is still scientifically obliged to employ the most appropriate method. A conservative and cautious approach can make empirical results more credible, particularly when research has a policy-specific destination. The following examples bring to bear the potential impact of data flaws and econometric choices on empirical findings and, perhaps, policies concerning the developing countries.

Several influential growth studies use constructed series for developing countries but fail to deal adequately with data problems. Devarajan *et al.* (1996) criticize these studies for using series constructed from World Bank reports on public investment in individual developing countries.[16] They blame the errors in such data for the sharp contrast between their findings that public investment in capital goods has a negative effect on growth and opposite findings by the studies they criticize. Devarajan *et al.*, however, do not question their own data, that are also constructed from reports by international organizations, even though their result reverses when they limit their sample to the developed countries with better quality data. The negative effect of public investment on growth that they report, therefore, can be an artifact of flawed data for developing countries. Here a policy change might be recommended based on analysis of bad data.

De la Fuente and Domenech (2000) argue that a recent counter-intuitive finding that educational investment does not affect growth may be an artifact of poor data quality. After revising and supplementing the data for a sample of OECD countries, they uncover a positive relationship between growth and the stock of human capital. The change in finding here has, obviously, a significant policy implication.

Nugent (1983) argues that the measurement error in survey data distorts the estimated relationship between income inequality and income level (Kuznets' inverted-U hypothesis) that many authors report. The errors are due to variations in survey response rates, selectivity bias in responses, and temporal invariance of income brackets despite changes in cost of living.

Fisman and Svensson (2000) examine the effect of taxation and bribery on firm growth in Uganda using a panel data set. The initial results suggest a negative and significant effect for taxation but none for bribery. After correcting for measurement error and outliers by using instrumental variable methods and outlier detection techniques, the effect of bribery on growth becomes significantly negative, while the tax effect is reduced. This is a great example of how examining data quality can alter policy implications of empirical research.

Tybout (1990) uses two methods to estimate indices of the return to scale, and the distance between the efficient frontier and actual output as well as the efficient factor mix and the actual utilization for five industries in Chile in 1979. One method corrects for measurement error, missing observations, and selectivity bias, and the other does not. He finds that the results are affected by the estimation choice.

Levy and Dezhbakhsh (2003) relate the size of the business cycle component of a country's output to its income level for 23 OECD countries and 35 developing countries. They find a positive relationship for OECD countries but none for developing countries. Suspecting that this could be an artifact of bad data, they revise their analysis for the developing countries using Summers and Heston's (1991) data quality rankings to identify problem cases and define instrumental variables. The revised results suggest that the income-cycle relationship also holds for developing countries.

The above anecdotes suggest that data quality and the choice of econometric method do, indeed, change empirical findings and their policy implications.[17] Whether such changes can redirect public and private business policy depends on the extent of research influence on policy formation. In cases where the influence is strong, altered findings can lead to policy change.

6 Concluding remarks

> If a man will begin with certainties, he shall end in doubts; but if he will be content to begin with doubts, he shall end in certainties.
>
> (Francis Bacon)

Empirical economic research not only shapes theory but also affects policies of the public and private sectors. Empirical findings concerning the developing countries are suspect, however, because of the low quality of these countries' data and the lack of attention to data problems in practice.[18] Indeed, the empirical findings in this area resemble the output of a production process with inadequate input and deficient production technology.

This study is intended to warn against the evils of bad data and provide a constructive criticism of current empirical practices. The evidence discussed here suggests that economic data for developing countries suffer from a variety of problems, some serious enough to invalidate empirical results if data inadequacies are not recognized in the analysis. A survey of leading journals in development and international trade reported here indicates, however, that most empirical studies do not take data issues seriously. They fail to acknowledge data problems and to use, accordingly, methods that can mitigate the effect of bad data. This apparent neglect has serious implications for empirical findings, especially those used for policy purposes. I discussed some of these implications drawing on exploratory evidence.

While the problem of bad data in developing countries cannot be resolved quickly, strategies can be adopted to mitigate the problem and diminish its undesired repercussions. Such strategies should promote collecting better data, developing better econometric methods for the analysis of inadequate data, and fostering better applications of existing econometric methods. Government agencies and international organizations that collect and maintain data shoulder the responsibility of improving data quality and availability. Making the best use of the available data is a responsibility of the empirical economists. Economics journals have the critical responsibility of setting high standards for empirical research that utilizes doubtful data and enforcing them.

Dewald *et al.* (1986) examined the role of replication in empirical economics and discussed numerous problems they faced in replicating articles published in the *Journal of Money, Credit and Banking* (the JMCB Project). Their findings were alarming enough to prompt some journals to require authors to submit their data for possible replication. Similarly, a debate about the serious limitations of policy-oriented research that draws on deficient data from developing countries can affect the refereeing policies of journals, leading to more solid norms. These in turn can affect empirical research both at the academy and agencies that sponsor policy-oriented research on developing countries. Moreover, such debate can attract the attention of policy makers and, consequently, draw more resources to data collection and compilation.

Notes

* I gratefully acknowledge helpful comments by Robert Chirinko, Milton Kafoglis, Manoucher Parvin, and Joseph Stiglitz, and research assistance by Soyong Chong, Erika Heaton, and Azita Samim. I am also thankful to the organizers of the Conference on Development Issues in the New Economy and particularly Melvin Ayogu and Don Ross. The responsibility for errors, however, rests alone with me.
1 Recently, economists have become increasingly involved in collecting data with longitudinal surveys intended to evaluate government programs.
2 The edited volume by von Braun and Puetz (1993) includes several accounts of microdata deficiencies in the area of food demand and consumption in the developing countries.
3 Greene (2000), for example, discusses the assumptions of the standard linear model.
4 Note that when all observations on a particular variable are missing we have an omitted variable problem which usually leads to biased estimation and invalid tests (see, e.g., Greene, 2000).
5 See, e.g., Hendry (1983).
6 Fuller (1987) is a valuable reference in this area.
7 The rank of each observation in a set of N observations is a number between 1 and N that corresponds to the location of that observation when the observations are ordered from smallest to largest.
8 An example of a classical estimator is the arithmetic mean commonly used to estimate the center of a probability distribution. The median and the trimmed mean, which is obtained by ignoring a percentage of the extreme points, are among the robust estimators of this location parameter.
9 Hettmansperger (1984), Hampel et al. (1986), and Rousseeuw and Leroy (1987) are excellent references in this area.
10 A case in point is the infamous CPI bias for the USA. The bias is neither IID nor uncorrelated with the regression errors that incorporate policy shocks. It may also contain an upward trend, given the positive error in inflation estimates.
11 The list of these organizations is long, but the IMF, World Bank, UN, OECD and WTO are among those who compile the most widely used data.
12 The book has a brief discussion of outliers in the general context of specification issues. The discussion, however, does not relate to data problems in developing countries.
13 I chose 1999 as the ending period, because at the time of survey some of the 2000 and 2001 issues were at binding and hence not available for review.
14 Theoretical articles that include parameter simulation, survey articles, and articles that report statistics from other studies without any analysis are not included in the empirical counts.
15 Inadequate use of econometrics is not limited to studies on developing countries. Dezhbakhsh's (1990) survey of four prestigious economic journals over

1982–1987 reveals that the most commonly used test for serial correlation in dynamic linear models is inappropriate for such applications. The most appropriate test in such a case is the least commonly used.

16 Two such studies are Easterly and Rebelo (1993), who admit their data contain 'substantial measurement error' but chose not to deal with it, and Barro (1991), who is concerned with the systematic measurement problems of the dependent variable, particularly for low-income countries.

17 While the examples provided here all relate to the developing countries, bad data also affects empirical findings reported for the industrialized countries; see, e.g., Goolsbee (2000) who shows that measurement error in the cost of capital in the USA reduces the estimated effect of taxes on investment by as much as a factor of four.

18 A related problem is the adequate implementation of policy, which can be equally harmful to the developing countries. Okeahalam (2003) examines this problem for the financial sectors in a number of African countries.

References

Abrevaya, J. and J. Hausman (1999). Semiparametric estimation with mismeasured dependent variables: an application to duration models for unemployment spells, *Annales D'Economie et de Estatistique*, 55–56, 243–275.

Ashenfelter, O., A. Deaton, and G. Solon (1997). Collecting panel data in developing countries: Does it make sense?, in K.F. Hallock (ed.), *The Collected Essays of Orley Ashenfelter, Volume 2, Education, Training, and Discrimination*, Economics of the Twentieth Century, Cheltenham, UK: Series, Elgar.

Atkinson, A.B. and A. Brandolini (2001). Promise and pitfalls in the use of 'secondary' data-sets: income inequality in OECD countries as a case study, *Journal of Economic Literature*, 39(3): 771–799.

Barro, R.J. (1991). Economic growth in a cross section of countries, *Quarterly Journal of Economics*, 106(2): 407–443.

Barro, R.J. and J.W. Lee (1996). International measures of schooling years and schooling quality, *American Economic Review*, 86(2): 218–223.

Bound, J., Z. Griliches, and B.H. Hall (1986). Wages, schooling and IQ of brothers and sisters: Do the family factors differ?, *International Economic Review*, 27(1): 77–105.

Casley, D.J. and D.A. Lury (1987). *Data Collection in Developing Countries*, second edition, Oxford: Oxford University Press.

Chow, G.C. and A. Lin (1971). Best linear unbiased interpolation, distribution, and extrapolation of time series by related series, *Review of Economics and Statistics*, 53(4): 372–375.

Cook, R.D. (1977). Detection of influential observations in linear regression, *Technometrics*, 19: 15–18.

De la Fuente, A. and R. Domenech (2000). *Human Capital in Growth Regressions: How Much Difference Does Data Quality Make?* Discussion Paper No. 2466, Center for Economic Policy Research, London.

Devarajan, S., V. Swaroop, and H. Zou (1996). The composition of public expenditure and economic growth, *Journal of Monetary Economics*, 32: 417–458.

Dewald, W.G., J.G. Thursby and R.G. Anderson (1986). Replication in empirical economics: the journal of money credit and banking project, *The American Economic Review*, 76: 587–603.

Dezhbakhsh, H. (1990). The inappropriate use of serial correlation tests in dynamic linear models, *The Review of Economics and Statistics*, 72: 126–132.

Easterly, W. and S. Rebelo (1993). Fiscal policy and economic growth: an empirical investigation, *Journal of Monetary Economics*, 37: 313–344.

Fisman, R. and J. Svensson (2000). Are corruption and taxation really harmful to growth? Firm-level evidence, Policy Research Working Paper WPS2485. World Bank, Washington, DC.

Fuller, W. (1987). *Measurement Error Models*. New York: John Wiley & Sons.

Goolsbee, A. (2000). The importance of measurement error in the cost of capital, *National Tax Journal*, 53(2): 215–228.

Gourieroux, C. and A. Monfort (1981). On the problem of missing data in linear models, *Review of Economic Studies*, 48(4): 579–586.

Greene, W.H. (2000). *Econometric Analysis*, fourth edition, Upper Saddle River, NJ: Prentice-Hall.

Griliches, Z. (1986). Economic data issues, in Z. Griliches and M.D. Intriligator (eds), *Handbook of Econometrics*, Vol. III, North Holland: Amsterdam, pp. 1465–1514.

Griliches, Z. and J. Hausman (1986). Errors in variables in panel data, *Journal of Econometrics*, 31(1): 93–118.

Hadi, A.S. (1992). Identifying multiple outliers in multivariate data, *Journal of the Royal Statistical Society, Series B*, 54(3): 761–771.

Hahn, J. and J. Hausman (2002). A new specification test for the validity of instrumental variables, *Econometrica*, 70(1): 163–189.

Hampel, F.R., E.M. Ronchetti, P.J. Rousseeuw, and W.A. Stahel (1986). *Robust Statistics, the Approach Based on Influence Functions*, New York: John Wiley & Sons.

Harvey, A.C. and R.G. Pierse (1984). Estimating missing observations in economic time series, *Journal of the American Statistical 3 Association*, 79(385), Theory and Method Section: 125–131.

Harvey, A.C., S.J. Koopmans, and J. Penzer (1998). Messy time series: A unified approach, in T.B. Fomby and R.C. Hill (eds), *Messy Data – Missing Observations, Outliers, and Mixed-Frequency Data, Advances in Econometrics*, Volume 13, Stanford, CN: JAI Press.

Hausman, J. (2001). Mismeasured variables in econometric analysis: problems from the right and problems from the left, *Journal of Economic Perspectives*, 15(4): 57–67.

Hausman, J. and W.K. Newey (1991). Measurement errors in polynomial regression models, *Journal of Econometrics*, 50(3): 273–295.

Hausman, J., J. Abrevaya, and F.M. Scott-Morton (1998). Misspecification of the dependent variable in a discrete response setting, *Journal of Econometrics*, 87(2): 239–269.

Hausman, J., W.K. Newey, and J.L. Powell (1995). Nonlinear errors in variables: estimation of some Engel curves, *Journal of Econometrics*, 65(1): 205–233.

Heckman, J. (1990). Varieties of selection bias, *American Economic Review*, 80(2): 313–318.

Hendry, D.F. (1983). Econometric modeling: the 'consumption function' in retrospect, *Scottish Journal of Political Economy*, 30: 193–220.

Hettmansperger, T.P. (1984). *Statistical Inference Based on Ranks*, New York: John Wiley & Sons.

Leontief, W. (1971). Theoretical assumptions and nonobserved facts, *American Economic Review*, 61(1): 1–7.
Levy, D. and H. Dezhbakhsh (2003). International evidence on output fluctuations and shock persistence, *Journal of Monetary Economics*, 50: 1499–1530.
Lewbel, A. (1997). Constructing instruments for regressions with measurement error when no additional data are available: with an application to patents and R&D, *Econometrica*, 65(5): 1201–1213.
Mankiw, N.G. and M.D. Shapiro (1986). News or noise: an analysis of GNP revisions, *Survey of Current Business*, 66(May): 20–25.
Morgenstern, O. (1963). *On the Accuracy of Economic Observations*, second edition, Princeton, NJ: Princeton University Press.
Mukherjee, C., H. White, and M. Wuyts (1998). *Econometrics and Data Analysis for Developing Countries*, London: Routledge.
Mule, H. (1993). Linkage between food policymaking, policy analysis, and data collection, in J. von Braun and D. Puetz (eds), *Data Needs for Food Policy in Developing Countries, New Directions for Household Surveys*, Washington, DC: International Food Policy Research Institute.
Nugent, J.B. (1983). An alternative source of measurement errors: an explanation for the inverted-U hypothesis, *Economic Development and Cultural Change*, 31(2): 385–396.
Okeahalam, C. (2003). Industrial structure, competition, and financial policy, Unpublished paper.
Penn World Table (2002). Center for International Comparisons. Online, available at: http://pwt.econ.upenn.edu (accessed 2003).
Rousseeuw, P.J. and A.M. Leroy (1987) *Robust Regression and Outlier Detection*, New York: John Wiley & Sons.
Rousseeuw, P.J. and B.C. van Zomeren (1990). Unmasking multivariate outliers and leverage points, *Journal of the American Statistical Association*, 85: 633–651.
Rozanski, J. and A. Yeats (1994). On the (in)accuracy of economic observations: an assessment of trends in the reliability of international trade statistics, *Journal of Development Economics*, 44: 103–130.
Ryan, K.F. and D.E.A. Giles (1998). Testing for unit roots in economic time series with missing observations, in T.B. Fomby and R.C. Hill (eds), *Messy Data – Missing Observations, Outliers, and Mixed-Frequency Data, Advances in Econometrics*, Volume 13, Stanford, CN: JAI Press.
Stiglitz, J. (2005). Finance for development, in M. Ayogu and D. Ross (eds), *Development Dilemmas: The Methods and Political Ethics of Growth Policy*, London: Routledge, pp. 15–29.
Summers, R. and A. Heston (1991). The Penn World Table (mark 5): an expanded set of international comparisons, 1950–1988, *Quarterly Journal of Economics*, 106: 327–368.
Tybout, J.R. (1990). Making noisy data sing: a micro approach to measuring industrial efficiency, Policy Research Working Paper WPS327. World Bank, Washington, DC.
Von Braun, J. and D. Puetz (eds) (1993). *Data Needs for Food Policy in Developing Countries, New Directions for Household Surveys*, Washington, DC: International Food Policy Research Institute.
Wooldridge, J.M. (2000). *Introductory Econometrics: A Modern Approach*, Sydney: South-Western.

World Bank (1997). *World Development Report: The State in a Changing World*, Washington, DC: Oxford University Press.

World Bank (n.d.). Economic Growth Research: Barro-Lee Data Set. Online, available at: http://www.worldbank.org/research/growth/ddbarle2.htm (accessed 2003).

Yeats, A.J. (1995). Are partner–country statistics useful for estimating 'missing' trade data?, Policy Research Working Paper WPS1501. World Bank, Washington, DC.

Part II
Special problems and applications

6 Regulation, enforcement and development

Jean-Jacques Laffont

1 Introduction

Public utilities such as postal services, telecommunications, transportation (roads, railways, maritime, airline), electricity, gas, and water are sometimes referred to collectively as economic infrastructure.[1] In this chapter, we provide an overview, using examples from several developing countries, of regulatory issues arising from the liberalization of public utilities in the face of globalization. To set the stage, we first review the characteristics of developing countries that have a bearing on the analysis of regulation and competition policy. These characteristics include the level of difficulty of raising money, the quantum of audit resources available, the strength of institutional checks and balances, more binding limited liability constraints, and the range of available commitment devices. Although we visit these issues briefly in the following sections, some of the themes are elaborated in this book in the contributions by Bates and by Stiglitz. Then we discuss ways in which regulatory agencies can be structured to render them pro-competition as well as the trade-offs in the unbundling of incumbent monopolies into the non-competitive (monopoly) and the competitive segments. Next, we present the regulatory rules applicable to the natural monopoly segment, followed by a discussion of the crucial issue of the management of the interface between the monopoly segment and the competitive segment. To keep the discussion comparable in size with the rest of the chapters in this book, we sidestep the treatment of competition policy and other complicated aspects of the management of the interface such as access pricing rules. We conclude with lessons on regulatory enforcement and economic development.

1.1 Cost of public funds

A useful concept for the discussion that follows is the marginal cost of public funds, that is, the social cost of raising one unit of funds. This cost includes a dead-weight loss because governments raise revenues by levying taxes that often are distortionary.[2] It is estimated that this dead-weight loss amounts to around 0.3 in developed countries, meaning that it costs citizens 1.3 units of account every time the government raises one unit. According to World Bank data, the dead-weight loss in developing countries is well beyond one. It has been estimated at 1.2 in Malaysia and 2.5 in the Philippines, while in Thailand it ranges between 1.2 and 1.5 (Jones et al., 1990).

The inefficiency of tax systems in developing countries and challenges of corruption combine to make it extremely difficult for governments to invest in infrastructure adequately. These factors also affect the cost of all types of public interventions, particularly regulation and competition policy. In developing our analysis we take the high cost of public funds as a given because of the many financial, human and political constraints that render the required tax reforms highly unlikely anytime soon.

1.2 Cost of auditing

An essential instrument of any regulatory (including competition) agency is the ability to audit costs. Yet, regulatory agencies in many developing countries are hampered by a lack of strong accounting and auditing systems (Trebilcock, 1996). This may be due to the lack of proper training programs; to the political and social difficulties that hamper the payment of incentive salaries to auditors to reward effort and discourage corruption; and to the inability to impose high penalties in cases of documented wrongdoing (because of the strong limited liability constraints of most economic agents). Many developing countries also suffer from widespread corruption due, in particular, to the low internal costs of side transfers. When two parties (such as a firm and an auditor or a bidder and the auction organizer) arrange a private deal, they must take into account the costs of being discovered and the need to use indirect compensation (which is less efficient than direct compensation). The cost of these side transfers is expected to be lower than in developed countries because punishments in developing countries are likely to be less severe or non-existent.

1.3 Limited liability constraints

Inefficient credit markets and the sheer lack of wealth make limited liability constraints more binding in developing countries. It is important to stress this point because many of the problems in regulation and competition policy result from difficulties in borrowing and attracting foreign capital. In addition, it is worth highlighting the complimentarity of general competition policy and good banking sector regulation. When the banking sector is inefficient and makes borrowing costly or impossible, an effective competition policy may destroy the rents that allow firms to invest, or may create instability.[3]

1.4 Institutional issues

Other characteristics that hamper public utility regulation concern the state of governance. In particular, two characteristics of developed countries that are often weakly present in developing countries are constitutional control of the government and the degree of ability to enter into long-term contracts. Weakness in the system of checks and balances makes the government an easier prey to interest groups and patronage than is the case in advanced democracies where the judiciary, public audit bodies, the separation of powers, and media independence all have a more substantive presence.[4] The preponderance of fledgling democracy and untested political institutions increases the uncertainty of future regulations and makes it difficult for the government and the regulatory institutions to make credible commitments to long-run policies. Consequently, the economic policies of developing countries are even more sensitive to ratchet effects and renegotiations.

Another shortcoming of developing economies is the weakness of the rule of law. Weak enforcement of laws and contracts biases contracting toward self-enforcing contracts or leads to costly renegotiations.[5] Finally, it is essential to stress that the liberalization and deregulation of public infrastructures in developing countries often fails to attract the level of foreign capital that is necessary. All the shortcomings highlighted above should be kept in mind throughout subsequent discussions because they complicate regulation as well as efforts to promote competition.

2 Structural issues

2.1 The structure of regulatory agencies

A first consideration in structuring the government entity that will have responsibilities for the regulation of utilities and general competition policy is whether or not these functions should be allocated to one integrated agency.[6] In this regard, recent experiences in Australia and New Zealand are enlightening.

New Zealand developed a very novel approach to regulation, relying only on general competition laws enforced by the courts and by an industry-wide competition authority. This approach was first used to regulate telecommunications and then electric power. The notion of self-regulation by industry was also introduced. In this case, industry participants form councils to negotiate the main rules and access conditions. Although New Zealand's experiment was not an immediate failure, the government recognized, after some years, that there was still a need for regulatory control of industries that are not competitive enough. Indeed, this proved necessary even in telecommunications, that is, the most competitive industry of the ones we are considering here. The concern is that 'light control' of the industry is not sufficient to contain abuse of dominant position. The outcomes in the number of cases brought before the courts indicate that rapid technological change and the technology intensive nature of the industry together complicate the task of trying to convict a firm of abusing dominant position. Moreover, the procedures involved make for very long delays. As a result, relying solely on competition laws has proved inefficient even when these laws are well developed and enforced. On the basis of this experience, therefore, we can conclude that eschewing regulation is not the right option. Besides, it seems somewhat odd to extend to economic activities that are distinguished by the absence of competition, the application of competition rules (as a substitute for regulation).

Integrating general competition policy and regulation into a single agency is only possible if the regulatory agency is a multi-industry one as in Australia. Australian regulation is organized around a federal multisector agency, specialized agencies, and regional regulation. The multisector agency, the Australian Competition and Consumer Commission (ACCC) is composed of sectoral and functional bureaus and coordination entities. The Commission deals with product safety, consumer protection, access, mergers and restrictive trade practices in all the sectors, including public utility sectors. Created in 1995, the ACCC has taken over a significant part of the duties of specialized regulators by acquiring responsibility for promoting competition in a larger sense. For example, the regulatory body responsible for telecommunications was closed after the creation of the ACCC. The Utility Regulators Forum, created in 1997, is responsible for coordinating regulatory activities within the ACCC. The Australian case involves integration at the federal level of regulation and competition, even with the active involvement of regional agencies in the process. This system can be contrasted with the United States, where multisectoral ruling takes place at the state level, specialized regulation is the rule at the federal level, and competition policy is dealt with separately.

The integration of regulatory agencies is an attractive option for developing countries because they face a severe shortage of adequately trained personnel. This is especially the case for the telecommunications, electricity and gas industries. While there are substantial economies of scope between the regulatory institutions of these industries, they seem much less important between regulation and competition policy. To avoid creating too powerful an institution, we would generally favor a separate competition agency and, except for very large countries, integrated regulatory agencies at the federal level. The only exception might be water that could remain at the local level. In general, technological intensity requires federal regulation to reduce costs, but accountability requires more decentralized institutions.

Good advice on this structural issue must recognize political constraints, initial conditions and industry specificities. The variety of solutions experimented within developed countries and the experiences of the different Latin American countries (Argentina, Chile, Peru, Brazil, Bolivia) suggest that the trade-offs are complex (see Box 6.1). They involve balancing differentiation versus coordination; creative versus destructive competition between regulators; better enforcement by local authorities versus better control by the government; local corruption versus federal corruption; industry-specific expertise versus sharing resources; and diversifying the risks of institutional failures versus coordination (Aubert and Laffont, 2001; Smith, 2000).

2.2 Industry structure

Although industries in the utility sector have operated as public or regulated private monopolies providing public services such as telecommunications, electricity, gas or transportation, segments of these industries are now viewed as potentially competitive. Some examples are long-distance telecommunications services and electricity generation. Other segments continue to be considered as natural monopolies because they are difficult to contest. This difficulty can arise from high switching costs confronting customers, thereby rendering them captive consumers. Alternatively, customers may have no choice because duplication of facilities is economically infeasible. An example is power distribution, the electricity transmission grid, railway tracks, platforms and signaling systems, and, to some extent, the local loop in telecommunications. These industry segments remain regulated and may eventually face new forms of regulation (discussed later in section three).

Three types of market structures can be envisioned for these industries: (1) vertical disintegration, (2) vertical integration, and (3) competition in infrastructures. Under vertical disintegration, the firm controlling the bottleneck (the natural monopoly segment) is not allowed to compete in the services using the bottleneck as an input. For example, the local telephone company owning the local loop is not allowed to compete in long-distance services using the local loop to access consumers. In the case of vertical integration, the firm controlling the bottleneck becomes one competitor among many service providers using the bottleneck as an input. Finally, in the case of competition in infrastructures, competition then takes place between vertically integrated firms, each of which controls restricted access points and provides services.

The comparison between the first two cases contrasts the economies of scope that vertical integration makes possible, and the problems of favoritism it raises. The bias in developing countries should be toward vertical disintegration because the economies of scope are likely to be independent of the characteristics of these countries (at least for given technologies), while favoritism is more difficult to counter.[7] The choice between case two and case three rests on a comparison of the fixed costs associated with competition in the provision of the 'bottleneck' (like local

Box 6.1

> **Specialization in Argentina**
>
> In Argentina, each sector restructuring was accompanied by the creation of a sector-specific regulatory agency, whereas the specific approach adopted by each sector was quite different. While the creation and staffing of the electricity and gas regulatory agencies followed international best practices and had no major problems in fulfilling their obligations, the experiences of the other regulatory authorities have been much poorer. The most problematic may have been the telecom and water regulators, where there are not only staffing problems but also concerns with the lack of transparency of the decision-making process. As for transport regulators, who have recently been merged into a single regulatory agency, the main issue has been the lack of independence.
>
> **A compromise between coordination and specialization: Bolivia**
>
> Bolivia's recently established regulatory system constitutes a balanced compromise between a multisector agency and specialized regulators. It is composed of sector-specific branches operating under the supervision of a coordination entity. The structure is very similar to that of a multisector agency with specialized bureaus; yet it affords more independence to the branches. This, in turn, makes it more acceptable to the ministries, which might be reluctant to turn their regulatory power over to a multisector agency. Such an organization may help reduce the threat of capture of regulators by the industry but may fail to insulate the agency from political interference in view of its strategic importance.
>
> **A mixed structure: China**
>
> Generally China has a mixed structure of regulatory agencies consisting of both industry-wide and sector agencies (ministries or departments) at both central and regional levels. According to the law, the State Development and Planning Commission (SDPC) is the government body in charge of price regulation of public utilities. Another major responsibility of SDPCs is to regulate market entry and investments in public utilities. There are also some sector specific ministries that complement the SDCP such as the Ministry of Information Industry (regulatory agency of telecommunications) and the Ministry of Railways. These are generally the implementation bodies.

Box 6.1 continued

Another structural feature of the Chinese regulatory agencies is the hierarchical structure between the central and local regulatory bodies. First, there are regional SDPCs along each layer of administrative governments. Similarly, there are some implementation bodies, either industry-wide or sectoral, at each local government level that complements regional SDPCs. The separation of powers between the SDPC and local SDPCs is that the former is usually in charge of the control of entry and investments for big projects and the approval of price adjustment proposals submitted by local SDPCs, while local SDPCs take care of smaller projects and make price adjustment proposals.

The general trend in the reform of regulatory structure is to delegate more and more of the regulatory power to regional governments. For instance, to provide incentives for the regions to make investments in electric power, the central government has given to local governments the authority to approve entry and investments in electricity generation. It also allows the local governments to make price purchase arrangements with independent power producers, subject to the approval of the SDPC. As a result of decentralization of regulatory power, installed generation capacity has increased rapidly and substantially so that China has solved since 1998 the shortage of energy problem, which plagued the economy for a long time. Similar decentralization and gain in clout by regulatory authorities have occurred to varying degrees in the telecommunications, gas and transport sectors.

With respect to the structural choice, at the national government, between industry-wide versus sector regulators, the trend in China is not clear. Until recently, the reform of regulatory agencies has focused on separating management from regulatory and policy-making functions and the attempts to set up independent regulatory agencies began only recently. Indeed, the government recently announced that an electric regulatory agency will be created, which is the first of its kind in China, at least judged by its name and status. However, this event arises within a specific institutional setting, because unlike telecom, railways, and transport, there is now no specific regulatory body in charge of electricity regulation in China.[8] Therefore, it is difficult to judge at this moment whether it will be another old style implementation agency just bridging this power gap or a real institutional innovation in the making, signaling that the government is determined to take a sector-specific approach, eventually removing electricity regulatory power from the SDPC.

telephony) and the gains one may expect from this competition (Auriol and Laffont, 1992). The comparison is skewed in a developing country context because the high cost of financing makes more expensive both the duplication of fixed costs and the information rents resulting from a monopolistic provision of the bottleneck.

These comparisons are further complicated by industry-specific dynamics that can lead to case 3 as in the telecommunications industry. Then, vertical disintegration may in fact slow down the emergence of competition among vertically integrated firms providing both local and long distance telephony. Recommending vertical disintegration may then be particularly inappropriate. However, for railways, gas, or electricity, unbundling the elements into separate enterprises may be recommended if competition in services is introduced.[9] Introducing competition may not be sufficient. It is also necessary to guarantee that quality control can be implemented economically, a commitment that is difficult to deliver in developing countries (LDCs).

In all the cases under discussion, there is a choice between a vertically integrated firm and shared ownership of the bottleneck by users who agree on rules for using it. The comparison being made is between the inefficiency of regulation and the free-rider problems of joint ownership. In a country where regulators are easily captured, one may favor the second alternative, despite the lack of consumer representation that it often entails. It turns out that undesirable as it is, lack of consumer representation is one of the least worrisome of the possible drawbacks in the second alternative; facility degradation is far more worrisome as its occurrence carries far-reaching adverse consequences ranging from derailments to power outages (involving in some occasions loss of human lives).

We close the discussion on industry structure mindful of the unresolved debate over whether developing countries can achieve a market structure (in the infrastructure sectors) supportive of competition given the often high economic rents demanded of LDCs by foreign investors in these sectors (see Box 6.2).

3 Regulation of natural monopolies

The regulation of natural monopolies requires finding a balance between efficiency and the cost of information rents. High-powered incentive schemes (such as price caps) which induce cost-minimizing behavior yield large rents to the most efficient firms, while low-powered incentive schemes (such as cost-of-service regulation) control those rents but create weak incentives for minimizing costs.

3.1 The high cost of public funds

As stressed in the beginning, a major characteristic of developing coun-

Box 6.2

Market structure of telecommunications infrastructure providers

Zambia aimed at a very competitive industry with two fixed-link telephony providers and three mobiles, but was unable to attract any investor. Ghana issued two licenses for fixed-link telephony but the weakness of regulation could not prevent foreclosure behavior by the incumbent monopolist so that the second operator is not operational. Côte d'Ivoire was criticized for granting a seven-year monopoly for fixed-link telephony, but the network is now expanding as scheduled. South Africa is allowing its carrier of carriers and signal distributor, Sentech, to enter into multimedia services. Both South Africa and Nigeria have licensed second national network operators but they are yet to become active.

The telecommunications sector in Peru was privatized in 1994 and a seven-year monopoly in fixed-phone services was granted to force large investments that increase coverage and penetration and allow for a smooth restructuring of tariffs. In 1998, the monopoly (Telefonica) and Peruvian authorities renegotiated the contract and opened all services to competition.

The structure of the industry in China

The general trend is to separate the monopolistic segment from the competitive ones. In other words, vertical separation is taken to be the mainstream restructuring form of industrial structure. For instance, mobile services were separated from the incumbent, China Telecom, in the restructuring reform of the telecom sector in 1998. In electric power, the government recently approved a new restructuring plan to separate generation from transmission and distribution even though transmission and distribution will remain integrated for a while. As can be expected, this move is driven by the desire to facilitate efficient regulation and prevent favoritism.

However, the government did not approach restructuring uniformly. Indeed other forms of industry structure such as vertical integration and competition in infrastructures have also been implemented or allowed to exist. In this regard, it is interesting to contrast the different restructuring approaches in electricity and telecommunications. In the power sector, entry in generation has been allowed to independent power producers since the mid-1980s, while the state power company owned not only the monopolistic transmission and

continued

Box 6.2 continued

> distribution networks but also competitive generation assets. Given the general situation of shortage of generation capacity, everything proceeded smoothly until excess capacity of generation and capacity constraints of transmission appeared in 1998.
>
> Thereafter, serious allegations of favoritism surfaced when the state power company no longer wanted to dispatch power from independent producers. Indeed, the power markets have become quite segmented among different regions such that power exchanges among provinces account for only about 20 percent of total transactions. This is considered unreasonable given the huge geographical differences, with Eastern China being the load center and having no generation assets and Western China being endowed with much of the resources for power generation (rivers and coal mines). Worries about the serious favoritism problem, particularly when more stations such as the Three Gorges Project are going to generate power soon, and the desire to build an integrated national market have contributed to speed up the restructuring reform in the power sector. Recently, the government approved a new reform package in which separation of generation assets from transmission and distribution is one of the main contents. That is, vertical separation will be adopted in the power sector.
>
> In the case of telecommunications, however, a different approach has been adopted from the beginning. More precisely, competition in infrastructures was created in the telecom sector. This has been implemented in two ways. On the one hand, entry was liberalized in the competitive services and competitors need to buy access from the incumbent. For instance, beginning in 1994 when China Unicom was created, competition was introduced in long distance, mobiles, and data services even though China Telecom still kept the dominant position in local services the access of which was needed by its rivals in competitive markets. It did cause some problems in creating competition in local services, because China Unicom, which can, as a matter of principle, provide local services, has until recently only employed network in three cities or regions, namely Tianjin, Chongqing, and Sichuan. Given the natural monopoly feature of local services, it should not come as a surprise. However, such an institutional arrangement did achieve an important policy goal, namely to increase the access of telecommunications services. Indeed, the penetration rate of fixed lines has reached 21 per 100 persons; in our view a remarkable achievement.
>
> On the other hand, competition in infrastructures has also been introduced through restructuring of the existing operators. After the

Box 6.2 continued

> implementation of major restructuring in 1998 in which operation was separated from the government functions and some services like mobile were divested, the Chinese government initiated a new restructuring reform in 2001. The main theme this time was to separate China Telecom on a geographical basis, namely dividing it into south part which inherited the brand name and north part which will be integrated with the China Netcom, originally a carriers' carrier and widely considered to be politically well connected. In addition, each company is allowed to enter each other's territory. After this round of restructuring, both China Telecom and China Netcom can provide long-distance and local services. Remember that China Unicom was granted a license in local services before but chose to exercise it only to a limited extent. It seems that the government is not convinced by the natural monopoly argument of local services.
>
> Driven by the desire to create competition in local services but also worried by the network expansion needs, this time the government has chosen the horizontal restructuring approach not only to create competition in the market but also to keep the market viable.

tries is the high cost of public funds. It is easy to see that this high cost calls for higher prices of the commodities produced by the natural monopoly and for lower-powered incentive schemes (high shares of cost reimbursement). Before presenting the intuitive reasoning for these results, it is important to emphasize that we are assuming here perfect monitoring of cost and full commitment of the regulator.

Intuitively, we know that higher cost of public funds means a higher cost of giving up rents and a higher cost of inefficiency. However, the relative cost of rents increases faster because when an additional rent is given up to a particular firm to support an efficiency improvement, the same incentive must also be provided to all other more efficient firms. The optimal regulation sacrifices some efficiency in order to decrease such rents. Thus, this is an argument in the direction of cost-plus schemes relative to fixed-price schemes or, in the language of regulatory theory, rate-of-return regulation versus price caps (see Box 6.3).

A higher cost of funds also means that it is more valuable to price above marginal cost, i.e., to use public utilities prices to finance fixed costs and the government's budget. In particular, it is a mistake to advocate marginal cost pricing for public utilities in developing countries.

The implied difference in pricing between developed and developing countries can be substantial, since a move from a cost of funds of 0.3 to 1 translates into a relative deviation from marginal cost, which is double in the second case. Since effort levels also decrease as cost reimbursement rules are tilted toward cost-plus schemes, marginal costs are higher and, therefore, prices should be even higher in developing countries.

3.2 Monitoring

The impact of monitoring on the power of incentives is quite different depending on the type of monitoring. Monitoring of *effort* generally enables the regulator to reduce the information rents and calls for higher-powered incentive schemes. A less-efficient monitoring technology will call for relatively less-powerful incentive schemes. Indeed, low incentives and monitoring are substitute instruments to extract the firm's rent. A decrease in the use of one instrument makes the other instrument more attractive. As a result, an increase in the cost of public funds induces low incentives both directly and indirectly (as explained above) through a decrease of the more costly monitoring.

We have emphasized so far the strong assumption of perfect monitoring of costs. In practice, however, costs are not perfectly observable and one must take into account the possibility of cost padding, i.e., the many ways in which a firm can divert money. Cost can now be increased by undue charges, which benefit the management and the workers. Analysis (Laffont and Tirole, 1993) shows that the imperfect auditing of cost padding calls for a shift toward higher-powered incentive schemes. In the extreme, if auditing did not exist, only fixed-price contracts would be possible. Indeed, they would be the only ones preventing unlimited cost padding by making firms residual claimants of their costs. It is therefore obvious that weak auditing technologies, as can be expected in developing countries, will result in an even higher desire to shift toward fixed-price mechanisms. This effect is reinforced by the savings in auditing costs resulting from fixed-price mechanisms in countries with a high cost of public funds (see Box 6.4).

The impact of the lack of auditing cannot be overemphasized. It is a crucial point, which conflicts with the findings of the previous paragraphs, but easily dominates the other effects. In the absence of reasonable accounting, price cap regulation is the only way out. It is only through price cap reviews that some cost elements can be brought in, leading to some cost-plus shift through the ratchet effect (see Box 6.4).

3.3 Hierarchical regulation and corruption

The next point to consider is the need to devolve regulation to the regulatory agencies or ministries. The main role of these institutions is to bridge partially the informational gap between public decision makers and the regulated firm. This gives rise to another issue, the possible capture of the

Box 6.3

Pricing of telecommunications in Côte d'Ivoire

In the 1997 concession contract, Citelcom was granted a seven-year monopoly for the services delivered by fixed-link telephony. The guidelines for pricing were as follows: in 1998, a price cap would maintain the global level of real prices with the possibility of adjusting by 10 percent each price. From 1998 to 2001, the price cap would require a 7 percent per year decrease of real prices. After 2001, the price cap chosen each year would guarantee a rate of return on capital to be negotiated, with the goal of reaching tariff levels and structures similar to those in Europe and in the neighboring countries. Indeed, in 2002 a rate of return of 15 percent was decided. Note also the following provisions: if after 2002 the rate of return exceeded 26 percent, the price cap could be revised downwards, but if after 2002 the rate of return was below 8 percent for at least two years, Citelcom could ask for an increase of the price cap.

About the high cost of public funds in China

The high cost of public funds in China may imply that it is better to finance the fixed cost and contributions to government revenues through tariffs rather than through general taxes. That is, industry-wide budget balancing should be maintained. In the power sector, for instance, prices were used to cover only operation and maintenance costs before 1992 and the investment costs were covered by the government through fiscal revenues. As a result, there was a lasting shortage of supply of power. Since then, electric tariffs have been raised to reflect full costs. More precisely, the Chinese government has implemented the so-called 'one plant, one price' policy, which is essentially meant to guarantee full cost recovery regardless of the financing structure.

This has helped to attract investments in the power sector. Another important case is in telecommunications, in which an installation fee was introduced in the early 1990s. Indeed, about one-third of each year's investments in network expansion were covered by installation fees. While this policy has been criticized a lot and the installation fee was eventually eliminated in 2000, many argue that China would not have been able to develop its telecom infrastructure so quickly without the installation fee policy. Still another example can be found in China's railways, where a special surcharge was levied on the top of tariffs to finance the huge investment costs, which guarantee the funds necessary for the rapid development of railway networks in China. Before this policy was introduced in the late 1980s, all capital expenditures of the railways sector had to be allocated from general taxes.

Box 6.4

> **Monitoring, auditing, and the choice of pricing rule in China**
>
> The weak monitoring and auditing system has major impacts on the regulatory policies in China. Presently, the Chinese government has chosen a kind of cost-of-service regulation with a strong cost-plus flavor, as in administered prices with generally neither upward nor downward flexibility. Moreover, historical cost standards are adopted and cost disallowances are rare. In theory, such pricing policy would need perfect observability of output or a good control system of monitoring and auditing, which are obviously not available in China. Constrained by such inabilities, the government must ask enterprises to make price-adjustment proposals and then approve their pricing policy. As could be expected, these regulatory policies provide no incentives for enterprises to cut cost. However, to appreciate the full impacts of such policies, one needs to realize that, like rate-of-return regulation, there are also lags between price adjustments.
>
> Moreover, these rigid prices have not been fully implemented due to the weak enforcement power of the government. A specificity of China is that competition takes place between public firms. The managers of these firms engage easily in excessive competition as their private benefits depend on the size of the firm more than on its profits. Due to these governance problems price cap regulation would not be effective and this explains the general use of rate-of-return regulation despite inappropriate accounting systems.

regulatory agency by the firm. Such collusion will occur with greater probability if the stakes of collusion are high, if the cost of side transfers between the firm and the regulator are low, and if no incentive mechanism is in place for the regulators.

The stake of collusion amounts to the information rent that an efficient firm obtains when the regulator hides the fact that it is efficient – the maximal bribe that a firm will be willing to offer to the agency. However, the bribe should be discounted by the price of internal transfers, which includes the cost of being discovered as well as the need to use often-indirect transfers that are less efficient. Capture is avoided if the agency is paid an amount larger than the discounted value of the stake of collusion when it reveals the firm is efficient (we will call this constraint the collusion-proof constraint).

In the simplest cases, the regulatory response to the fear of capture is to satisfy the collusion-proof constraint at the lowest possible cost. This includes shifting optimal regulation toward cost-plus schemes to decrease the stake of collusion, and improve monitoring to increase the cost-of-side transfers.

Three features of developing countries call for even higher shifts toward cost-plus mechanisms. First, we can expect a lower cost of internal transfers because of less stringent monitoring of illegal activities. Second, incentive payments to the agency are more costly because of the higher cost of public funds. Third, it may be politically more difficult to create such strong incentive payments.

So far, we have dealt with a case where the optimal regulatory response entails no corruption. If we extend the framework to a case where, for example, regulators are more or less susceptible to being corrupted (some requiring low bribes, others requiring higher bribes), it may be optimal to let some corruption occur if the proportion of regulators requiring low bribes is small enough. Creating incentive payments, which suppress the corruption of this type of regulator, would be too costly because the high payments required to fight corruption would have to be incurred even for the other type of regulators (for whom it is not necessary). Then, the same features of developing countries, which militate in favor of low-powered incentive schemes (high cost of public funds, poor auditing technologies), suggest that it is optimal to let more corruption happen at equilibrium.

Therefore, the effect of corruption appears complex. If we consider corruption of cost auditing, it calls for higher-power incentives, but if we consider corruption in information reporting, lower-powered incentives are required.

3.4 Commitment

Let us consider now the important issue of commitment, more specifically, the fact that governments in developing countries have even less credibility to commit to long-run regulatory rules than those in developed countries.[10] A lack of commitment puts the ratchet effect into motion. Faced with incentives in the first period, firms fear that taking advantage today of these incentives (efficient firms make more money by having low costs) will lead to more demanding incentive schemes in the future. A way to commit credibly to not expropriate rents in the future is to learn nothing today about the firms' efficiency. Instead of offering, as in the static case, a menu of contracts with variable sharing of overruns, which induces self-selection, the extreme attitude is to offer a single contract, which induces under-effort of the good type and higher-than-first-best effort of the bad type. The inefficiency created by the lack of commitment is the inappropriate provision of effort levels over the various periods, which has no simple interpretation in terms of the power of incentive schemes. In the case of linear schemes, it can be shown (Freixas *et al.*, 1985) that the ratchet effect pushes toward high-powered schemes, which create higher rents in the first period to induce the revelation of types. More generally, the less commitment ability there is, the less the regulator should try to separate types, particularly if the cost of public funds is high (see Box 6.5).

Regulators' lack of ability to commit can be mitigated by the repetition of their relationship with the firms and the building of a reputation of not expropriating rents derived from future efficiency improvements.[11] No general analysis exists of how easy commitment is, depending on the type of regulatory regime. Regulatory institutions must be particularly scrutinized in developing countries for their ability to provide long-run incentives through their power of commitment, since a major goal is to attract foreign investment. For example, price capping has been pushed in the Western world as a way to provide high-powered incentives. However, price caps are regularly renegotiated, while a commitment to a fair rate of return might be less prone to costly renegotiations (Greenwald, 1984).[12]

Box 6.5

Enforcement failures in telecommunications

In Ghana, the incumbent monopoly for fixed telephony, which was not allowed to enter the mobile business, eventually did enter the market and used all kinds of tactics to delay interconnection. In Tanzania, the regulator attempted to enforce regional mobile licenses. However, the dominant operator, Mobitel, argued that its license was national and launched service in an area where the regulator tried unsuccessfully to shut down the operator.

In Côte d'Ivoire, the incumbent monopolist priced access for competing public phones in a way that foreclosed entry. The regulator intervened in 1998 to set a minimum price for the call boxes to allow entry. However, until recently the incumbent refused to adjust its prices.

In China, the regulatory officials openly admit that price regulation is not as effective as it used to be. Even though administered prices without any flexibility are officially imposed, price wars are common. In China's mobile phone sector, the receiver-pays principle is currently in place. However, many cases have been reported where the caller-pays principle is applied, albeit illegally. While the government has punished and corrected some cases, the practice has not been eliminated. Similar occurrences have been reported with regard to IP phone services, where competitive pressures have led to dramatic price cuts in comparison to the official prices. It seems that the Ministry of Information Industry can do nothing but to let it happen. There are also indirect price cuts in the form of free airtime and subsidized handsets, which are illegal but frequent.

3.5 Weakness of the rule of law

Enforcement of regulatory rules is poor in developing countries for two reasons. First, enforcement is costly, and optimal enforcement decreases with the cost of public funds. Second, the principal–agent paradigm with full bargaining power attributed to the regulator does not fit the reality of developing countries. Note that weakness in the bargaining position at the renegotiation stage calls for increased investment in enforcement. Finally, corruption of the enforcement mechanism itself or of the regulatory mechanism calls for less enforcement. Thus, the weakness of the rule of law in developing countries is not only due to poor human resources, it is also part of an optimal regulatory response.

3.6 Financial constraints

Financial constraints compound the difficulties of asymmetric information in many circumstances. The basic intuition can be stated in simple moral hazard control problems with risk neutrality. Moral hazard in a delegated activity can be controlled without giving up a rent to the agent if penalties are possible even when the observation of the performance is noisy. However, if such penalties are not possible because of limited liability constraints, only rewards for good performance can induce appropriate effort levels, i.e., information rents must be given up. The more severely binding are the financial constraints, the higher are the proportion of rents to be surrendered.

Both the severity of financial constraints and the high cost of public funds favor a shift toward less powerful incentive schemes in developing countries. The irony of the situation is that, even though these countries should make more effort to emerge from underdevelopment, inducing effort is much more difficult in developing countries.

3.7 Summary

Section three has detailed many arguments that favor a move toward less powerful incentive schemes (and, therefore, an acceptance of a tolerable level of production and allocative inefficiency) in developing countries. However, the use of performance evaluation to improve the fundamental trade-offs between efficiency and rent extraction presumes a perfect, or at least unbiased, auditing of that performance. The main argument against such advice is that the distribution of knowledge about cost details is biased in favor of the producer. Additionally, monitoring is both costly and can be highly imperfect in many developing countries. Therefore, fixed-price mechanisms, which obviate all the monitoring costs, are favored.

Thus, we may distinguish three stages of development concerning regulation. In the first stage, the auditing mechanisms are so poor that powerful incentive schemes should be advocated. They promote short-run efficiency in activities that are immune to ratchet effects. However, they strongly favor ex-post inequality (since the efficient types make more money than the inefficient ones). Additionally, they encourage some types of corruption of regulatory and political institutions, and they are costly for the rest of the economy because they create a money drain toward the regulated monopolies. This first stage should be used to develop a good auditing system. Once in place, one can move rather discontinuously to stage two of development by promoting less-powerful incentive schemes for the reasons explained above. Then, as development continues, the optimal solution is to move slowly toward more-powerful incentive schemes in stage three. The quality of regulation in each of these stages depends critically on the ability of the government to commit credibly to the implementation of the schemes.

4 Conclusion

Liberalization, competition, and regulatory policies in tandem are recent developments, still in an evolutionary stage. Historically, competition policy has existed to govern what was then considered competitive economic activities, while regulatory policies were meant to take care of specialty and monopoly trades such as banking and utility respectively. On the other hand, liberalization of economic activities in general, as part of the globalization ideology, has generated hybrid structures that continue to challenge architects of market governance mechanisms.

This unfinished business of charting the 'policy handbook' has left many relevant policy questions on market governance unanswered. For developing countries, ever playing catch up and generally trailing the global trend in market liberalization, the data necessary to permit rigorous interrogation of the theory and conjectures bearing on the various questions of liberalization and governance are yet to be collected. Available results from developed countries do not easily generalize because institutions and therefore context matters. Case studies and theory are the only available tools that can be used under these circumstances, but this should be done with a lot of caution, in particular because the economic theory relevant for developing countries is so far only sketchy.

Notes

1 We exclude from consideration so-called social infrastructure such as education and health or financial infrastructure.
2 The dead-weight loss depends on the type of tax used because the tax systems are not usually optimized.
3 Mishkin (1997) concludes that 'developing countries may need to move slowly in financial liberalization in order to keep a lending boom from getting out of hand'.

4 See Besley and Burgess (2001) for an empirical study of government responsiveness to media activity.
5 It should be noted though that this weakness has in some cases been exploited to advantage by multinational corporations in escaping product liability, ignoring warranties or other legal obligations. This aspect of the weakness is often not mentioned but is in practice exploited widely.
6 Useful readings on the design and structure of industries include Abdala (2001) on Argentina, and Berg and Gutierrez (2000) on Brazil.
7 This should be balanced with another consideration, which is the importance of transaction costs, which will be higher in case 1 due to costly enforcement of contracts and the non-credible commitments, which produces constant renegotiations. See also Ordover *et al.* (1994). The idea of weak or absent commitment is not limited to developing economies. Besley and Coate (1995) provide a more general discussion of efficiency and inefficiency in political equilibria with a related dynamic model of infeasibility of commitment. Laffont and Tirole (1993) have also noted the problem of long-term commitment in a representative democracy. Another consideration in countries with small market size is that in some industries such as electricity, a vertical structure may provide the only feasible industry configuration capable of attracting the interest of foreign investors.
8 The Ministry of Water Resources and Electricity was restructured and disappeared in 1998 and the regulatory functions were taken over by the State Economic and Trade Commission, another government agency, which mainly takes care of the management of state-owned enterprises.
9 In large countries, competition between vertically integrated firms with reciprocal access rules is possible.
10 Useful readings include Heller and McCubbins (1996), Henisz and Zelner (2001) and Levy and Spiller (1996).
11 See Gilbert and Newbery (1988) for a model of infinitely repeated contracting in which some collusive equilibria do not exhibit the trading inefficiencies associated with shorter horizons.
12 However, one can also commit to a fair renegotiation of price caps.

References

Abdala, M. (2001). Institutions, contracts and regulation of infrastructure in Argentina, *Journal of Applied Economics*, 4: 217–254.

Aubert C. and J.J. Laffont (2001). Multiregulation in developing countries, Mimeo IDEI.

Auriol, E. and J.J. Laffont (1992). Regulation by duopoly, *Journal of Economics and Management Strategy*, 1: 503–533.

Berg, S. and L. Gutierrez (2000). Telecommunications liberalization and regulatory governance: lessons from Latin America, *Telecommunications Policy*, 24: 865–884.

Besley, T. and R. Burgess. (2001). *The Political Economy of Governmental Responsiveness: Theory and Evidence from India*, Mimeo, London School of Economics.

Besley, T. and S. Coate (1995). *Efficient Policy Change in a Representative Democracy: A Dynamic Analysis*, Working Paper, Princeton University, May.

Freixas, X., R. Guesnerie, and J. Tirole (1985), Planning under incomplete information and the Ratchet Effect, *Review of Economics Studies*, 52: 173–192.

Gilbert, R. and D. Newbery (1988). *Regulation Games*, Working Paper No. 8879, Berkeley: University of California.

Greenwald, B. (1984). Rate base selection and the structure of regulation, *Rand Journal of Regulation*, 15: 85–95.

Heller, W. and M. McCubbins (1996). Politics, institutions, and outcomes: electricity regulation in Argentina and Chile, *Policy Reform*, 1: 357–387.

Henisz, W.J. and B.A. Zelner (2001). The institutional environment for telecommunications investment, *Journal of Economics and Management Strategy*, 10: 123–147.

Jones, L., P. Tandon, and I. Vogelsang (1990). *Selling Public Enterprises: A Cost Benefit Methodology*, Cambridge: MIT Press.

Laffont, J.J. and J. Tirole (1993). *A Theory of Incentives in Procurement and Regulation*, Cambridge, MA: MIT Press.

Levy, B. and P.T. Spiller (1996). *Regulations, Institutions, and Commitment: Comparative Studies of Telecommunications*, Cambridge: Cambridge University Press.

Mishkin, F. (1997). Understanding financial crises: a developing country perspective, in M. Bruno and B. Pleskovic (eds), *Annual World Bank Conference on Development Economics*, Washington, DC: World Bank.

Ordover, J., R. Pittman, and P. Clyde (1994). Competition policy for natural monopolies in a developing market economy, *Economics of Transition*, 2: 317–343.

Smith, W. (2000). Regulating utilities: thinking about location questions, World Bank Summer Workshop on Market Institutions, Washington, DC.

Trebilcock, M. (1996). *What Makes Poor Countries Poor? The Role of Institutional Capital in Economic Development*, Toronto: University of Toronto.

7 Good ideas and human welfare
Big Pharma versus the developing nations

Alex Rosenberg

The conflict between the holders of patent rights in antiretroviral anti-AIDS medicines and the interests of a significant proportion of the population of the Republic of South Africa represents a set of problems of increasing gravity for everyone. We can expect repeatedly to face the same problem over the foreseeable and for that matter the unforeseeable future, nationally and internationally, in the developing nations and in the developed ones. Moreover, it is a practical problem whose optimal solution involves so many imponderable considerations and so much potentially contested theory – descriptive and normative – that solving it requires little short of an international crash program by welfare economists, political theorists, and moral philosophers. In this chapter, I make a philosopher's first stab at a possible solution.

The problems associated with the conflicting interests of the holders of patent rights in antiretrovirals from the developed world and the welfare interests of persons infected with HIV in the developing world are the tip of an iceberg that is getting larger. Imagine the potential conflict raised by the discovery of a cure for or vaccine for malaria, or somatic genetic resistance to major illnesses of the third world due to impure water supplies? Imagine the temptations even in developed nations to expropriate gene-chip technology when it provides a cheap, easily replicated, instantaneous tool for diagnosing each individual's 'inborn errors of metabolism', and perhaps even synthesizing the required bioactive molecules in situ. The short-term saving to national health systems of expropriating such technology are potentially budget balancing by themselves. The prospects of ever increasing biochemical and especially genomic innovations in health care are accelerating very rapidly, practically ensuring that the choice faced by the Republic of South Africa will recur again and again in the future, with ramifying consequences even for those without any direct stake in the matter.[1]

Here I want to sketch the nature, magnitude, and solutions of two of the problems raised by the important discoveries and inventions – let's call them good ideas – emanating from the revolution in applied molecular biology. The first is the question of what policy should, from the disinterested point of view, be adopted to adjudicate the conflict between maintaining intellectual property rights and the immediate human welfare benefits of abrogating them. This is an abstract philosopher's question about what, independent of self-interest, we ought to do. The second question may be more important than the first. It is a question of what the owners of intellectual property should do, in their own interests, in light of the fact that regardless of whether they have an untrumpable moral right to their intellectual property, it will be taken away from them in the interests of large numbers of people who need their property and cannot pay a market – or perhaps any – price for it. Their problem, the problem of 'Big Pharma' as we might call it, is what international institution to design and support that will induce these large numbers of people and the states that represent them to refrain from abrogating the rights of intellectual property.

1 The welfare economics of good ideas

Good ideas are the biggest problem in developmental economics, or the economics of growth, and therefore in welfare economics as well. They present so big a problem that it is often treated by developmental economists as if it doesn't exist, or is none of their business, and they may be right to do so. Once land, labor, and current capital are fixed, diminishing returns to scale will always limit total output of whatever it is that people want and need. As Malthus noticed, holding land and capital constant, population increase by itself must ensure ever-increasing emmiseration owing to the increasing supply of and diminishing returns to labor. But Malthus did not reckon with technological change, i.e., with the provision of ideas about how to increase the efficiency of land, labor, and capital inputs in producing output. Good ideas are not just the most important variable for increasing production over time. All increases in the productivity of land (physical capital), labor (human capital), and capital (capital), both separately and together are due to good new ideas. Even narrowly construed, the rate of return on technological investment alone appears to be huge.[2]

But good ideas are quintessentially unpredictable. A famous jazz musician answered the question 'Where is jazz going?' by replying 'If I knew, I would be there already!' As philosophers have regretfully reported, there is no logic of discovery, nor for that matter a psychology, sociology, still less an economic theory that identifies the causal variables responsible for the appearance of good ideas. Accordingly, developmental economists traditionally described technological change as an 'exogenous shock', the cause of the 'residual' leftover component of the data about economic growth which they cannot explain (Solow, 1957). Endogenous growth theory – the account of how an economy grows and what institutional arrangements may abet or hinder such growth – thus seems just to ignore the factor economists recognize as the ultimate and sole source of all economic growth: at most endogenous growth theory introduces forces familiar to economists (e.g., imperfect competition, human capital, levels of R and D investment by government and firms, international trade barriers, von Neumann/Morgenstern uncertainty) that treat good ideas as a desired outcome – a component of the 'objective function' – while going on to the more tractable and academically impressive task of deriving general equilibrium results for model economies adorned by these institutional forces (Romer, 1990).[3]

Of course it's no criticism of economic theory that it cannot make the appearance of good ideas an explanatory variable; no one can, with the possible exception of some future neuroscientist. And not even the neuroscientist can make the provision of good ideas a matter of prediction. That is the point about the jazz musician, and one recognized by philosophers since Popper, who used it to argue that a predictively powerful social science is impossible (Popper, 1957: vii–viii). Besides Popper's ('logical' and controversial) argument for the unpredictability of an innovation, there is the fact that good ideas interact 'strategically', not parametrically, and there is no stable equilibrium toward which the production of such ideas moves. Like a move in a strategic game without a unique Nash equilibrium, one good idea (e.g., Coulomb's law, circa 1840) generates a cascade of interacting improvements that if anything increases the unpredictability of subsequent good ideas (from Coulomb's Law to the microprocessor in 120 years). The complete unpredictability of which, when and where good ideas will be produced means that there is hardly any way to assure their provision by any centrally planned, coordinated or controlled means.[4]

The failure of central planning – whether private or public – to provide efficiently or even at all for good new ideas is a direct consequence of their inherent unpredictability. It is rarely possible to identify and still less to solve a specific intellectual problem merely by throwing money at it from a central source, and it is never possible to do so efficiently. Only the individual person closest to the research frontier has both the relevant information and the incentive to recognize an opportunity to solve a problem and when and how to do so. The central planner is never identical with that individual. Maximizing the provision of good ideas requires maximally decentralizing the decision-making power about investing in their production. One thing that economists since Hayek have of course emphasized is that the *only* institution capable of providing relevant information to those who can make the best use of it is the price system of a free-market economy. A price system is an information-transmission device and one that most efficiently harnesses individual self-interest to provision of good ideas and other things that people really want instead of what planners with the best will in the world think they want.

A free-market price system optimally provides the information required at the most decentralized level required to produce new ideas. But the free market is not sufficient to insure optimal provision, owing to features which good ideas share with that other source of market-failure – the public good. Even more than public goods, good ideas can be optimally consumed by one person without depriving anyone else of the benefits of consuming the good idea. In economist's parlance, once a good idea has been produced the marginal cost of another copy of a good idea is either zero or the price of a stone tablet, a piece of parchment, paper, or a floppy disk. The upshot is of course that as with public goods, a perfectly competitive market will not provide the optimum level of good ideas.

In the case of public goods, the welfare economist's solution to the problem of provision is central planning and government coercion. Since this will not work for good ideas, the solution has been to privatize good ideas, make them intellectual property and provide their originators with patent rights. The analysis is straightforward. A market economy without patent rights will not provide the optimum level of welfare it is capable of providing to its participants. Seeking to invent and/or discover new labor-saving or welfare-increasing ideas about how to organize or reorganize matter takes effort, time, and resources, incurs opportunity costs, and is risky: there is no assurance of success. For many inventions and discoveries, no one has an incentive to undertake the efforts without the assurance of returns; everyone has the incentive, however, to watch others and simply copy any idea others develop that will enhance their welfare. If you expend resources to invent something, say crop rotation for example, others can freely copy if it is observed to work, they will free ride on your efforts. No rational agent wants to take needless risks or be a sucker, so among economically rational agents, there will be a sub-optimal supply of new ideas. But the problem is worse. In a competitive economy without intellectual property rights, some new inventions and discoveries may give their discoverers great advantages if they can keep the innovations secret and so restrict their use. If everyone knows this, many will seek the solution to some problems, in the hope of securing a competitive advantage over others. What happens when one among these many discovers the solution? To reveal the solution to all is to surrender the competitive advantage. If the secret is successfully kept, the others will continue to invest in seeking a solution, thus wasting the economy's scarce resources. The discoverer cannot sell the discovery to those who could make use of it to their own advantage and that of the other economic agents, thus wasting more of the economy's resources. Moreover, it will usually cost the discoverer something to keep the secret, and of course at least some agents will employ resources to engage in industrial espionage to uncover good ideas that others were keeping secret. Result, still more waste of productive resources, and economic inefficiency, which in a market economy makes at least some people, and sometimes even all people, worse off than they would otherwise be.

The absence of intellectual property rights among economically rational agents results in serious under-investment in ideas it is hard to keep secret and serious over-investment in ideas it is easy to keep secret. The introduction of patent rights in such an economy is a welfare-increasing solution to this problem. It is not a solution that optimizes the efficiency of the market, it is merely one that increases its efficiency. It is not an optimal solution for two reasons: most obviously because a patent right is a monopoly, and there is a standard economist's argument to show that monopolies result in welfare losses – the so-called 'dead weight loss' which perfect competition avoids. Less obviously, the monopoly is never quite equal to the level which optimizes the rewards to innovation, since it is always less than the total surplus in the whole economy created by the innovation. Patent rights are a so-called 'second-best' solution because without them the welfare loss to the economy is greater than with them – fewer good new ideas and too much investment in duplicate research, hiding, and stealing results of research. But with patent rights there is still some loss by comparison to the optimum allocation of resources in the economy. An alternative to patent rights that more closely approached the welfare optimum allocation of resources to invention and discovery in the economy would be preferable. But there have long been reasons to think none is available. Accordingly we adopt the second-best solution. A patent is an exchange. The discoverer makes the idea public so that everyone who can improve their productive efficiency by using the idea can easily learn of its existence, thus reducing the amount of resources wasted in duplicating ideas kept secret, making industrial espionage pointless and saving money the innovator would have had to spend to keep the good idea secret. In return the innovator is allowed the exclusive right to sell the innovation for a period of time, after which the right expires and anyone can use the idea without payment. The exclusive right to sell is the monopoly, and the amount of time it can be exercised must be long enough to repay the costs of research, especially for ideas it is easy to copy and hard to keep secret, and the amount of time must be short enough to prevent the monopolist from destroying more of the consumers' surplus than is necessary to motivate research for good ideas.[5]

Some recent work in economic theory suggests that there is an alternative to granting patent rights, which is at least as good and may be better from the point of view of welfare economics (Shavell and van Ypersele, 2000). A system of government rewards for innovation in which payments depend on demand for the products produced by employing the innovation would avoid the deadweight loss resulting from the limited time monopoly accorded to the new ideas owner, and might avoid the under-investment problem that granting the monopoly results in as well. Under this system, the incentive to invest in producing new ideas is the government's payment of a reward. The innovation is sold to competitors at marginal cost so there is no deadweight loss and the incentive to innovate may be closer to optimum if the reward is set equal to the market surplus. It can be shown that a system of governmental rewards to innovators would be superior to a patent system if the government knows enough about the market demand for goods produced using the idea, and if the level of incentives required to get people to invest heavily enough in the invention and discovery of new ideas is not too great.

It is relatively easy to see that despite the soundness of the 'theoretical result' that a system of rewards for new ideas is preferable from the point of view of welfare efficiency, practical difficulties and the great distance of the real world from the economist's idealizations limit the attractiveness of this proposal. In connection with the present problem of whether we abrogate intellectual property rights in the interests of large increases in short-term welfare, the alternative of a reward system is largely irrelevant.

There is to begin with the very large scale of governmental involvement which always raises transaction costs and introduces rent-seeking behavior (AKA, corruption) on the part of bureaucrats, and those who can influence their conduct. The second problem is the requirement that the government secure accurate information about the level of demand for all the products employing an innovation to be rewarded in order to determine the level of reward to the innovator. The potential for misrepresenting demand, improperly increasing demand, added to the costs of measuring demand, will be large. Opportunities to manipulate the market in order to secure higher rewards would be particularly tempting when the product embodying the good idea is cheap to produce – e.g., a pill or a piece of software – and can be purchased heavily by the agents of the ideas owner to secure a reward which may exceed the goods production cost. Notice that a patent scheme places the burden of determining demand on the owner of the good idea, and the burden of rewarding it on purchasers, who have incentives to measure or predict supply and demand accurately. Of course there are some transaction costs of a patent system (the patent office and the patent courts) and opportunities to improperly influence its distributions of income. But a patent system's greater reliance on individuals to pursue their own interests directly, instead of through an intervening government, is generally more efficient than alternatives. As noted, the most efficient system for recording and responding to information about consumers' demands and producers' costs is a market price system. Patent protection relies on such a system more directly if not more fully than does governmental reward.

Most important for our present purposes, the reward scheme and the patent scheme share several salient features which make them pretty much equivalent. Notice, they both accord ownership to the inventor of the good idea and pay for its exploitation. But we are interested here in the question of whether there are circumstances that make it permissible or obligatory to forgo such payments; it does not matter by whom. Second, both the patent system and the reward system reflect national and not international institutions. Just as one nation's patent laws do not have force in other countries, one nation's reward system cannot compensate for a good idea's uses in other countries. In both cases there is a serious problem of securing enforcement and uniformity across developed, developing, and underdeveloped countries with differing needs and interests, who may be unwilling to subscribe either to a patent agreement or a fund for rewarding ideas employed in their jurisdictions.

In what follows I will focus on a patent system as the closest to a practicable solution to the problem of assuring the continued flow of good new ideas. But my claims will apply almost equally to a reward system, should that be more optimal.[6]

2 The political philosophy of good ideas

I believe that a welfarist theory is the only normative basis for institutional design, and in what follows I shall employ it.[7] Welfarism provides a far more compelling argument for according individuals intellectual property rights than for according them any other property-rights. Indeed, so strong an argument as to make *intellectual* property rights – unlike *chattel* property rights – all but untrumpable, no matter what the near-term costs of so entrenching them. Or so I shall argue.

A welfarist argument is one that underwrites a certain policy, institution or outcome on the grounds that it enhances human welfare more fully than available alternatives. Welfarism is a highly controversial political philosophy, owing to its denial that some individual human rights are so morally important that they can never be sacrificed for improvements in welfare, no matter how large. Let us set this problem for Welfarism aside on the reasonable grounds that intellectual property is not one of these human rights untrumpable by considerations of welfare.[8] If the only reason to adopt patent rights is their contribution to human welfare, then it is obvious that such rights cannot conflict with human welfare, that when faced with a choice between honoring such rights even though this reduces welfare, and abridging such rights to enhance welfare, abridgement always wins. Moreover, if a scheme for more nearly approaching the optimum level of investment in new ideas, and so enhancing human welfare, is available, intellectual property rights must be abridged.

Now it seems that nothing could be more obvious than that honoring the patent rights of 'Big Pharma' in the antiretroviral drugs cannot make for greater enhancement in human welfare than abrogating those rights and making such medicines widely available in the developing world. The choice faced by the government of South Africa was, from a moral point of view, a 'no brainer', no?

Well, from the point of view of the committed welfarist, who weighs all moral choices in the light of how the alternatives will affect human welfare, the answer to this question is very far from obvious. The confident affirmative answer to the question can only be based on narrowing the time frame within which we calculate human welfare. Thus, it is a 'no brainer' to conclude that in the immediate and near term human welfare is better served by abridging patent rights in antiretroviral drugs. Once we lengthen our horizon, however, the question becomes much more complicated, and it does so against a number of different dimensions.

The source of the problem is that (a) once patent rights in a pharmaceutical product are abrogated in order to meet the needs of those who cannot pay monopoly prices for them, disincentive effects on investment in innovation set in; (b) these effects will be long lasting or even permanent; and most important (c) it is in the nature of scientific innovations that they are completely unpredictable, and more consequential in their welfare-enhancing effects than any other human activity. Consequently, the medium-term and long-term costs of abrogating patent rights are impossible to quantify or measure in any detail but must, very probably, be huge.[9]

Points (a) and (b) require little argument. (c) both requires some further explanation and argument. But once its ramifications are clear, welfarist arguments against abrogation of intellectual property rights become evident. First, once innovators anticipate that their property may be expropriated when relatively large short-term welfare needs require it, innovators will shift their investments and investigation to those innovations of interest only to the smaller numbers of wealthy people in the developed world who can afford to pay monopoly prices for the innovations. In the case of Big Pharma this means a focus on diseases exclusively of the rich: baldness, impotence, wrinkles, etc. Second, experience with hyperinflation, an inconsistent legal environment, and other sudden departures from settled expectations, always have a persistently chilling effect on participants in a market. They know that even after one of these sudden departures has been concluded, it may occur again. Once the genie is out of the bottle, it is hard to get him back in.[10]

Combining even a slight tendency for (a) and (b) to obtain with the truth of (c) is what makes the abrogation of patent rights so grave a matter. (c) is in part the claim that no other factors are more responsible for improvements in human welfare than intellectual innovation – good ideas. Quite independent of the theoretical claim about decreasing returns to scale of all other factors of production, the claim is close to patently obvious that good ideas are the chief source of welfare-improvements in the history of the world, certainly since the invention of the steam engine, and at an accelerating rate since 1900. Unlike the rest of nature, there is no limit to the stock of new ideas, just because they are not material, and they enable us to rearrange the same quantities of matter endlessly with ever *increasing* return to scale. Consider the implications of Moore's law, that

Good ideas and human welfare 133

the memory capacity of microchips doubles every 18 months; consider that the computer power available for delivery anywhere in the world in less than five days for less than $1000 by mail-order would have cut the cost and time of completion of the Manhattan Project which built the first atomic bombs by a year or more and cut perhaps a billion dollars in 1945 money (50 billion dollars in 2000 money) from the cost.[11] Consider the decrease in infant mortality and the increase in life spans in the developed world over the last century compared with previous centuries. Consider the improvement in human welfare consequent to the invention of mosquito netting, or consequent to the invention of an efficient mechanical process for fabricating it. All these quality-of-life changes are the direct consequence not of opening up new territory or extracting more of the same raw materials, or of increases in labor inputs resulting from population growth. They are all due to good ideas, and good ideas that build on other good ideas. Electricity, the incandescent bulb, the vacuum tube, the cathode ray tube, the transistor, the integrated circuit, the microchip, each is an unanticipated new idea that required its predecessor but also greatly enhanced its predecessor's value. Once we grant the overwhelming importance of intellectual innovations to improvements in welfare, the ramifications of any step that discourages investment in them becomes manifest.

Welfarism is a form of 'consequentialism' in moral decision-making: it holds that the morally best course of action is the one that maximizes future welfare or minimizes future 'ill-fare'. One classic objection to consequentialist theories such as Welfarism is the evident fact that we cannot see very far into the future and so it is difficult to tote up the costs and benefits of alternative courses of action and choose the welfare maximizing one. Accordingly Welfarism is attacked as a policy which cannot be implemented with any confidence. When it comes to weighing up costs and benefits for human welfare of significant disincentives to intellectual innovation, however, this objection has little force. Indeed, we can be confident that the very reverse of its conclusion must be the case. No matter how little we can foresee even the near-term consequences, the long-term benefits of commodifying good ideas must exceed the costs.[12] This policy must be chosen come what may.

3 How long is the long term?

The question of whether we should forgo property rights in good ideas in order to enhance human welfare, or in order to avoid reducing it thus becomes a question about how to trade off the short-, medium-, and long-term effects on human welfare. Let us agree that in the short term, in the immediately foreseeable future, abrogating Big Pharma's property rights in the design of antiretroviral anti-AIDS drugs will result in a net increase in human welfare: the lives of millions of people – including many infants and young children in the Third World – will be saved, the economies of these countries will remain viable, their healthcare systems will not collapse under the burden of the AIDS epidemic. And the only 'downside' will be a reduction in the income of the much better off residents of the developed world who own shares in Big Pharma, are employed by it, or otherwise directly benefit from doing business with it. Indeed, we can anticipate some short-term benefits to the developed world from the Third World's abrogation of First World patent rights: the flow back of cheaper antiretrovirals through a grey market will lower the cost of these drugs for all who need them, rich or poor, and so thereby also increase short-term welfare in the developed world.

But what of the medium term and the long term? Well, as Keynes famously noted, in the long run, we are all dead, so we can disregard the costs and benefits that will emerge from abrogation in the long term. This leaves the medium term. How long is that? One generation, two, three? It is clear that in several important areas of national and international policy debate, the near term is a matter of several, and perhaps even many generations. Consider in particular the debates about environmental and ecological issues: how to dispose of nuclear waste material, closing the hole in the ozone layer, protecting rainforests, global warming, pesticide use, protection of endangered species, exhaustion of water, petroleum, and other scarce resources. In each of these cases the relevant time frame varies from centuries to millennia. In each case, it is recognized that the short-term cost–benefit calculation favors the exercise of (largely property) rights by living people that impose costs (externalities) to be paid by future generations who will not be able to exercise the rights. Nevertheless, the medium-term costs, measured in consequences up to 25 generations (500 years) into the future in the case of nuclear waste storage for example, are agreed by most participants in the debate to swamp the short-term benefits.[13]

To illustrate the problem of the short term versus the near term in the case of intellectual property rights, assume that the population of the world will reach some fixed upper limit, say 10 billion, within the next half century and then remain there. Assume also that the total quantity of arable land, refinable mineral and non-mineral reserves, etc. will remain fixed thereafter. Attach a convenient number to the total level of welfare of this generation: say, 100 units of welfare, distributed probably unequally across the 10 billion people. Now assume the unequal proportions remain constant while the total welfare increases in each subsequent (20 year) generation by 10 percent (i.e., 0.5 percent per annum) as a result of the continual provision of patented good ideas and their implementation. At the end of six generations, the index number for total welfare in the population would reach 161.05 units; at the end of 13 generations, the index number would reach 311.68. Suppose, however, that there is a disease rampant in generation one and patent rights in some pharmaceutical needed to treat the disease are abrogated, for that generation only, resulting in a 20 percent increase in welfare in generation two, owing to increased survival, good health, and the benefits they confer on children, and a decline from 10 percent to 9 percent in per generation welfare increases thereafter owing to the chilling effect on intellectual innovation resulting from the abrogation of patent rights in generation one. These assumptions are liberal as regards the benefits of abrogation in generation one, and may be quite conservative as regards the costs of abrogation in subsequent generations. The result of the 20 percent increase in welfare at generation two and the 9 percent increase in welfare for every generation thereafter, would after 13 generations equal 311.68 units, just slightly less than preserving intellectual property rights in generation two and not enhancing the welfare of those who need but cannot purchase the intellectual property rights in question.

It may be that the numbers assigned to these variables are quite unrealistic. Indeed, it may be held that human welfare does not admit of cardinally measurable units in dollars, euro or rands, or utiles of happiness. Perhaps this is correct. But even if the numbers attached are notional, provided they are non-zero there will always be some generation after which all future generations' level of welfare will be lower if we abrogate intellectual property rights. And after this generation the amount of welfare forgone will increase from generation to generation time without end. Even if the immediate advantage to abrogating intellectual property rights is a doubling of welfare and the subsequent cost is a tenth of 1 percent decrease in the provision of new ideas, at some point in the future the welfare trade-off will turn against abrogation. As for the claim that the quantities in question have no cardinal values, it is certainly true that money cannot buy happiness, nor does it vary in a linear way with welfare, but it can purchase lower infant mortality, longer lifespan, fewer hospitalizations, more human flourishing generally, and most other components of welfare. This is why per capita income is an imperfect but useful measure of welfare. The problems the assumption that welfare is measurable raises are common to all welfare-enhancing policies, and not ones that undermine the present point about the medium-term consequences of abrogating intellectual property rights.

Of course one could postpone the generation at which the costs of abrogating intellectual property rights exceed the benefits of preserving them by 'discounting' the welfare of future generations. One could hold that the welfare of a generation as yet unborn should not be a variable in any cost–benefit calculation, or if it is, it should be reduced by some constant or variable factor, in the way that future income is 'discounted' to determine its present value. But there is no ground in Welfarism, or many other acceptable normative bases for policy decision, for discounting future lives.[14] We may well not have an interest in distant future people, or more likely each of us may well have an ever-diminishing interest in our descendants as the proportion of our genes they share declines, but this is a morally irrelevant consideration. When it comes to political philosophy, blood is no thicker than water.

Here is an argument for discounting future lives, which though not welfarist might nevertheless give the political philosopher pause, especially if he or she takes John Rawls (1971) seriously. Suppose you are placed behind a veil of ignorance, so that you do not know in which generation you will find yourself when the veil is lifted. As a self-interested agent would you choose a policy which (subject to maximum qualifications) trades increased welfare in generation n for a permanent decrease in the improvement of welfare in an indefinitely large, not to say infinite, number of generations thereafter? Well, you might do so under one condition. Behind the veil of ignorance you might choose the one generation improvement at n in exchange for a permanent reduction in the rate of improvement thereafter, if (and it is a big 'if') generation n's level of welfare is below some minimum, the one time improvement in its level of welfare raises its welfare above the minimum, at the cost of reducing the rate of increase in the future, but the level of welfare of future generations is always above that minimum. Then behind the veil of ignorance, not knowing whether we were to find ourselves in generation n or a later generation, we would choose policies which have this effect. And this is a conclusion to which Welfarism must accommodate itself.

It is probably the case that in the past, perhaps before the industrial revolution, the general level of welfare throughout the world was below a minimum which would have made abrogation of intellectual property rights in exchange for short-term welfare improvements morally permissible. But even if the feasible levels of production and distribution of welfare-enhancing goods and services were once below the minimum level in question, it is highly debatable that they are now below that level. What is not debatable is that current inequalities in distribution of these welfare-creating goods and services condemn many actual people to a level of welfare below the minimum in question. So, from a welfarist point of view, the question becomes that of choosing among those policies which will bring the largest numbers of people currently living at least up to the minimum at the cost of the smallest reduction in the rate of welfare growth for generations thereafter. Ironically, the crucial premise of the argument that the greatest *increase* in immediate welfare will be brought about by abrogating the intellectual property of 'Big Pharma' is at the same time the crucial premise in the argument that doing so will bring about the greatest long-term *reduction* in the rate of welfare growth. For the only reason to think that expropriating good ideas will have the greatest positive effect on short-term welfare is to admit that innovations, inventions and discoveries are the most powerful engines of medium-term welfare improvement. To bring current people above the minimum permissible level of welfare there are many policies from which we might choose – schemes of redistribution, education, public service, industrialization, civil rights and liberties, education for women, pollution abatement, etc. – each of which could raise the same number of people or even the very same individuals above the welfare minimum. None of them can have medium-term costs as great as those to be borne consequent to a reduction in the provision of good ideas.

'Yes but people are dying now who might be saved by these drugs which they cannot afford.' I agree that this is a compelling reason to do something now. But from the point of view of a moral theory which values present lives and future ones all equally, and given the facts about the welfare impact of good new ideas, this compelling plea is not a morally compelling reason to abrogate intellectual property rights. It is much more plausibly a reason to abrogate *traditional* private property rights over moveable chattels, which can be bought and sold in something approximating a competitive market and whose proceeds can be used to purchase innovative ideas – such as antiretroviral drugs – at their current monopoly prices. For the provision of new ideas is, as a sheer brute empirical fact of the matter, a far stronger engine of welfare improvement than is the protection of private chattel property from taxation or expropriation.

4 The political economy of intellectual property

Regardless of how iron clad is the moral argument for why we should all respect intellectual property rights, the fact is that at some point the temptation to abrogate these rights in the interests of a nation's citizens must become overwhelming to a government which their citizens choose. For governments famously are prepared to sacrifice long-term benefits, especially other people's long-term benefits, in order to secure election and reelection, if not to avoid unconstitutional and even violent overthrow. Developing nations with endemic problems of disease and without an infrastructure capable of producing marketable new ideas, or much else the developed world is prepared to pay for, have an ever-increasing temptation to free-ride on the discovery and invention of good new ideas, especially in health care, generated in the developed world.

It is therefore in the interests of Big Pharma to put incentives in place among developing nations to respect their intellectual property rights. This is a problem rather more restricted to Big Pharma than it is one facing other multinational businesses whose chief asset is intellectual property, for two reasons: first, other forms of intellectual property, software for instance, cannot be employed without substantial expenditures on hardware. Since it is easier to restrict access to hardware, the temptation to free-ride by pirating software is somewhat easier to police than chemical formulae. Furthermore, it is unlikely that first world opponents of globalization, international capitalism, and the World Trade Organization, are likely to attack companies engaged in monopolistic pricing of their rap music videos. On the other hand, Big Pharma must deal with the fact that not only are its assets in good ideas subject to expropriation in the developing world, but its business practices may come under scrutiny if not restriction, in Big Pharma's home markets, through the action of First World advocates for Third World health development.

Protecting their intellectual property requires Big Pharma to design and support institutional arrangements that give potential free riders an interest in preserving patent rights. This is also an interest of all those in the developed world who will benefit from the discovery of treatments for diseases they share with inhabitants of the Third World or who benefit from improvements in the quality of life in the Third World. Bear in mind that these improvements will be both huge and completely unpredictable, to the degree that they hinge on the provision of good new ideas. As we have seen, centralized international solutions to the problem of providing good new ideas are unfeasible. The provision of particular good new ideas cannot be centrally planned.

There is another desideratum which may be harnessed by Big Pharma to secure acquiescence in property rights for the good ideas it wants to keep. Even while retaining their property rights in good ideas, Big Pharma is not likely to focus on the diseases of the developing world. If their research produces treatments for these diseases, it will be the result of serendipity. It is in the nature of the case that many treatments result from serendipity. So even without focusing on diseases of the Third World, Big Pharma may produce such results. On the other hand, it would motivate respect for Big Pharma's patent rights in wrinkle creams if such respect were tied to support for research into diseases of the poor, instead of the rich.

The solution is not going to be found in paying taxes to governments – national or supernational – to subsidize research in diseases of the developing world. Over the long term internationally subsided not-for-profit research institutes of the sort that brought us the Green Revolution will not solve this problem. Recall, new ideas are unpredictable. The search for them must be maximally decentralized and must harness individual initiative and information. And consider recent history. Although the funding system of the US National Institutes of Health, the National Science Foundation, the Howard Hughes Medical Foundation, the (UK) Wellcome Trust, and similar public and private agencies have a strong record of identifying and fostering innovation in basic science, the scientists they support did not make much of a contribution to pharmaceutical development until governmental policy (in the form of the Dole–Bayh act in the US) held out the prospect of monetary reward for doing so. More significantly, the history of scientific innovation in the Soviet Union, especially in the life sciences and high-tech sector should be an object lesson in the failure of governmental policy and central planning to produce good new ideas. Over its last 20 years, the Soviet Union could not even copy good ideas, let alone produce them.[15]

So, to begin with, members of Big Pharma need to impose a tax on their own earnings with which to fund an international venture-capital institution – Third World Pharma – to invest in new research and development efforts in the developing world. These efforts must take the shape of private companies in which shareholding employee scientists have serious incentives to focus on good ideas that are useful in the developing countries where they are working.

These firms would retain intellectual property rights in their discoveries and inventions. The participating scientists would have to have strong stakeholder or shareholder incentives to focus on those problems that promise to combine near-term solubility and widespread welfare payoffs for the regions in which these scientists work. And the nations within which these firms operate will have to have an aggregate (but not a disaggregated) stake in the returns to intellectual property of these firms' discoveries. It is this stake in the returns to intellectual property which give developing nations an incentive to respect the intellectual property of Big Pharma, and this constitutes the reward to it for its investment in Third World Pharma.

The governments of individual Third World nations would secure rights to direct the investment decisions of this venture-capital institution, in return for enforcing intellectual property rights in their jurisdictions. But decisions about what areas to invest in would be made by Third World Pharma operating as a for-profit venture capital style business. Returns to the fund would be determined by market demand for products produced as a result of its investments. Its beneficial owners – Third World nations – would therefore have an incentive to make sound 'business decisions' about investment, and block attempts by coalitions of members to hijack the fund into making investments which do not have prospects for optimal returns. Individual consortia of scientists in developing nations would make proposals to Third World Pharma for support in exchange for equity interests in the intellectual property they produce, and the scientist's consortia will themselves secure income only from the property rights in discoveries and inventions they produce. In order to ensure that these consortia focus their research on problems endemic to the developing world, and do not simply compete to seek cures for diseases of the rich, their incomes would have to be limited only to revenue from sales in their home markets, or regional markets – nations with the same health concerns. This would focus research on innovations that are affordable and in real demand in developing countries. Thus, all participants would have strong incentives to devote resources to producing and exploiting intellectual property with direct useable benefits for Third World health.

There is however a 'catch'. In order to work, this plan must impose restrictions on the freedoms of individual scientists not hitherto considered acceptable. To secure able potential scientists and train them requires resources. Third World Pharma could certainly identify potential candidates and support their training in scientific centers, whether in the first or third worlds. And these scientists could make binding commitments, in exchange for training to return to their countries of origin and participate in consortia supported by Third World Pharma. But the fact is, such commitments are not practically enforceable. As demonstrated by the 'brain-drain' of physicians, scientists, and technically talented people from the Third World to the First World over the past half century, despite immigration regulations, support agreements, temporary visas, etc., enforcing such obligations is extremely difficult. It is not just that individuals who have trained in developed countries often do not want to leave, but many of the institutions which offered them training do not want the foreign-born scientists to leave! They have become too valuable as contributors to the institutions which trained them. Both parties – the individuals and the institutions – make efforts to circumvent policies designed to return trained persons to nations which need their skills. This is an outcome that will unravel the proposal. Students that Third World Pharma sends to labs in universities and companies in the developed world would want to stay, and the best of them would be invited to stay. Successful and creative scientists who have returned to their country of origin will be sought out and hired to return to the developed world, to universities, and for that matter to Big Pharma.

The problem is not just restricted to this proposal of course. Indeed, it reflects an issue on the horizon of First World/Third World relations over the near term as aging populations in the developed countries make the immigration of younger workers imperative. We can anticipate over the medium-term future the following sort of condemnation of the developed world, especially of the United States, which has long afforded the easiest immigration access – both legal and illegal – in the developed world. As populations in the developed world age, the proportion of people securing pensions will increase while the proportion of employed persons paying for these pensions will decline. In Western Europe the ratio will soon be 1:2. The easiest solution to this problem is the large-scale immigration of productive persons from developing countries, who will do better in the developed world, will generate economic benefits in these countries and will pay taxes to support pensions in these countries. (Indeed if they are illegal immigrants they may pay taxes without securing benefits.) The long-term effect of such free immigration will be to widen the disparities in human capital between countries and further exacerbate inequalities in welfare among them. After all, it is the healthier, stronger, more intelligent, ambitious individuals who successfully make their way over obstacles to new places. If what has been said above about the importance of good new ideas to economic growth and development is correct, and if by and large smart educated people have more good ideas than others, the free movement of people around the world is an even larger threat to human welfare than the abrogation of intellectual property rights.

Here are fundamental human rights, not just intellectual or real property rights, coming into conflict with considerations of human welfare. It is all well and good to argue that in the long run, just like free trade in everything else, free movement of people will even out disparities by attracting each person to his or her most productively efficient calling and location. To repeat Keynes' mantra, in the long run we are all dead. Medium-term solutions will always fill the vacuum left by the long term. In the past these conflicts have always been settled by expropriation of property, abrogation of rights, sometimes with and sometimes without compensation. It will turn out to be something of an irony if those who now advocate open access to First World economies and societies for immigrants of ambition, energy, and initiative fleeing from the poverty of their countries of origin begin to demand restrictions on such movement of people, in order to prevent developed nations from sucking these nations dry of their most productive assets.

Short of enforced prohibition of free movement by just the sort of people whom citizens of developed countries should want to immigrate, it is hard to identify a solution to this potential conflict between human rights and welfare. On the other hand, the establishment of a Third World Pharma with sufficient resources to enable many such people of ambition, energy, and initiative to find intellectual and material reward developing good new ideas that would otherwise not emerge, could not make this problem worse.[16]

Notes

1 The fact that the aim of the Republic of South Africa was not to provide antiretroviral drugs to the estimated 30 percent of the population likely to need such medicines to survive, but simply to lower all drug prices in order to effect health care savings, does not reduce the significance of the problem. In fact, the reluctance of the government to respond effectively to the AIDS/HIV problem is more than disturbing. So is the markup at which 'Big Pharma' prices its drugs (Cleary and Ross, 2002).
2 See Griliches (1957) for an influential early exploration of how great is the excess of benefits over costs that is produced by good ideas.
3 This program of research in development economics substantiates the analysis of centrality of general equilibrium analysis throughout theorizing in many branches of economics I have advanced repeatedly (see Rosenberg, 1993) and which has been widely decried by economists as exaggerated.
4 This is not to deny that they can be generically fostered, as by the US National Institutes of Health or National Science Foundation. But even the success of these institutions is a testimony to the importance of maximally decentralizing research decisions to the individual laboratory researcher.
5 It is quite likely in the case of Big Pharma at present all of these variables are set at too generous a level, particularly in light of the indirect subsidy provided by the US NIH, DOE, and NSF through university research support they were able to exploit (Cleary and Ross, 2002). Accordingly, the number of years usually accorded their patent protections is too great, and the return on their investments is probably well above the level required to induce them (see Nordhaus, 1969).

6 Some have and will respond to this analysis by decrying the 'commodification' of good ideas it reflects and pointing out that over the historical past, it has not been necessary to incentivize people to produce good ideas. The best ideas, pure science for example, are produced in an environment of strongly institutionalized communism, as Robert Merton noted three generations ago. In reply it should be noted, first, that over the last 400 years the social institution of science has incentivized and rewarded those who provide good ideas with fame, prestige, security and in many cases financial reward. Second, many important good ideas were produced in response to the provision of money prizes – e.g. the method of determining longitude at sea. Third, the costs of providing good new ideas, as well as the benefit they provide, have become so much greater in recent years, especially in health care, that commodification is a small price to pay for assuring their continued and ever-increasing rate of provision.

7 I recognize that the theory has many problems, in particular the problem of reconciling it with our convictions about untrumpable human rights and justice, and about the nature of welfare. For an introduction to them see Hausman's contribution (Chapter 3). Suffice it to say that competing theories have more severe problems. Among the problems welfarism faces, I cannot include those raised in Hamilton's contribution (Chapter 10). Perhaps the least controversial obstacle to adopting Hamilton's position is that there is no incentive-compatible way of institutionalizing the needs/preferences distinction which his view requires.

8 In particular I reject as obscurantist the argument attributed to Hegal that intellectual property is an expression of the innovator's person or character and I reject as tendentious the claim of some natural rights theorists that one has a natural right to the immediate creation of one's self.

9 This may be expressed as an expected value calculation: even if the probability of some good idea's appearance is low, the product of a low probability and a huge money or welfare pay-off must itself be huge.

10 On the general point of the role of trust in governmental promises see Bates (Chapter 2) and Nattrass and Seekings (Chapter 9).

11 Which is not to say that the Manhattan Project produced a net increase in human welfare. See the brief discussion of the welfare cost of good ideas in note 12 below.

12 Welfare reducing innovations, from gas to nuclear weapons to biotoxins may be held up as counter-examples to this claim. 'Good ideas' – like nuclear power – with unintended consequences may be even more serious counter-examples. It is, however, clear that a system of property rights in innovation is the one most likely to induce the provision of new ideas that will help solve problems like nuclear waste. Innovations designed to reduce human welfare are another matter, and their rate of provision is probably independent of any property scheme for ideas or chattels.

13 In making recommendations for the storage of nuclear waste in the USA, the National Academy of Sciences adopted a planning horizon of 10,000 years (500 generations).

14 Notwithstanding the huge problem this generates (see Parfit, 1984).

15 Note that among its policies was a reward-payment system something like the one discussed earlier, which did not elicit a sufficient supply of such innovations.

16 For comments on previous drafts I am indebted to Don Ross, Allan Buchanan, and Marion Hourdequin. Research for this chapter was begun while I was a senior visiting fellow at the Center for Social Philosophy, Bowling Green State University in 2000. I am grateful for its support.

References

Cleary, S. and D. Ross (2002). The 1998–2001 legal struggle between the South African government and the international pharmaceutical industry: a game – theoretical analysis, *Journal of Social, Political and Economic Studies*, 27: 445–494.

Griliches, Z. (1957). Hybrid corn: an exploration in the economy of technological change, *Econometrica*, 25: 501–522.

Nordhaus, W. (1969). *Invention, Growth and Welfare*, Cambridge, MA: MIT Press.

Parfit, D. (1984). *Reasons and Persons*, Oxford: Oxford University Press.

Popper, K. (1957). *The Poverty of Historicism*, London: Routledge.

Rawls, J. (1971). *A Theory of Justice*, Cambridge, MA: Harvard University Press.

Romer, P. (1990). Endogenous technical change, *Journal of Political Economy*, 98: 70–102.

Rosenberg, A. (1993). *Economics – Mathematical Politics or Science of Diminishing Returns*, Chicago, IL: University of Chicago Press.

Shavell, S. and T. van Ypersele (2000). Rewards versus intellectual property rights. Working Paper, Harvard Economics Department.

Solow, R. (1957). Technical change and the aggregate production function, *Review of Economic Statistics*, 30: 214–231.

8 The WTO, unfair trade and development

Don Ross

1 Philosophical preliminaries

There may not be many points of consensus over what best promotes economic development, but here is one that has formed over the past decade: the institutional context matters a lot. This represents the single greatest shift in economic thinking about development since World War II, for there once was an almost equally clear consensus that institutions *do not* matter, since capital was supposed to be able to find its way through and around them, whatever they were like, to the magnet of highest returns. I know of no significant group of economists who believe that anymore. To this extent, development theory is *not* just the cacophony of rival opinions it might appear to be when the grain of analysis is drawn more finely.

But of course we *do* require finer grains of analysis when debating policies, including policies for the design of the all-important institutions. In this essay I will focus on one of these institutions, the World Trade Organization, and on the ethical criticisms to which it is regularly subjected. My contention will be that most of that criticism has, so far, been of very limited use to the promotion of development, because it has been insensitive to the dynamics of bargaining, including ethically informed and guided bargaining.

The stalking horse for my argument will be the reflections of a leading moral philosopher, Peter Singer, who devotes about a quarter of his 2002 book on globalization, called *One World*, to the shortcomings of the WTO. I choose Singer for the role of foil for two reasons. First, while his analysis is organized around the main themes of the populist criticisms heard against the WTO, Singer channels them through careful reasoning and attentiveness to facts. Thus, for example, he scrutinizes the evidence for a proposition dear to the hearts of self-styled 'anti-capitalist' activists, that globalization in general, and the WTO regime in particular, have made poor countries materially worse off, and rejects it. This is not to say that he supports the opposite proposition; rather, he argues that the facts we would need to justify either generalization are not to hand. Arguing with ideologically committed people who are interested only in facts that support their preconceptions is tiresome. Singer is worth arguing with because he is not such a person. Second, I share enough of Singer's background moral assumptions that when I enter into this debate with him, our disagreements are really *about* the WTO, and not about wider issues in moral philosophy that are logically prior.

Let me begin, then, by stating these background assumptions. Like Singer, I am a consequentialist. That is to say, I believe that the moral status of a political, social, legal, or economic policy or institutional framework should be assessed by reference to its impact on actual human welfare, not against its conformity to abstract deontological principles. I do not assume that material welfare is all that matters. However, I *do* assume that if an effect of implementing a suggested moral principle were reduction of, or stagnation in improvement of, average human material welfare, given the present actual and soon-to-be-actual global population level,[1] this would constitute overwhelming evidence against the acceptability of that principle. I also join Singer in assuming that the welfare of all people in the world should be weighted equally in choosing principles for designing policies and institutions. Specifically, I assume that nationalism, of a kind that allows people to prefer policies that benefit their co-nationals to the detriment of, or in indifference to, the welfare of foreigners, is *prima facie* immoral. Putting this in terms that will be familiar to philosophers, I reject 'communitarianism' as a *fundamental* principle. I of course accept that membership in communities is a very important part of most people's well-being, and that for that reason we ought not to prefer policies or institutions that *gratuitously* disrupt communities. But I assume that communities have no moral standing in and of themselves, over and against the welfare of their actual members. Thus, if most members of some ethnic, national or regional community would be better off, by their own lights, were that community to disappear, then the extinction of the community in question would not be a morally relevant loss (all else being equal).[2]

In this chapter, I will use the concepts of 'welfare' and 'well-being' interchangeably. I do not share the view of Sen (1999 and elsewhere), let alone the more extreme version of the view expressed by Hamilton in Chapter 10, that people can be made better off against their own preferences. This is mainly because I do not believe that the tyrannical effects of paternalism can realistically be controlled if it is allowed a conceptual foot through the door, given all our inductive evidence about human moral and factual reasoning. I therefore prefer to ban paternalism outright by requiring that actual, subjective preferences of all people, as expressed in their actual behavior, be fully respected in moral reasoning and bargaining. I would add, against Hamilton's contention that 'needs' should be weighted heavily against mere 'wants', that I cannot imagine how any broadly democratic institutional mechanisms that tried to capture this distinction could avoid incentivizing people to promote their *merest* 'wants' into 'needs'. I thus believe, as a factual matter, that insofar as a policy regime sought to implement Sen's or Hamilton's ethical framework, it would further encourage rent-seeking behavior; and that is about the last thing we should want to see. (Indeed, speaking as a philosopher with some considered metaphysical opinions, I do not really understand how Hamilton's distinction between 'wants' and 'needs' could be made consistent at all. Very competent philosophers, such as Braybrooke (1987), have attempted this and, in my view, failed.)

Among authors represented in this book, my meta-ethical position is thus close to that of Rosenberg (though I do not agree with him that any moral considerations count against discounting the utility of future generations at some argued and non-arbitrary rate based on preferences of actually living people). I agree with Hausman in Chapter 3 that we must be careful to take wealth effects into close account when performing cost–benefit analyses, but I think there is a widespread exaggeration of the extent to which economists are usually ethically insensitive in practice when they recommend policies based on such analyses. In my experience, most development economists are morally sophisticated people who are relatively good at empathizing with the poor because they know quite a bit about them.

Finally, by way of general preliminaries in stating my background moral assumptions, I do not join Singer in his famous (and thoroughly argued) view that a utilitarian evaluation should directly weigh the interests of all sentient creatures. I instead follow the framework of Binmore (1994, 1998) in believing that (cognitive) ability to bargain is crucial for establishing a claim to a moral stake, and that all who cannot bargain – animals, infants, soon-to-exist people, and the severely cognitively impaired – have morally relevant interests only to the extent that their well-being matters to the well-being of actual bargainers. Fortunately, I think there are good reasons (carefully examined by Binmore) for believing that where institutions for bargaining are morally and economically well designed, the interests of non-bargainers with capacities for suffering will generally be quite strongly represented.[3] Where my disagreement with Singer on this question matters to my arguments in this chapter, this will be noted; and I will confine my case against him to questions on which it does not matter.

2 The WTO as a *prima facie* good

On, then, to consideration of the WTO. At first glance, it would be expected that to a consequentialist as described above the establishment of the WTO, with its actual institutional rules and procedures, would have constituted an improvement for the prospects of developing countries. The GATT (General Agreement on Tariffs and Trade) process that the WTO replaced had been one that significantly affected developing countries and least-developed countries (LDCs), simply by significantly affecting the global economy in general, but in which most of them had no participation. These countries (henceforth, for brevity, to be referred to collectively as 'non-OECD countries'[4]) were generally exempt from the constraints of GATT, and in this respect could be conceptualized as free riders on it (Schott, 2000). However, what they got for 'free' was mainly a 'right' of dubious benefit: they could pursue import-substitution policies if they chose. I need not argue against Stiglitz (Chapter 1) that this could, given the right mix of *other* policies and factors, like hard-working populations and high domestic rates of savings, have been useful in some cases. It is highly unlikely, however, that it provided a *net* benefit against the fact that, as non-participants in the GATT, non-OECD countries could profit from international trade only when and as OECD countries chose to allow them to, for self-interested economic or strategic reasons.[5] If some countries were permitted, for political reasons, to shelter their 'infant industries' behind protective walls when they had no *institutionalized* negotiating power, it is hard to see how *more* institutionalized negotiating power could have harmed them under otherwise unchanged political circumstances.

As Singer emphasizes, the most important way in which the WTO plays an institutional role independent of the policy choices of its member governments is through the operation of its Dispute Settlement Body (DSB). DSB panels are essentially trade courts. As with other courts, their rulings will tend to be no fairer, against a given abstract ethical standard, than the rules they enforce. I will turn to issues around the fairness of current trade rules below. First, however, we should ask whether the DSB has been *procedurally* unfair. This question can itself be further analyzed into two subsidiary ones. The *consequences* of DSB procedures, as I will also discuss in more detail later, inherit lopsidedness directly from the global imbalances in economic power. However, there is no evidence that the DSB magnifies this imbalance by being biased toward the *cases* of OECD countries (Hudec, 2002). Evaluated as a court, the DSB seems to be in ethical circumstances quite similar to those of domestic courts in modern democracies. That is, it is *legalistically* fair in its procedures, but avoids confronting or dealing with, at least systematically, the fact that legalistic fairness is compatible with special exploitation of court procedures and outcomes by those disputing parties who have more resources.

Again, I will return to the details of all this later. For the moment, I want just to make the following point. To the extent that poor people within societies, or poor nations in the world, face a choice between a legalistically fair court system, however far short of a higher standard of fairness the consequences of its operations might fall in practice, and no court at all, the first is their better option. Prior to the establishment of formal dispute settlement procedures (which began under the GATT but which required voluntary participation by *both* sides prior to the WTO regime), poor countries could not even *have* trade 'disputes' with industrial ones. Richer countries determined trade rules and practices among themselves and poorer countries lived with the consequences. Some could, and did, exploit their strategic significance in the Cold War to extract reciprocal concessions, but this was entirely an accidental and passing historical basis of (limited) power. The fact that the DSB exists, and that an OECD country can anticipate losing a case before it to a non-OECD country if the former *simply* acts in its self-interest without regard to treaty obligations, must constitute *some* minimal gain in influence to poorer countries. It is for this reason, along with the fact that under the WTO non-OECD countries are at least party to the making of trade treaties (even if they are distinctly weaker parties), that I said above that the transformation of the GATT system excluding most poor countries into the inclusive WTO constituted a *prima facie* good for poor nations.

Of course, being a merely *prima facie* good is the weakest possible sort of good. The WTO as a whole, or the DSB in particular, could be *prima facie* goods for non-OECD countries and still be practically irrelevant, or even net bads, for poor countries if negative implications of their practices cancel out or overwhelm the good they promote through awarding an increased voice in formal bargaining and disputes. That the WTO and the DSB give non-OECD countries formal representation in trade bargaining and dispute resolution establishes only one point of importance: if we were persuaded that the current system ought to be scrapped on grounds of its unfairness, a return to the pre-Uruguay status quo could only constitute an improvement if poorer countries are better off pursuing autarchy, or at least radical import-substitution policies, than they are in *some* kind of integrated commercial relationship with the rest of the world. *No* persuasive economic analysis suggests that attempted autarchy is anything but disastrous for development, and *no* democratic or semi-democratic non-OECD government believes otherwise. I will therefore assume from here on that when we argue about the WTO, we are arguing about reforming it rather than abolishing it.

3 Unfairness in world trade rules

So what *are* the main respects in which the current world trading system is 'unfair'? And how is this unfairness directly manifest in the operations of the WTO? Let me try to provide a summary descriptive catalogue. First, though, to avoid a lengthy philosophical digression on the analysis of 'fairness', I will just operationally stipulate a sufficient, but not necessary, condition for it weak enough to be non-controversial. I will call a practice, institutionalized norm, rule, or policy 'unfair' if it requires special, *ad hoc* rationalization to be defended even by reference to the prevailing ethical norms of those whose interests it best favors, and even if the people with these interests do not regard highly unequal distributions of wealth *per se* as implying *any* unfairness. If something is unfair even against that standard, then it is unfair against *any* standard that allows *anything* to count as 'unfair'.

And, yes, even by this standard the world trading system is unfair. Almost all advocates of freer trade defend it by reference to broadly Ricardian logic: welfare is best promoted if countries and regions can exploit their comparative advantages. The comparative advantages of non-OECD countries lie almost exclusively in lower labor costs, longer and wetter growing seasons (in most cases) for agricultural products, and direct access to some valuable natural resources. An ethical perspective according to which the WTO improves on the GATT because it makes non-OECD countries party to trade bargaining and dispute resolution cannot consistently deny that this improvement substantially consists in bringing trade practice into increasingly better conformity with this minimal Ricardian logic. Yet every general source of poor-country comparative advantage listed above is systematically undermined by the policies of OECD countries and (ethically) defended by special pleas. When any non-OECD country successfully invades a new OECD market on the basis of a comparative advantage in labor costs, then unless it returns substantial profit shares to OECD-based investors – and even this provides no guarantee – it can expect its new products to be met with anti-dumping actions or other disingenuous 'safeguards'. Non-OECD agricultural products are systematically shut out of OECD markets, while subsidized OECD agricultural products drive down profits from farming even *in* non-OECD countries. Whereas genuine dumping – below-cost pricing *not* resulting from efficient exploitation of comparative advantage – is almost non-existent in manufacturing or services, where non-OECD countries find themselves routinely accused of it, the flow of subsidized agricultural products into poor countries really *is* dumping. Trade in commodities most nearly approaches freedom under the rules, but in the context of widespread tariff escalation[6] this amounts to *special* defense of OECD comparative advantage. In general – as in the trade in services agreement (TRIMS), and with respect to intellectual property protection rules (TRIPS) – existing multilateral treaty provisions promote comparative advantages that OECD countries tend to have, and neglect or suppress comparative advantages that non-OECD countries tend to have. This is unfair by even the weak standard – as the overwhelming majority of economists agree and emphasize.

It is often pointed out that non-OECD countries interfere with one another's exploitation of comparative advantages even more than OECD countries do. This is true, as even a well-informed source with no self-interested reason to stress the point, South African Finance Minister Trevor Manuel (2003), acknowledges. Furthermore, they often do so by means of the same disingenuous semantics over 'dumping' that rich countries resort to. However, from the perspective of an evaluation concerned with *fairness*, rather than efficiency, this is beside the point. Failure among a group of countries to achieve Ricardian improvements *in general* is unfortunate (for them), and may typically result from (unfair) influence of domestic rent-seekers within the countries in question; but it does not constitute unfairness in the network of relationships among these countries. What is unfair to non-OECD countries in the current international trading system is that it systematically promotes OECD countries' comparative advantages while systematically failing to promote non-OECD countries' comparative advantages. It is not – at least as envisaged in the multilateral processes of the WTO – simply a consequence of a generalized failure of bargaining to crawl toward Pareto-efficient outcomes, as with the inefficiency of trade outside the OECD. It is a direct consequence of power imbalances which the logic of the process, by the norms that justify it according to all participants, is supposed to undermine or at least aim at discounting. To try to make this point as clear as possible: *most* multilateral trade relationships, outside of regional common markets, may be messes from the Ricardian perspective, but not all messes are *made* messes *by* being *unfair*. The rules enforced by the DSB *are* partly made problematic by being unfair.

We may analyze the WTO's institutional role in this unfairness into two components. First, there are aspects internal to treaty-making processes and to the contents of existing agreements. Trade in agriculture has not yet been brought within the regime, and as of this writing all progress toward incorporating it has stalled. This is despite the fact that a crucial part of the basis on which the WTO was created was a commitment by OECD countries that agricultural trade rules *would* be regularized. The standing definition of 'dumping' in the Uruguay Round Agreement is uselessly flexible and economically incoherent (Jackson, 1997; Messerlin, 2000), thus inviting its manifest abuse. The nuts and bolts of multilateral negotiation go on in so-called 'Green Room' sessions to which most poorer countries are not invited, lack the political clout to force themselves into, and would lack the resources for full participation in on an ongoing basis even if a red carpet were rolled out for them (Tussie and Glover, 1993). At WTO Ministerial meetings, where treaties must be ratified, time pressures and procedural rigidity hamper the evolution of fluid logrolling dynamics that might enable poor countries to profit from vote selling. This makes it extremely difficult for them to change the status quo, even incrementally.

Second, DSB procedural features contribute to prevailing unfairness. Poorer countries lack resources to prepare or argue cases as thoroughly or professionally as OECD countries (Delich, 2002), something that is always a source of unfairness in any strongly legalistic process. Dispute resolution is widely regarded as slow (Messerlin, 2000). Since an ongoing dispute pending resolution is typically more damaging on the margin to a poorer disputant, this incentivizes non-OECD countries to avoid disputes by making concessions, rather than to stand on the law and try to win them.

DSB panels may not recommend, in the first instance, specific remedies that would constitute compliance with their decisions; if an aggrieved party regards a response by its opponent as insufficient under treaty obligations, it must open a new procedure. This of course increases the capacity of stronger parties to drag issues out and thus reap the rewards of greater patience – the basic source of power in any bargaining relationship. In any case, poor countries can seldom find retaliatory measures that significantly damage, and thus effectively sanction, rich countries whose policies seriously harm them; and given Ricardian logic, retaliation by means of withdrawal of concessions – what victory at the DSB allows – at best hits the opposing party by means of hitting oneself.

An obvious way to inquire into the extent to which the WTO could be improved as an institutional engine for fairness is to ask whether and how the structural problems just catalogued could be reduced by reform. I will return to this in the final section of the chapter. First, however, I want to turn to Singer's ethical critique, and ask to what extent it encourages us to even ask these questions. My contention will be that it mainly does not, that it instead distracts our attention toward issues of distinctly secondary importance, if not outright irrelevance. Since, as I indicated above, Singer is among the most careful and responsible ethical critics of the WTO, this implies that most of the populist ethical skepticism he filters through better analysis is that much further beside the point of really helping non-OECD countries.

4 Singer's charges

Singer makes three main ethical charges against the WTO. These are:

i The WTO's mandate, and the structure of representation in its procedures, lets commercial values trump all others.
ii The WTO undermines (ethically legitimate) national sovereignty.
iii The WTO is undemocratic.

As noted earlier, he also considers a fourth charge, that WTO agreements and DSB rulings have made poor countries and/or poorer people within countries, worse off, but finds that known facts are inadequate to decide for or against the accusation.

On the fourth issue, I am prepared to be a *bit* less cautious than Singer. Only one part of the world, sub-Saharan Africa, has actually slid backwards *since* being integrated within the WTO system. Some other parts – central Asia and the Middle East – have slid backwards while *not* integrated within the system.[7] Eastern Europe experienced a period of increased impoverishment *before* integration, but has been doing better as it has been integrated. Latin America, quite strongly integrated, has at worst been stagnant over the period since Uruguay, though this is likely too pessimistic an assessment for the region in general.[8] In the two countries where a massive proportion of the world's poor are concentrated, China and India, increased integration has coincided with impressive growth. Inequality within these countries has probably increased, but I know of no persuasive evidence that the poorest have become *worse* off. Singer is certainly right that establishing causal relationships in global-level macroeconomics is extremely difficult, so any confident pronouncement on these matters *must* outrun available evidence.

I suggest that, in general, we can and should side-step this issue in a way that does not occur to Singer. Stiglitz (Chapter 1) argues that we have little empirical evidence that 'Washington consensus' macroeconomic policies have consistently promoted growth. I here take no stand on this argument. What *is* clear, however, is that the IMF and the World Bank are genuinely powerful institutions whose policies have surely made some significant difference, though probably of equivocal valence in different instances. Now, to the extent that trade liberalization as encouraged within the mandate of the WTO is seen as part of a broader 'Washington consensus' agenda – which is the context in which Singer considers his fourth issue – the kind of assumption I just granted to Stiglitz in the cases of the IMF and World Bank is much harder to justify with respect to the WTO. The history of the WTO to date, for reasons I will discuss below, has mainly been one of failure to achieve Washington-style objectives. I refer here not only to the fact that no real progress has been made in (global) multilateral trade negotiations since the conclusion of the Uruguay Round. It is also the case, as I will discuss in connection with Singer's issues (i)–(iii), that implementation of the Uruguay Agreement has done at least as much to promote unintended *non*-Washington-style ends as those its OECD-based champions expected. In general, I will contend, the WTO has accomplished so little of an *intended* nature, in an unequivocal and coherent policy direction – something for which the WTO Secretariat is *not* to blame – that it would be surprising if we did or could find data implicating it strongly in global-level welfare changes in any consistent direction. I thus broadly concur with Singer's reluctance to pronounce on his fourth issue, but not just, or even mainly, because of missing data. I think that Stiglitz is right, when trying to assess Washington-consensus macroeconomics, to focus his attention on the IMF and the World Bank and say little about the WTO. One *can* argue – though I am not prepared to endorse the conclusion without many qualifications – that the IMF and the World Bank have often been hijacked by special OECD-based (especially American) interests. However, a vessel without a captain or a clear route to anywhere, which I will contend the WTO mainly has been, is not open to hijacking in the first place.

5 'Democracy', voting, and logrolling

The charges numbered by Singer as (ii) and (iii) are often not distinguished by critics. As noted above, Singer is, like me, an ethical globalist. So are most 'left-wing' popular critics of the WTO. In their frame of values, if the WTO weakened national sovereignty this would not constitute an ethical objection in itself, so long as the transferred sovereignty were being ceded to democratically constituted and globally representative groups. (ii) constitutes an ethical concern just in case we suppose that national governments, where they are democratic, are the appropriate vehicles for representing people's interests. In that case, (iii) then becomes the closely focused objection that WTO procedures do not weigh countries' influence by reference to their relative populations: OECD countries have far more influence than their population shares warrant, and small countries have the same number of votes – one – as much larger ones.

Though some radical critics of the WTO imagine that some sort of direct community representation would ideally bypass national governments,[9] this is not what Singer advocates. He argues that ethical national policies, which should be pressed on international institutions by democratic member governments, would regard dictatorships or narrow oligarchies, except where these can *demonstrate* popular support arising from customary legitimacy,[10] as not entitled to trade national resources or to base claims for increased weight in international voting bodies on their population sizes. I agree with him on this, though the idea requires a careful theory of political legitimacy that is cognizant of the difficulties involved in applying it to cases of economically *powerful* governments – whose policies affect the rest of the world regardless of whether the rest of the world treats them as fully legitimate – and which may be sensitive to ranges of popular interest while violently blocking democratic reform. China of course furnishes the litmus test here at the moment.

Within this frame, we can take charge (iii) as referring to the decision-making structure of the WTO itself. In practice, the WTO operates by consensus: every member has a nominal veto. Singer says that this represents 'a very strange view of democracy' (2002: 75). Relative to national and local governance rules, it of course does. But it is maintained for an important reason that Singer never considers. It is highly unlikely that most electorates in mature and economically powerful *democracies* would permit their own legislatures to be overruled by international votes on policies of importance to them. The WTO would simply collapse if votes of its Ministerial Council *imposed* trade policies on the United States or the European Union. This fact would be of no *ethical* moment – though of overwhelming political moment! – if it simply resulted from the fact that most people are not ethical globalists (in the sense of weighting interests of foreigners and co-nationals equally in their ethical judgments). But *ethical* globalism does *not* necessarily imply international political majoritarianism. American and European economic and legal policies, by virtue of American and European wealth, are of far greater interest to non-Americans and non-Europeans than, say, Egyptian ones. If the rest of the world *could* dictate American or European trade policies it would have large incentives to actually do so, even where such dictation was not mainly *ethically* motivated. While I do not think that a convincing argument can be made that it would be unethical for developing countries to try to determine American policy by votes if this were possible, it is equally far from obvious that Americans would be responding *unethically* if they resented this and opted to secede. They would surely be able to argue convincingly that such a scenario would be heavily biased in favor of redistribution of wealth *independently* of whether particular redistributive policies actually enhanced global welfare.

Singer would not find this objection persuasive, on grounds that a global utilitarian ethic would deny the Americans or Europeans a veto in judgment over what does and does not enhance global welfare. But then I think the following consideration is relevant. We have plenty of experience with the actual workings of democracy in federal arrangements. Failures to respect power balances in assignment of regional vetoes have had baleful consequences for *everyone's* welfare in federations, over and over again. Sometimes regions adopt morally unacceptable policies and should be overridden, as in the case of the American South before the Civil War and again after Reconstruction. However, *many* policy disputes are not *mainly* ethical disputes; many arise simply from asymmetric information. No one knows how to make procedural rules that will allow vetoes in 'mainly ethical' disputes but not in others, because no one knows how to delimit 'mainly ethical' subjects of dispute in advance.

If we had an effective world government, so that the issue with respect to national vetoes was no *more* difficult than the issue of regional vetoes in federations, we would in any case be in a world far removed from the one in which we now contemplate reform of the WTO. (That is, if an argument for reforming the WTO turns into an argument for nothing less than world government, we have allowed the subject to change.) If, for the sake of still being able to talk about real policy issues, we confine ourselves to a world where trade rules are made by multilateral negotiations among sovereign states, then it amounts to diversion of useful critical energy, at best, or unethical institution-wrecking, at worst, to press for abolition of vetoes in the hands of the economic powers whose policies largely *determine* world welfare levels. And then it could hardly amount to democratic reform to urge that the economies no one can live without keep their vetoes while smaller economies lose theirs. I take it that nobody would be inclined to hold up the United Nations Security Council as a model of a *democratic* structure (even if large-power veto rights are a good idea there for other reasons).

As Singer of course recognizes, veto rights in the hands of less powerful countries, taken individually, are nominal in any case; Burkina Faso cannot *really* block a multilateral agreement all by itself. Now, this will seem at first glance to be the antithesis of democracy, as Singer suggests: it is the UN Security Council arrangement after all! But this is not in fact the case. As vividly demonstrated in the recent Cancun Ministerial meeting, a coalition of countries large enough to be economically significant to everyone else[11] *can* block agreement. In principle, it is the fact that everyone knows this, combined with the fact that trade treaties are 'single undertakings' across the whole range of issues on the agenda, that is supposed to incentivize all countries to *negotiate*. The consensus principle and the single undertaking principle structure WTO negotiations as a logrolling process. It is an under-appreciated fact that logrolling dynamics have at least one *democratic* virtue in their favor: they encourage revelation by negotiating parties of their preference *intensities* instead of just their preference *orderings* (see Stratmann, 1997). If Switzerland has little interest in policies that affect the world price of cotton, it is *not* a principle of democracy that it ought to have a vote of the same weight on this question as Benin. In a logrolling environment it effectively will not: Switzerland might cede its marginal preference on this question to West African countries in return for their support on questions concerning the regulation of trade in banking services. Not only can logrolling dynamics be more democratic than majoritarian ones, they also, in any organization where members' commitments to the organization's rules are politically vulnerable, enhance stability by opening wider ranges of paths to equilibrium.

In practice, logrolling has not gone very well in the WTO since the Uruguay Round. But far from objecting to the *principle* of logrolling, by opposing the consensus practice on 'democratic' grounds, my view is that we ought to be asking how we could make institutional adjustments that would allow logrolling to *work*. Singer is quite right in drawing attention to the green room process, for there is no doubt that a major barrier to effective logrolling has been the fact that non-OECD countries tend to get excluded from detailed bargaining until too late in the process. Since most of them do not take part in the details of agreement drafting, they rationally adopt the second-best approach of forming blocs around issues of principle, such as, at Cancun, resistance to the so-called 'Singapore issues' favored by the OECD, and then seeking to roll this very *large* log, as a single issue, against the even heavier matter of general reform in agriculture. The problem is not that these are not the appropriate sites for reciprocal concessions that need to be managed if the WTO is to succeed. The problem is that logrolling, like much market haggling, requires *tatonnement* and antes of small change. Green room discussions are suitable for this; Ministerial Council meetings are not. But most non-OECD countries, as discussed above, are unrepresented in green rooms.

I have just defended the consensus principle on pragmatic grounds, not (directly) ethical ones. My point in doing so, in the context of an argument about ethics, is to emphasize that appeal to highly general ethical values, such as 'democracy', fails to speak to the considerations that actually *matter* to whether poor countries are able to benefit from the WTO. The relevant sense of 'democracy' at the WTO can be operationalized as follows: we will have good reason to think that we've made an advance along democratic lines if non-OECD countries, as the weaker parties, start to become less frustrated with the process and its outcomes. My contention is that if lively logrolling dynamics could be brought about, they would; whereas, if majority or weighted voting were used for decisions, there is no reason to expect this. Therefore, advocating a more standard democratic decision-rule for the WTO for the sake of its fairness is mistaken.

I take a similar stance on the general issue of green room reform. If green rooms were *official* WTO institutional fora, then the limited participation in them would obviously be objectionable on democratic grounds – unless, like the consensus principle, they facilitated greater weight being given to poor countries' interests indirectly. However, the very fact that green rooms are *not* official fora, and thereby lack any objective institutional basis for participation in them, is just what makes them 'old boys' clubs' – a standing image for democratic resentment. There are a number of serious proposals on the table within the WTO for creating official drafting committees that would indeed have a kind of direct democratic legitimacy that green rooms cannot. However, it must be recognized that no rules can prevent the governments of the OECD countries from talking with one another in private whenever they like (which is continuously). Nor can anything prevent their joint view from carrying immense weight whenever they have one. This simply results from their economic power. If an ethical objection to the WTO turns out to just be a disguised objection to power imbalance itself, then we will again have changed the actual subject of discussion from institutional reform to moral metaphysics. Remaining on topic, then: note that any new drafting mechanism intended to partly supplant the green rooms had better *not* insist on a representativeness principle pushed so far that OECD countries will treat its deliberations far less seriously than they do their private conversations, for then the new mechanism would come to be perceived as irrelevant and would serve to further *emphasize* poor-country exclusion. 'They have a place to talk out their ideas,' it will be said, perhaps sometimes with a smirk.

Morality *does* demand that we do not make a sham of multilateralism by failing to provide resources allowing poor countries to maintain proper, and properly prepared, representation in Geneva. (Perhaps we might also move WTO Headquarters to Nairobi or Mumbai; as Singer notes, Geneva is among the most expensive cities on the planet. And it would surely not hurt if negotiators passed hovels, broken streets and hungry street children on their way to green rooms.) I will return to this issue at the end of the chapter, when I describe some reforms to the WTO that certainly should

The WTO, unfair trade and development 157

be advocated – and, in every case, *are* being vigorously advocated *now*, by the staff and using the resources of the WTO and its sister institutions, especially the World Bank.

6 The WTO and national sovereignty

Let us now turn to Singer's charge (ii), that the WTO undermines national sovereignty. For reasons given at the beginning of the previous section, we need only consider the sovereignty of democratic governments here, since, for globalists like Singer and me, sovereignty is of no value unless it promotes welfare, and dictatorships are hardly ever *net* promoters of welfare when evaluated against democratic alternatives.[12]

Singer argues that the WTO in fact does undermine national sovereignty. He endorses the popular contention that if WTO rules oblige national governments to reduce tariffs and domestic subsidies and harmonize their regulations on foreign ownership of businesses and assets, this reduces their discretionary power and 'in the eyes of the left, makes it too easy for global corporations to do as they please' (2002: 74). Singer provides no arguments for this, other than to cite an unfortunately chosen example. The example in question is the South African Government's 1998–2001 legal conflict with the Pharmaceutical Manufacturer's Association (PMA) over the former's attempt to abridge some patent protections on drugs. (I use the vague phrase 'abridge some protections' because exactly *what* the Government wished and intended to do was subject to several interpretations, including different interpretations at different times by the Government; see Cleary and Ross, 2002.) Singer says that the PMA based its case on appeal to TRIPS provisions, and rightly notes that the US Government supported the PMA's interpretation of TRIPS until American AIDS activists led it to abandon this stance for political reasons. However, Singer mistakenly claims that the PMA dropped its court challenge to South Africa's patent-abridging measures because of 'public outrage'. As Cleary and Ross (2002) show at length, there are several things, important things, wrong with Singer's version of events here (which, in fairness to him, was also the popular media's version, both in South Africa and elsewhere). First, it was clear from the outset that the *measures* referred to in the South African legislation challenged by the PMA were legal under TRIPS; the core of the PMA's contention was that the legislation gave a *vague* domain of administrative authority to the Minister of Health, thereby creating unfair business uncertainty. More importantly, the PMA withdrew its case when the Government *conceded* the only point under contention by agreeing that the Minister would not interpret the Act so as to allow compulsory licensing (but only parallel importation) of patented drugs. The PMA allowed the Government to *claim* victory because, had the case reached court, AIDS activists who had been appointed *amicus curiae* were in a position to expose highly deflated profit claims on anti-retrovirals by the drug companies – and *neither* the PMA *nor* the Government wished to argue in public over AIDS drugs. In light of all these complications, the case implies nothing one way or the other about the impact of TRIPS on national sovereignty.

Of course, there are various other cases described in a large public literature in which multinational corporations are supposed to have put pressure on governments to comply with WTO obligations. I am, however, unaware of any that bear close scrutiny. Certainly, OECD governments regularly exert pressure on each other, and on non-OECD governments, on behalf of their investors. WTO provisions are sometimes cited, along with anything else that might be convenient, when political-economic strong arms are being dressed in legalistic rationales. Multinational corporations, however, generally go to considerable lengths to stay on good terms with governments, including non-OECD governments, because the former have sensitive and valuable public reputations to protect, and the latter hold strong cards with respect to influencing public perceptions. Many governments prefer dealing with multinationals, for reasons having nothing to do with the WTO, because they generally pay higher wages than domestic corporations and because they are usually better placed to provide locational and other political offsets that are valuable to politicians. While scandals involving agents of multinationals, especially those tendering for government contracts, are recurrent episodes in developing countries, there is no reason to believe, based on reviewing actual cases, that WTO rules have the slightest causal relation to this.

Attempts by governments to coerce each other over trade and investment are a feature of human history throughout its recorded length. What is novel about the GATT/WTO regime, especially since its full multilateral flowering with the Uruguay Agreement, is that it facilitates coordination among governments in influencing investment patterns to a degree hitherto unknown on a global scale. As Steven Vogel (1996) has shown generally, deregulation has almost invariably involved complex bargains between governments and corporate interests that have allowed the former to promote industrial policies by new means, and without incurring expensive management liabilities that strain national accounts. (Those who fear for loss of government sovereignty often forget that indebtedness can restrict policy discretion more severely than any other single impediment. Public ownership of, or extensive subsidies to, utilities and large industries are almost *invariably* drains on the public purse.) Ronald Jones (2000) has applied this general point specifically to international trade dynamics in the post-Uruguay environment. A deep source of government power is capacity to control the location of economic activity. In the absence of multilateral trade coordination of the sort that the WTO regime, along with regional trade agreements, makes possible, governments seeking foreign investment may find themselves in competitive inducement races, which lower their individual bargaining power. By grouping together as, in effect, a regulatory *cartel*, the world's governments *as a sector* can substantially *increase* their power.

The specific nature of WTO treaty agreements compounds this. In each GATT round up to and through Uruguay, *average* tariffs were sharply reduced, but governments retained discretion over which of their productive sectors would be the sites of the reductions. This has incentivized industries around the world to bid, using political and policy favors (and sometimes, of course, illegal bribes), for preferred slots in tariff reduction schedules. Governments collect the substantial political rents anted in such bidding. The fact that only governments have the power to launch anti-dumping actions, or invoke other WTO-sanctioned safeguards, gives them yet another source of power for which industries rationally pay them.

When I alluded, earlier in this chapter, to the absence of a clear macroeconomic or political-economic policy direction steered by the WTO since its inception, the dynamics described above are partly what I had in mind. They are distinctly *not* the sorts of outcomes that Ricardians or free-marketeers – or Mike Moore, the most visible public face of and source of energy in the WTO during his tenure as Director-General (see Moore, 2003) – had in mind when they celebrated the conclusion of the Uruguay Agreement. The other main respect, of course, in which the WTO has not successfully driven a liberalizing agenda lies in the fact that it has had difficulty driving *any* agenda because the cartel members have been unable to agree on extensions of their original treaty, as evidenced by the breakdowns in Seattle and Cancun. The proliferation of regional and bilateral deals has contributed to the difficulties, since the value of such deals to signatory governments – especially non-OECD governments – lies precisely in gaining special market access from which competitors are frozen out. The better a given government's bilateral and regional arrangements from its own point of view, the less enthusiastic it will become about multilateralism, an attitude that will be shared by domestic producer interests that undertake investments based around the country's special access.

In evaluating the claim that the WTO undermines national sovereignty, we must also ask what governments might actually wish, importantly, to do that the WTO is supposed to interfere with. Every government on the planet presently gives preference, using thickets of loopholes and special exemptions clauses in the Uruguay Agreement, to domestic producers (especially of services) where internal bargaining over rents leads them to want to. Stiglitz, in Chapter 1, worries about loss of freedom by non-OECD governments to limit short-term capital flows. However, given the highly incomplete status of the TRIMS Agreement, the relevant part of the Uruguay package here, it is hard to see how this worry, to the extent that it is legitimate, has much to do with the WTO. I think there is indeed a strong case to be made that short-term volatility in capital flows into and out of small non-OECD countries is a problem. However, it is far from obvious that pressure from OECD governments, let alone from the WTO, is the main obstacle to tackling it. When Malaysia interfered with such flows in 1998, it was sharply criticized in the OECD but not stopped. Governments must live with crises caused by sudden outflows because, in most cases, they find periods of high inflows politically irresistible for domestic reasons. When the South African Rand rose dramatically during 2003 on the back of capital inflows attracted by high interest rates, it was the *corporate* sector that publicly fretted over damage to its export revenues, while labor unions celebrated the increasing spending power of their members. The South African Reserve Bank lowered interest rates much less, and much more slowly, than either corporate interests or economists urged. But governments and central banks cannot have it both ways, enjoying inflow surges without risk of outflow surges. Again, the relevance of the WTO to this issue is, unless TRIMS comes to be substantially broadened and strengthened by agreement, minimal.

Singer emphasizes two particular respects in which he fears interference with sovereignty that he can specifically link to international trade rules. As an environmentalist, he is anxious about the fact that these rules restrict countries' rights to refuse imports of products harvested or extracted in ways that might be ecologically harmful. As a person of the left, he is also concerned that attempts to incorporate labor standards into the WTO treaty have so far been largely unsuccessful. Indeed, these two fears are the main basis of his charge (i) against the WTO, that it encourages 'economic' values to trump 'non-economic' ones, which I have not yet considered.

Singer rightly notes that resistance to incorporation of environmental and labor standards has come mainly *from* non-OECD governments, on grounds that such incorporation would disproportionately threaten their comparative advantages – thus amplifying the very dimension along which I have agreed that current trade rules are unfair. He acknowledges the point, but severely underplays it – not mentioning, for example, that non-OECD anxiety about environmental and labor-standards measures was a *main* cause of the breakdown of the 1999 Seattle Ministerial session – and applies nothing like his usual argumentative rigor to consideration of it. Admitting that stricter environmental and labor standards in trade rules 'could' impinge on non-OECD comparative advantage he rhetorically asks, '[B]ut what is the alternative?' (2002: 95). This is surely not good enough. Less expensive labor, and much lower regulatory costs faced by companies, are the *overwhelmingly* greatest sources of non-OECD comparative advantage, the *main* reasons why anyone trades with or invests in them *at all* (except in commodity extraction, where Singer's environmentalist concerns are *also* engaged in a way troubling to non-OECD interests).

As I mentioned in the first section of this chapter, I disagree with Singer's belief that there are intrinsically valuable things besides human welfare (specifically, in his case, animal welfare). I of course agree that biodiversity and a healthy ecology are important *to* human welfare, but that is *why* I think they are important. Now, pursuing this disagreement here, were I to try to do so adequately, would take me too far away from topics in development economics and too deep into metaphysics. The ultimate basis of my disagreement with Singer is that I consider it to be a metaphysical fact, forced by considerations of coherence with a broader scientific world view, that there are no values to be 'found' in the world independently of what collective bargaining among agents reveals. In particular, that inflicting or tolerating suffering by sentient beings is wrong is not such a fact. (For the reader interested in the relevant arguments, I recommend Binmore, 1998.) Animals cannot bargain, nor can unborn or infant people. If current adult people wish to bargain on their behalf, I wholeheartedly encourage them, but then such wishes are to be treated as aspects of the welfare of those people. The fact that I can go no further (here) into this topic of controversy with Singer means that I cannot claim to *wholly* answer his case for worry about the WTO. I do insist, however, that in his failure to seriously consider the conflict between his favored 'non-economic' goods[13] and the economic welfare of people in non-OECD countries, he dodges what ought to be the *toughest* issue for most people who think that policies giving overwhelming emphasis to economic growth are in some degree wicked.

Let me conclude this section with a forthright value claim. Each person gets only one finite life. If that life is stunted and blasted by poverty, especially poverty against which the person has no effective remedy because of the actions and attitudes of other people, this is a moral atrocity. In the present world, only terroristic behavior, mainly perpetrated by some governments, is as or more morally objectionable than failure to take poverty-alleviation seriously. For reasons I have given in this chapter, I therefore think that an ethical stance that would undermine the WTO instead of supporting its own efforts at reform of the global order is morally irresponsible at best and outright immoral at worst. Now, as I said at the outset, Singer joins me in favoring reform of the WTO, so I am not accusing him of either moral irresponsibility or immorality. (There are many other commentators, regularly heard from, who I would so accuse.) However, for reasons I also hope to have made clear, I don't think that focusing on highly abstract charges like Singer's (i)–(iii) is a potentially productive way of promoting poverty alleviation at the global level.[14] Instead, we should begin by concentrating on *specific* ways in which current practice is unfair, and try to effect *specific* institutional reforms. Development economists, including those who work for the WTO (and the other global economic institutions) have given careful thought to many such reforms – unlike, I regret to say, philosophers. I will conclude this chapter by listing some of the best suggestions (among those that are relevant to the aspects of unfairness I have considered here).

7 Improving the WTO

The list of reforms I will now enumerate must, for reasons of space, be a *mere* list. I will not be able to provide arguments for and critical discussions of each one. In many cases, however, the considerations that would make them improvements are self-evident. In any event, my purpose in listing them is mainly to indicate how much more substantive they are than anything that follows from mere abstract reflection. (A reader seeking a more comprehensive and less rushed survey should consult Hoekman and Martin, 2001.)

Most of the unfairness associated with the WTO results simply and directly from power imbalances. Power imbalances, in turn, stem primarily from differential economic resources. Therefore, the most important reforms for which moral critics of current trade rules and practices should press involve commitment by OECD countries to provision of meaningful technical assistance to non-OECD ones. Rhetorical pledges to such commitment are widespread in WTO statements and agreements – especially the Doha Declaration and associated documents – but run far ahead of institutionalized actions.

Those who are morally concerned about trade rules and practices can begin by lobbying their governments to supply much higher funding levels for the United Nations Council on Trade and Development (UNCTAD) and the International Trade Centre (ITC), since these agencies have demonstrated strong competence, within their existing budgets, in enhancing the bargaining capacities and access to information of non-OECD negotiators. Two multilateral initiatives, the Joint Integrated Technical Assistance Program for Selected Least-Developed and Other African Countries (JITAP, 1996) and the Integrated Framework for Technical-Related Assistance, Including Human and Institutional Capacity Building to Support Least-Developed Countries in their Trade and Trade-Related Activities (IF, 1997), have recently been strengthened and expanded following acknowledgment by OECD governments that, as a result of their own insipid and miserly support to UNCTAD and the ITC in implementing them, their initial results have been inadequate (Luke, 2002). Since those aspects of the plan that UNCTAD and the ITC *were* able to roll out *have* been effective – contributing to the success of developing countries in making their strategic weight felt at the Seattle, Doha and Cancun Ministerial sessions – disappointments with these initiatives do not imply that they should be given up on; quite the opposite (ibid.). These programs merit still further broadening and deepening, to extend them to non-OECD countries throughout the world, and to promote leadership roles in their implementation for middle-income developing countries who can profit from them by being funded to partner with the trade agencies in steering them.

OECD countries can and should provide other forms of technical assistance directly through the WTO, and through government-to-government commitments. Especially important are efforts to enable non-OECD countries to harmonize and modernize their Customs facilities and procedures (Staples, 2002) – since problems in this area are a major source of deadweight trade barriers – and to be able to identify, verifiably demonstrate and seek redress for unintended or underestimated implementation costs imposed on them by the TRIMS and TRIPS agreements. Direct financial assistance can and should be provided to ensure that all WTO members can maintain adequately sized and budgeted delegations in Geneva on a full-time basis. In concert with this, WTO Headquarters could be moved to a less expensive site in a non-OECD country, with appropriate infrastructural support provided. Measures such as these all amount simply to shifting more of the costs of enhanced fairness to OECD taxpayers. Persuading them of their obligations in this regard obviously requires moral argument, of the sort that Singer has been in the forefront of articulating. However, the relevant moral arguments are much more likely to be effective if they are accompanied by demonstrations that such specific measures as have been properly implemented to date have paid off efficiently – as they have. Equally importantly, the arguments should be linked to emphasis on Ricardian logic – reminding OECD citizens that building richer markets abroad enhances their own opportunities for exporting their goods and services – rather than in tones suggesting that existing trade institutions are morally corrupt.

'Throwing money at' problems is *not* always an ineffective way to solve them, *where* we have both empirical experience of, and decent economic models to explain the dynamics of, specific types of applications in which extra resource infusions multiply good effects without drowning them in new rent-seeking opportunities. I have been listing some such types of application. Another is provision of expensive legal resources, through global trust funds, for non-OECD countries bringing cases to the DSB. Friends of fairness should relish the idea that when teams of lawyers from quad countries examine the legal briefs and arguments accompanying cases brought by Ghana or Surinam or Papua New Guinea, they might find them prepared by legal firms with Manhattan or Chicago addresses. The value of the resulting fair fights would surely exceed the admitted costs of rents to the lawyers.

Numerous other measures for improving DSB procedures have been suggested (see Jackson, 2000 and Delich, 2002 for surveys). Countries that have won cases should be able to appeal to compliance review panels within short time periods after remedies have been identified; ideally, such panels should be constituted by the original panels that considered the cases in question, and invested with binding writ. Time frames for *all* DSB procedures can and should be shortened. The DSB could and should encourage *collective* retaliation against countries found to be in breach of their treaty commitments, as this is one of the few ways in which the imbalance in sanctioning capacities can be addressed. Another is to allow countries that win DSB cases over breaches in one trade mode to respond by withdrawing concessions in another. If Pakistan is harmed by a Japanese tariff, it might not be able to worry many Japanese by use of a countervailing tariff of its own; but withdrawal of a concession to Japanese firms under TRIMS, or abrogation of a Japanese patent right under TRIPS, might keep some extra lights on after hours in Tokyo. (In 1996–1997, Ecuador attempted exactly this in a dispute with the EU over banana exports. The resulting DSB opinion did not close the door on such measures, but spun a substantial cloud of confusion through hesitant and opaque reasoning (see Delich, 2002)). Finally, Hoekman and Mavroidis (2000) have suggested that a kind of 'special prosecutor's' office be established by the DSB, which could expedite case assessments and encourage 'out of court' settlements, especially in cases where alleged economic damages are small.

It is not widely appreciated that by comparison with its sister organizations, the IMF and the World Bank, the WTO Directorate has relatively little ability to exercise policy influence, because its staff and discretionary budget are tiny. This makes the animus directed at the organization by radical critics ironic; if it tried to be a site of special economic manipulation independent of its member governments, it would find its capacity for fomenting conspiracies greatly limited. In fact, the WTO Directorate is the one player on the scene that is straightforwardly incentivized to try to broaden both the reach and the fairness of WTO agreements. Developing countries and their supporters should therefore press for its strengthening.

A general aspect of current trade practice that magnifies power imbalances is structural failure to tote up *all* injuries to parties other than those represented by particular non-OECD governments when the latter come into conflict with OECD producer interests. For example, when regional trade agreements (RTAs) cause trade diversion that negatively impacts third parties, they have no recourse through the WTO. A new institutional procedure that addressed this could substantially blunt the potentially disastrous dynamic, discussed earlier in this essay, by which RTAs create new rent-seeking coalitions opposed to multilateral progress, and which become wedges by which non-OECD interests are set against each other. Similar logic underpins what would likely be the single most effective (politically feasible) measure for combating the plague of anti-dumping actions. If WTO members agreed to harmonize their procedures in domestic anti-dumping inquiries so that domestic users (especially industrial users) of the imported products under scrutiny were automatically represented in official considerations of dumping allegations, then at a single stroke the *systematic* interference with market access caused by this 'safeguard' would be addressed, and non-OECD governments could expect to find procedurally implicated allies *within* the political bargaining dynamics of OECD countries (Finger, 2002).[15]

This last suggestion leads directly to a more general point. Moral critics of the WTO usually direct their arguments, as Singer does, to an abstract and generalized 'moral conscience'. That this is the typical mode of address adopted by philosophers is unsurprising; they are supposed to be professionally concerned, first and foremost, with the logical power of arguments, independently of considerations of audience. However, this can and does encourage failure to recognize that objectively sound arguments can be effective economic weapons if they help to isolate *special* burdens of moral responsibility in interest sectors much more specific than 'OECD citizens' or 'wealthy people' in general. For example, I think it unlikely that meaningful reform in agricultural trade rules – the single most urgent area of manifest current unfairness – will happen until and unless the non-OECD countries and their friends launch a carefully planned, concerted and well-financed public-relations campaign in OECD countries that clearly paints subsidized agricultural interests as the outrageously successful rent-seekers they are. It is a clear and demonstrable fact that their rent-seeking not only does grievous harm to poor countries, but also damages OECD consumers by raising food prices and by burdening tax bills with (*very* large) subsidy costs. However, it is difficult to make these dry efficiency considerations into vivid and culturally contagious images of the sort that the modern advertising industry is skilled at producing. But philosophical argument can soundly press the conclusion that wealthy, subsidized and inefficient farming corporations in OECD countries are *morally vicious*. A philosopher who fastidiously objected to seeing the conclusions of his or her *good* arguments turned into politically effective slogans, sound-bites, ditties and images would thereby, I suggest, show questionable commitment to the seriousness of the moral case he or she makes. Let us *advertise* against rich-world rent-seekers – starting with farmers – and do what we can to make them targets of cultural derision. We can begin by not mincing words: they are stealing (since that is what rent-seeking is) staggering quantities of money from the world's poorest people.

There is a tradition in moral philosophy, especially in radical moral philosophy, of regarding advocacy of incremental structural reforms to institutions as missing what is truly morally serious by compromising with a bankrupt status quo. Of course, if someone is convinced that they have a good case for regarding trade for profit among private business interests, in general, as a wicked thing, then they will not be persuaded by anything I have said. But it is equally unlikely that such people will persuade OECD electorates to adjust their moral priorities, so however much television excitement they create, their political importance is minor. Fortunately, many moral critics of the WTO base their cases on the fact that too little is being done, too slowly, about poverty. If such critics are sincere, they should contrast in their imaginations two possible mass-media advertising campaigns. One would hector whole OECD societies for being selfish and hypocritical about the value of genuine, global, democracy. Another would emphasize that various narrow interests – and not, mainly, the multinational corporations in which millions of people make their livings – are being allowed to prevent the WTO from fulfilling its mandate to improve global welfare. Which of these campaigns would be more likely to change the minds of citizens in wealthy countries? Until these minds are persuaded, the interests of poor countries will continue to be damaged by the stalemate over agricultural trade, by preposterous anti-dumping findings, and by demands that poor countries implement complex reforms for which they lack infrastructural capacity. It is not even necessary to go outside the current institutional framework in pursuit of significant changes to benefit the environment. For example, as Esty (2000) points out, it would be fully consistent with the mandate of the WTO to pursue zero worldwide tariffs on environmental goods and elimination of (presently extensive) non-tariff barriers on environmental services. Such a measure would almost certainly be of more long-term environmental benefit than complaining that national governments, when they meet with one another to discuss world welfare, focus too narrowly on 'economic' issues.

It is good that a leading moral philosopher like Singer has put the case for a cosmopolitan and consequentialist ethic of globalization. What follows from such a case, however, when couched only in terms of very abstract values, is frequently non-obvious. Singer's discussion is in one sense at the level of institutions: he morally evaluates the WTO. But in holding it up only to the light of highly abstract principles, with little attention to the strategic wisdom its design embodies, he gives the impression that direct conformity to the principles is the road to goodness for the institution. Here, I have been disagreeing with this. The WTO can contribute to an ethically better world mainly by being made more *effective*. Let us all – economists, philosophers, and citizens alike – avoid using an ethical perspective to make the best the enemy of the good. With millions of lives waiting for opportunities to be *good* lives, this would itself be unethical.

Notes

1 The point of this qualification is as follows. It is generally easier, in a world of scarcity, to raise average material welfare levels if population shrinks. This fact can provide a utilitarian basis for quite radical forms of environmentalism. Now, I am not against policies designed to control or reduce population levels where there are reasons to think that these are causing harm to actual people. Unlike environmentalists, however, in a comparison between two hypothetical worlds with equal levels of average human well-being, I regard the world containing more people as better (all else being equal). Furthermore, the concept of 'actually living' people must be interpreted generously, so as to include those people who are bound to *become* actually living given reasonable extrapolations of current demographic trends, and given reasonable assumptions about how quickly non-coerced human behavior can respond to policies that might reduce rates of reproduction.

2 This part of my view is not based on ontological individualism, which I reject for reasons discussed at length in Ross (forthcoming, 2004). It is based on what I regard as an empirical fact that agents more internally complex than human individuals cannot be coordinated adequately for the maintenance of the minimal level of preference stability necessary to make ethical evaluation meaningful. This is not to say that human individuals *are not* internally complex or that they generally or naturally have stable preferences. Ethics is hard because people are very complex indeed. My view is that complex units much larger than individual people evolve too chaotically and dynamically to be sites of values clear enough for first-order moral imputation.

3 Note that I do not say they'll always be *effectively* represented. Even non-charismatic animals presently have *strong* representation, but these representatives lose a lot more battles than they win. The only useful response to this by animal welfare advocates is effort at developing better bargaining strategies. If the impact of a short-term better strategy were to diminish human welfare in significant ways, I would oppose it, because I would expect the long-term impact to be politically self-defeating. I think that unhappy people will go on abusing animals, so doing favors to animals requires making people happy.

4 This is an imperfect label, because the OECD now includes some countries, like Turkey, that are economically worse off than some non-members, like South Africa. However, I think this basis for marking the distinction is still less misleading, among available *convenient* markers, than any other.

5 I think that Stiglitz, in drawing lessons from the policies that carried the Asian tigers up their development trajectories, gives insufficient attention to the special historical circumstances that made them possible. The United States and Western Europe had powerful incentives during the Cold War to control protectionist impulses where Asia was concerned. It is far from obvious that OECD countries now have similar incentives, at least ones likely to be politically effective, with respect to Latin America, Africa, or Central Asia.

6 Tariffs are said to *escalate* when their *ad valorem* rates go up as products incorporate increased value added in assembly.

7 A number of Middle Eastern countries, and a minority of Central Asian ones, are WTO members. However, *all* of the backsliding in key development indicators in these regions has occurred in the non-WTO members, with the exception of a very recent member, Georgia.

8 The boom-and-bust dynamics in recent Latin American economies make all assessments in the case of the region as a whole highly sensitive to one's choice of a baseline year for measurement.

9 Some remarks of Hamilton's in Chapter 10 suggest this view. I take it that the view is not supposed to just be the truism that many countries might change their constitutions or political practices so as to function more democratically than they now do. Rather, it is the charge that representative parliamentary systems, the standing form in most countries that are not overtly dictatorships, are flawed in principle and might be replaced by something like tribal consensus or stakeholder seminar models of collective decision. I invite anyone who has been involved in institutional decision-making through stakeholder consensus to explain how such a model could be practical on a large scale except where and as it devolved back into parliamentary form as stakeholders' leaders constituted themselves as elected Executive Committees. It should give critics such as Hamilton pause that developing countries have demanded that NGOs promoting 'social reforms' be accorded *less* involvement in DSB Appellate Body deliberations, rather than more. Models of so-called 'republicanism' (e.g., Pettit, 1997) aim at fundamental political reform in a communitarian direction, but I find also that they fall short on many key transactional details. The most persuasive model

of political reform I have encountered is that of Binmore (1998), which I think might provide for the valuational framework in which more democratic economic policies, of the sort advocated by van Parijs (1995), could feasibly arise.

10 *Perhaps* Jordan, Nepal, or Brunei would constitute instances of this; though perhaps not. It is highly unlikely that Saudi Arabia or Swaziland would do so.

11 Some countries, as noted above, *do* constitute real veto-wielding blocs of one; the US and Japan, for example. Precisely because the consensus principle *forces* negotiation, however, and implies that nothing at the WTO ever *is* brought to a formal vote, there is useful ambiguity about who *really* (as opposed to nominally) has a veto. Does Canada, for example? No one knows – and it's best that we never bring the question to test.

12 Note that I am *not* saying that dictatorships never raise welfare levels. The Chinese dictatorship has clearly done so since 1978. As Stiglitz (Chapter 1) reminds us, non-democratic regimes presided over the rise of most of the Asian tigers. Finally, there is the dismaying case of Germany in the 1930s, where living standards improved substantially under Hitler's criminal order. My claim is rather that, given the rent-seeking that is endemic to dictatorial structures, if democratic government were politically feasible in the circumstances where dictatorship and growth have coincided, then growth would have been higher, at least in the long run, under democracy. The Asian tigers probably were able to stay on their growth paths *because* they became democratic; and Hitler's Germany was heading for economic crisis when it launched the war because the dictator, for political reasons, refused to allow *any* unemployment or to depreciate an over-valued currency (Kaiser, 1980).

13 I put 'non-economic' in scare-quotes here because I deny, for reasons I cannot go into here, that the idea of a non-economic good makes coherent logical sense. See Ross (forthcoming, 2004).

14 Singer might reply here by emphasizing the value of abstract, general criticisms for establishing *regulatory ideals* against which specific policy reforms should be motivated. I agree that that is exactly what moral philosophy is for. However, I claim that an effective regulatory ideal should emerge *from* reflection on feasible strategies and be developed in reflective equilibrium with specific policy alternatives. Promotion of moral ideals as a priori instruments for testing policies tends to condemn incrementally helpful improvements along with the status quo it aims to change, and thereby often does more harm than good. The fact that many left-wing critics of the WTO favor its abolition on moral grounds is precisely a case in point.

15 For example, the recent suspension of morally and economically outrageous steel tariffs by the US Government, though crucially influenced by pressure brought to bear through the DSB, was made much more likely by the fact that industrial consumers of steel in America, such as the automobile industry, threw their political weight into the argument.

References

Binmore, K. (1994). *Game Theory and the Social Contract, Volume One: Playing Fair*, Cambridge, MA: MIT Press.

Binmore, K. (1998). *Game Theory and the Social Contract, Volume Two: Just Playing*, Cambridge, MA: MIT Press.

Braybrooke, D. (1987). *Meeting Needs*, Princeton, NJ: Princeton University Press.

Cleary, S. and D. Ross (2002). The 1998–2001 legal struggle between the South African government and the International Pharmaceutical Industry: a game-theoretic analysis, *Journal of Social, Political and Economic Studies*, 27: 445–494.

Delich, V. (2002). Developing countries and the WTO dispute settlement mechanism, in B.M. Hoekman, A. Mattoo and P. English (eds), *Development, Trade and the WTO*, Washington, DC: World Bank.

Esty, D. (2000). Environment and the trading system: picking up the post-Seattle pieces, in J. Schott (ed.), *The WTO After Seattle*, Washington, DC: Institute for International Economics.

Finger, J.M. (2002). Safeguards, in B. Hoekman *et al.* (eds), *Development, Trade and the WTO*, Washington, DC: World Bank.

Hoekman, B. and W. Martin (eds) (2001). *Developing Countries and the WTO: A Pro-active Agenda*, Oxford: Blackwell.

Hoekman, B.M. and P.C. Mavroidis (2000). WTO dispute settlement, transparency and surveillance, *The World Economy*, 23: 527–542.

Hudec, R. (2002). The adequacy of WTO dispute settlement remedies, in B. Hoekman *et al.* (eds), *Development, Trade and the WTO*, Washington, DC: World Bank.

Jackson, J. (1997). *The World Trading System*, Cambridge, MA: MIT Press.

Jackson, J. (2000). Dispute settlement and a new round, in J. Schott (ed.), *The WTO After Seattle*, Washington, DC: Institute for International Economics.

Jones, R. (2000). *Globalization and the Theory of Input Trade*, Cambridge, MA: MIT Press.

Kaiser, D. (1980). *Economic Diplomacy and the Origins of the Second World War*, Princeton, NJ: Princeton University Press.

Luke, D. (2002). Trade-related capacity building for enhanced African participation in the global economy, in B. Hoekman *et al.* (eds), *Development, Trade and the WTO*, Washington, DC: World Bank.

Manuel, T. (2003). Africa and the Washington consensus: finding the right path, *Finance and Development*, 40: 18–20.

Messerlin, P. (2000). Antidumping and safeguards, in J. Schott (ed.), *The WTO After Seattle*, Washington, DC: Institute for International Economics.

Moore, M. (2003). *A World Without Walls*, Cambridge: Cambridge University Press.

Pettit, P. (1997). *Republicanism*, Oxford: Oxford University Press.

Ross, D. (forthcoming, 2004). *Economic Theory and Behavioral Science, Volume One: Microexplanation*, Cambridge, MA: MIT Press.

Schott, J. (2000). The WTO after Seattle, in J. Schott (ed.), *The WTO After Seattle*, Washington, DC: Institute for International Economics.

Sen, A. (1999). *Development as Freedom*, New York: Anchor.

Singer, P. (2002). *One World*, New Haven, CT: Yale University Press.

Staples, B. (2002). Trade facilitation: improving the invisible infrastructure, in B. Hoekman *et al.* (eds), *Development, Trade and the WTO*, Washington, DC: World Bank.

Stratmann, T. (1997). Logrolling, in D. Mueller (ed.), *Perspectives on Public Choice*, Cambridge: Cambridge University Press.

Tussie, D. and D. Glover (1993). Developing countries in world trade: implications for bargaining, in D. Tussie and D. Glover (eds), *The Developing Countries in World Trade*, Boulder, CO: Lynne Riener.

Vogel, S. (1996). *Freer Markets, More Rules*, Ithaca, NY: Cornell University Press.

van Parijs, P. (1995). *Real Freedom For All*, Oxford: Oxford University Press.

9 The 'new (global) economy' and inequality in South Africa

Nicoli Nattrass and Jeremy Seekings

1 Introduction

What does the 'new economy' mean for South Africa? The answer depends in large part on what is understood by this trendy but vague term. Is the 'new economy' simply a catch-all phrase to describe the 1990s boom in the USA – or does it signify a new stage in capitalist development in which the conventionally understood economic laws no longer apply? The issue boils down to whether the extraordinary advances in computer technology and the Internet comprise a heartland technological revolution that is transforming the way in which entire economies function, or whether their powers of diffusion and transformation are more limited. For those who believe the former, it follows that high-income developed countries, being on the right side of the 'digital divide', will leap ahead on the basis of an absolute comparative advantage – whilst poorer, less developed countries, sink ever faster behind. The new (global) economy is thus portrayed as a place of increasing differentiation and absolute immiseration. For a middle-income country like South Africa (with reasonably good telecommunications and information technology) the issue thus becomes whether the economy clings to the coat-tails of the winners, or sinks with the losers.

Whilst there is no doubt that the power of the networked computer has revolutionized the lives of most people in the developed world, it is as yet unclear to what extent this has filtered through into actual improvements in economy-wide productivity. Well-known 'new economy sceptic' Robert Gordon (2000) has pointed out that multi-factor productivity only grew at 0.6 per cent per annum between 1972 and 1995 – despite twenty years of the so-called 'information revolution'. He dismisses the jump in productivity growth to 1.8 per cent per annum between 1995 and 1999 as a function of a faster-than-trend increase in output, and argues that most of the increase in productivity occurred within the durable manufacturing sector – especially those parts producing computers and peripherals (Gordon, 2000). Oliner and Sichel (2000), however, argue that because computers comprised a relatively small proportion of the capital stock, their contribution to productivity growth would have been minor until the mid-1990s (when, in their view, the true revolutionary impact of the new economy became apparent in the statistics).

If there is still significant room for doubt about the strength and importance of the new economy for the USA, then it would appear that talk about the impact of the new economy on the global distribution of income is little more than excited speculation. If (as Gordon suggests) new economy technologies are more important in some sectors than others, then it does not necessarily follow that all countries have to cross the 'digital divide' in any total sense in order to benefit from international trade. For example, computer-aided design has been around for many years in the clothing industry, but that has not stopped low-wage developing countries from competing aggressively in international markets (albeit at the lower value-added end). Global inequality may well rise (as the high-income countries reap the rewards of new economy technologies), but countries competing with less cutting-edge technologies and in lower value-added product lines will not necessarily become poorer as a result.

As new economy technologies diffuse unevenly through national economies and across international borders, workers and entrepreneurs in all countries experience differentially the opportunities and pain of structural adjustment. How an economy responds to the emerging international order has a major impact on who benefits or loses (relatively or absolutely) – and who is marginalized altogether. This chapter focuses on the impact of the new (global) economy on the national (rather than international) distribution of income – paying particular attention to South Africa.

In the case of South Africa, globalization and technological change has coincided with an increasingly skills-intensive employment structure, sluggish growth, growing unemployment (particularly among the unskilled) and rising inequality. However the causal connection between trends associated with the new (global) economy and domestic employment is difficult to establish – especially given the coincident decline of the mining industry, the democratic transition in 1994, and the adoption of conservative macroeconomic policies from the mid-1990s.

For this reason, attempting to isolate statistically the impact of the 'new economy' forces of globalization and technological change on employment and inequality in South Africa is probably not all that helpful an approach. Instead, this chapter describes how the international sector, together with the mediating impact of labour market institutions and domestic economic policies, may have shaped employment and distribution. Section two below considers the relationship between globalization and employment, section three explores the independent and mediating role of domestic economic policy choices, and section four concludes with a discussion of the implications for distribution in South Africa.

2 Globalization, employment and inequality in South Africa

Increasing globalization (understood here simply as the growth in international trade and capital flows) is typically understood to be a feature of the 'new economy'. Such globalization has had (and continues to have) a powerful effect on South Africa. It can be argued that globalization helped bring about the end of racial discrimination, and even apartheid itself. The apartheid growth path was based on import-substitution, and high tariff barriers helped compensate those businesses whose costs were raised by apartheid policies (Nattrass and Seekings, 1997). But by the early 1970s, it was clear that this growth path had run out of steam and that South African firms had to become more competitive if they were to survive international competition – and that meant a more rational (i.e., less racially structured) use of human resources. Domestic protest and mobilization against the racist system was key to the downfall of apartheid, but economic forces were powerful allies of democratization.

The international anti-apartheid movement and global financial pressures no doubt also contributed to change. The drying up of foreign direct investment, the impact of financial and trade sanctions, and sustained capital outflows from the mid-1980s onwards sent a clear message to the apartheid regime that a democratic transition was required. The fall in the gold price from the mid-1980s onwards also increased the economic pressures on the state, and in this regard too, global economic forces were largely responsible. The increasing sophistication of the global capital market meant that gold was no longer the only hedge against inflation. This has had a dampening impact on the price and hence on the value of South Africa's gold exports. Likewise, increasing integration of global capital markets has given investors greater opportunities and options for capital flight (see Chapter 1). This was a problem for the apartheid regime from the mid-1980s onwards, and remains a threat for post-apartheid South Africa.

Soon after democratization in 1994, the last vestiges of statutory racial discrimination were removed in South Africa. But the new government inherited a society where inequality could not be reduced to race alone and persisted in the face of formal political equality. The best available data suggests that the Gini coefficient remained stable or even edged up during the 1990s, as inter-racial inequality continued to decline and as intra-racial inequality rose sharply (Nattrass and Seekings, 2001; Whiteford and Van Seventer, 2000). The racial wage gap remains high, but is now explained primarily by factors other than overt discrimination, such as differences in education and skill, location (urban or rural), union membership and economic sector (Schultz and Mwabu, 1998a, 1998b; Moll, 2000; Lam, 1999).

Since the early 1980s, the African trade union movement has boosted

African wages – particularly at the lower end of the wage distribution. But, to the extent that this encouraged firms to shed labour, overall inequality would have increased as the number of households with no access to wage earnings rose.[1] Unlike other middle-income developing countries, South Africa has an undeveloped and limited informal sector (Nattrass, 2000a). Informal earnings are pitiful and the sector does not provide an alternative source of unemployment for most of those losing their jobs.[2] It is thus unsurprising that unemployment has become an important determinant of inequality and poverty in South Africa (Leibbrandt *et al.*, 2000; Seekings, 2000). The decline in formal employment (see Figure 9.1) and rise in unemployment in the 1990s (Nattrass, 2000a) is thus of serious concern.

What role has international trade and technological change played in shaping this emerging pattern of employment and inequality in South Africa? Is international competition to blame for the fall in employment and the rise in unemployment and inequality? Evidence from recent economic history indicates that there is no necessary reason why developing countries should experience increasing inequality as a result of participation in the international economy. In the 1960s and 1970s, the highly performing Asian economies dominated the low-wage, labour-intensive end of international trade. As manufacturing exports expanded rapidly, labour was increasingly drawn out of lower-value added sectors and into manufacturing. Over time, the manufacturing sector itself started moving into higher value-added product lines – a process aided by targeted industrial policies (Weiss, 1998) and the fact that most workers had a basic education (Wood, 1994). Wage flexibility appears to have kept unemployment low and steady, and a more rapid rise in productivity than wages (up until at

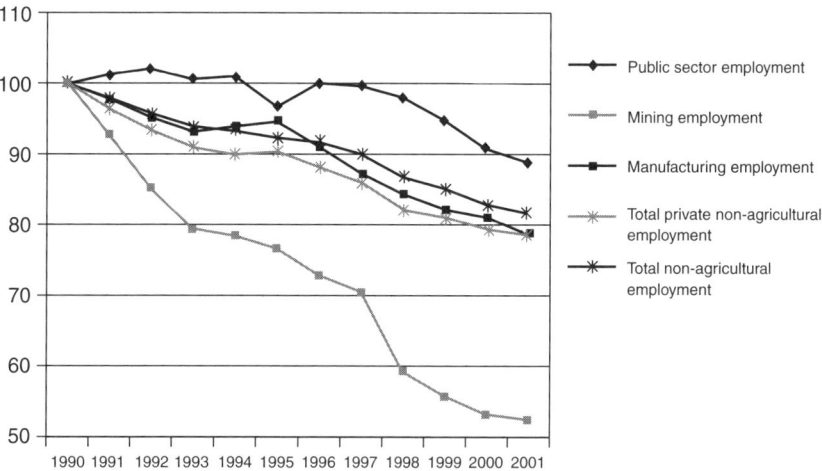

Figure 9.1 Trends in non-agricultural formal employment in the 1990s (data from the South African Reserve Bank).

least the mid-1980s) helped fuel investment and growth (World Bank, 1993; Perry, 1995). Strong growth in output and employment ensured that wages and living standards rose. Growth, to an important extent, was thus shared growth.

Like Latin America, South Africa started removing protective barriers in the 1980s. This process was given further impetus through renewed trade liberalization in the 1990s (see overview in Edwards, 2000 and Fedderke et al., 2000). Current trade policy is strongly committed to increased openness (RSA, 1996), but the extent to which this has been translated into a decrease in effective protection remains unclear (Edwards, 2000; Tsikata, 1998), particularly during the past few years.

By the time that South Africa and Latin America started liberalizing their trade regimes, low-wage countries like Bangladesh, Indonesia, Pakistan and China had moved into the lower-value-added end of the international market. There are now established and strong competitors at all levels of the value-chain. To compete in any sector or niche-market means ensuring that the ratio of costs to productivity is better than the international standard. With regard to low-wage, labour-intensive production, the choice is often one of constraining wage increases (because wages account for a substantial part of costs). Alternatively, competitiveness can be forged through changes in workplace organization, improving relations between firms, and changes in technology. The cost, however, is a shift away from labour-intensive production, and rising demand for skilled labour, and falling demand for unskilled labour.

There is evidence that trade with low-wage developing countries has reduced the demand for relatively less-skilled labour in high- and middle-income countries (Wood, 1994, 1995, 1997; OECD, 1997). Although there is still controversy regarding how much of the decline in demand can be placed at the door of international trade, there is widespread agreement that trade with low-wage countries is at least one contributing factor. As Wood (1997) observes, 'the debate is now over the magnitude of the effects, with their direction – adverse to unskilled workers – being largely agreed'.

This has unfortunate implications for growth in middle-income countries. In contrast to the East Asian growth path followed two decades earlier, increased openness and trade liberalization in Latin America appears to have been accompanied by slower employment growth and widening wage inequality (World Bank, 1993; Morley, 1995, 2000). Latin America, with its relatively developed industrial structure, found itself entering global markets with intermediate ratios of skilled to unskilled labour (Wood, 1997) and unable to compete in low-wage labour-intensive product lines. This problem, as manifested by a general decline in the demand for unskilled labour, appears also to have been experienced by other middle-income countries (Dirwan and Walton, 1997). As discussed below, similar trends are evident in South Africa.

2.1 Trade liberalization and employment in South Africa

To the extent that trade liberalization results in structural adjustment, short-term job losses are inevitable. Ideally, trade liberalization should facilitate rapid structural adjustment so that those workers who lose jobs obtain new ones in rapidly expanding industries. However there is little evidence that rapid and significant short- or medium-term job creation has resulted (or will result) from trade liberalization. According to the Industrial Development Corporation's multi-sectoral general equilibrium model, trade liberalization in South Africa will have resulted in a net job loss of 1.7 per cent in manufacturing and a fall in output by 2002 (reported in Bell and Cattaneo, 1997). More recent estimates by Edwards (2000) indicate that import penetration reduced employment by 9.1 per cent in ultra labour-intensive industries, and by 2.4 per cent overall between 1993 and 1997. The study concludes, however, that once the positive (direct and indirect) impact of export expansion on employment is taken into account, the net impact of international trade on employment was to raise employment by 1 per cent over the period (Edwards, 2000). Fedderke et al. (2000) came to similar conclusions.

Both the Edwards and Fedderke et al. studies rely on decomposition techniques that estimate separately the impact of international trade, demand and technology. As is the case with most international studies that decompose changes in sectoral production in this manner, Edwards found that technological change was the main factor behind the declining demand for labour. However, as Wood (1994) has argued, such studies do not take into account the possible connection between globalization and technological change: if firms change technology as part of 'defensive innovation', then the effect of the technological change should be attributed to trade rather than technology as such. In recognition of this problem, Edwards checked to see if there was a statistically significant relationship between trade and technology, and found there was. This suggests that the impact of trade on employment was greater than indicated by the conventional decomposition methodologies (Edwards, 2000). The ILO (1999) has also made the connection between trade and technological change by attributing employment losses mainly to a 'process of "rationalization" or "downsizing" which might occur as a reaction to increased international competition'.

Input–output analysis has clearly shown that export growth has boosted employment growth in some labour-intensive sectors like transport and services. It is nevertheless still worrying that South Africa's exports are becoming more capital- and skill-intensive (Bell and Cattaneo, 1997; ILO, 1999; Edwards, 1999) and thus not contributing much directly to employment growth. Indeed, the ILO found that employment losses were greater in capital-intensive export industries (-7.7 per cent) than in import-competing industries (-5.5 per cent) between 1994 and 1997 (1999). This could well be a result of the higher wage increases that occurred in the export sectors relative to the rest of the economy over that period (*loc. cit.*). Tsikata attributes South Africa's 'paradoxical' export structure to South Africa's 'comparatively high wage level [relative to productivity] which puts it at a competitive disadvantage in low-wage, unskilled-labour-intensive activities' (1998). Nattrass (1998a) makes a similar argument and provides evidence that South Africa's manufacturing wage productivity ratio is comparatively high.

The rise in skill and capital intensity of South Africa's exports, together with increasing import penetration in labour-intensive and ultra-labour-intensive industries, suggests that the forces Wood (1997) hypothesized were acting on middle-income Latin American labour markets are making their presence felt in South Africa. Ultra-labour-intensive imports from low-wage countries have grown sharply, whereas South African exports in these categories are contracting. There is evidence that South Africa is moving towards more (intermediate) skill-intensive product lines, with technological change in manufacturing resulting in an increased demand for skilled labour (Standing, 1997). The demand for skilled workers (particularly in the information technology sector) has been rising, and the general shift towards capital-intensity has further increased the demand for skilled workers, and reduced the demand for unskilled workers (Bhorat and Hodge, 1999). This does not bode well for the prospects of expanding low-wage employment for currently unskilled unemployed people. As such, it also does not bode well for the reduction of inequality.

The impact of international competition on employment is mediated by labour market institutions. There is evidence that South Africa's wage-setting machinery acts to protect unskilled wages, and to serve the interests of larger-scale, more capital-intensive firms at the cost of smaller, more labour-intensive firms (Moll, 1996; Nattrass, 2000b). Larger firms use more capital-intensive techniques, achieve higher labour productivity, and hence pay higher wages than smaller firms. Collective bargaining in South Africa takes place at industry level in bargaining councils, and the resulting minimum wages are extended across the entire industry by the Minister of Labour. As bargaining councils are dominated by large firms, the bargained wage is more likely to suit capital- rather than labour-intensive activities. Compulsory extensions of collectively bargained agreements to non-parties thus probably harms labour-intensive firms and activities, and hence reduces labour absorption in manufacturing.

As trade liberalization continues, labour-intensive firms and sectors will come under increasing competition from imports from lower-wage countries. As wages are prevented from adjusting by minimum-wage floors, the result is likely to be further job shedding in labour-intensive sectors.

2.2 Capital flows and other dimensions of globalization

Globalization, of course, amounts to more than just trade liberalization. Typically it refers also to increased capital flows and to the integration of domestic stock markets. Globalization has gathered pace in South Africa with regard to both these dimensions. In 1994, South Africa underwent significant capital account liberalization with the abolition of the dual exchange rate system and capital controls on non-residents. There has also been a gradual liberalization of exchange controls on South African residents and the introduction of 'asset swap' arrangements has allowed for greater outward investment by institutional investors. The regulatory environment for foreign direct investment (FDI) improved in 1995, with the abolition of discriminatory non-resident shareholders' tax and most limits on the repatriation of hard currency.

FDI picked up during the 1990s, especially in 1997 when Telkom (the telecommunications service provider) was privatized. The IT telecoms sector attracted the greatest share of FDI in the period 1994–99 (Heese, 2000). Unfortunately, most FDI between 1994 and 1999 was in the category 'mergers and acquisitions' (60.4 per cent), with only 16.7 per cent being classifiable as new productive capacity (ibid.). This, together with the collapse in FDI in 2000, does not bode well for economic growth.

Foreign purchases of equities on the Johannesburg Stock Exchange increased nearly eighteenfold between 1991 and 1997, but this was mainly of a short-term nature, and it injected greater volatility into the financial and foreign exchange markets (ILO, 1999). Outward investment increased during the 1990s, as South African institutional investors diversified their portfolios, and as some companies chose to open up offshore business activities. While net portfolio investment was positive for most of the 1990s, it became sharply negative in 2000. As Stiglitz warns in Chapter 1, capital flows are fair-weather friends which cannot be relied upon to finance a sustainable growth strategy.

The balance on the financial account (which comprises net direct, net portfolio and net other investment) was mildly positive in the 1990s, but dropped sharply into negative territory in 2000. The low level of capital inflow probably reflects the lack of confidence in the South African economy, and the high cost of South African capital – which has encouraged large South African conglomerates to list overseas (see, for example, Fleming Martin, 2000).

What are the implications of globalization for distribution? Given that net capital inflow is typically a small fraction of GDP, it is unlikely that capital flows can be directly linked to distributional changes associated with globalization. However, to the extent that capital is now more mobile, and firms have greater options as regards where to locate their businesses, this 'exit threat' will affect the employment response of firms facing competitive pressures from factors such as trade liberalization.

3 Globalization and the domestic policy content

The impact of globalization is contingent on the state of the economy and the domestic policy context. Well co-ordinated trade, labour and macroeconomic policies can lessen the pain of the adjustment associated with trade liberalization, whereas inappropriate policies can exacerbate it (Stiglitz, 2002). As discussed below, there are indications that South Africa's domestic policy environment was not conducive to employment growth. In this regard, some of the negative repercussions of globalization for distribution should be laid at the door of policy makers.

Since the mid-1990s, the South African government has pursued orthodox economic policies of deficit reduction and fiscal discipline. In this regard, they followed the Washington Consensus position espoused by the Bretton Woods Institutions (Stiglitz, 2002). The architects of South Africa's 'Growth, Employment and Redistribution' (GEAR) policy assumed that investors would respond quickly and well to the lower deficit, and to the government's commitment to continued deficit reduction (RSA, 1996). The assumption was that the positive impact of increased investor confidence on investment would outweigh the negative impact of tighter fiscal policy on demand – and hence investment. In other words, they assumed that investors were more anxious about the prospect of macroeconomic instability brought about by an over-rapid increase in demand, than they were about sluggish spending and poor sales.

Has it worked? On the 'positive' side, the fiscal deficit target was reached, and inflation fell to lower levels than predicted. However, the drop in the deficit was not accompanied by lower interest rates – indeed, the real bank rate rose sharply – and private investment has remained sluggish. This is consistent with the warnings of economists across the ideological spectrum that GEAR would reduce demand, and that private investment would follow demand downwards, rather than compensating for it (see, for example, Gibson and Van Seventer, 1995; Nattrass, 1996; NIEP, 1996; NLC, 1996; Standing et al., 1996: 33; Samson, 1997). It is also consistent with evidence that aggressively anti-inflationary components of stabilization packages have undermined, rather than supported, growth (Stiglitz, 1998). The GEAR modellers were almost certainly unrealistic in their assumption that business confidence would rise (drawing investment up with it) once the GEAR policies had been announced to the business community.

However, not all of South Africa's poor growth performance can be laid at the door of GEAR. From early 1998, the economy suffered from the contagion effects of the Asian crisis, which affected growth in ways that could not reasonably have been predicted. But it appears that South Africa's growth performance was significantly worse than that of other middle-income countries, and worse than that which would have been predicted solely on the basis of changing world market conditions (Weeks,

1999). This implies that the GEAR strategy exercised a major, and independently negative impact on growth and investment.

Another reason why the GEAR targets were not met may have been because the GEAR strategy was not implemented consistently, particularly with regard to labour-market policy. In sharp contrast to the labour-market vision outlined in GEAR, the government passed various pieces of legislation that increased the costs of employing labour[3] and extended minimum wage floors. Promised reforms to existing labour laws – such as amendments to the mandatory extension of collectively bargained agreements to non-parties – did not materialize.[4]

According to evidence from the OECD (1999), countries that have undergone macroeconomic stabilization and trade liberalization without addressing labour market rigidity have found the experience costly in terms of unemployment. South Africa is unlikely to be an exception. As shown earlier, instead of generating jobs, GEAR has presided over significant job losses (see Figure 9.1). Although much of the decrease in employment in mining and agriculture cannot be blamed directly on GEAR, it is nevertheless feasible that co-ordination failures between fiscal, monetary and labour-market policies could be exacerbating unemployment (Nattrass, 1998b). And, even with regard to short-term poverty-relief employment programmes, the government appears not to be able to deliver on the jobs front. Although great plans were trumpeted about short-term job creation for the unemployed in public works programmes and the like (e.g., RSA, 1998), the government (with the exception of the Department of Water Affairs) has had little success in deploying what little funds were actually allocated for such purposes.

As discussed earlier, there are reasons to believe that increased international trade with low-wage countries has reduced the demand for less-skilled labour in both high- and middle-income countries, including South Africa (although the extent of the fall in demand remains moot). This suggests that countries can either respond by allowing relative unskilled wages to fall, or by protecting unskilled wages – in which case, unskilled unemployment will rise (at least in the short term). If welfare is provided to the unemployed, then the adverse distributional consequences of higher unemployment can be ameliorated. In South Africa's case, where support for the unemployed is available only to a fraction of the workforce (and for a limited period only), the contraction of employment can widen inequality and have devastating effects on households.

Industrial policy has been broadly supportive of industry facing competitive pressures as a result of globalization (see, DTI, 1995; 1998). The main thrust of the policy support has been to facilitate recapitalization (to allow for best practice techniques to be introduced) and to promote productivity improvements. However, such interventions have encouraged greater capital-intensity, and have not been (directly) supportive of employment growth (Kaplan, 2003).

There does not appear to be a case for slowing down trade liberalization in South Africa – although there is a case for better policy coordination, especially between macroeconomic, trade and labour market policy. One of the most oft-cited 'lessons' from international experience is that openness (or at least producing for the export market) is good for growth,[5] and, as noted earlier, recent South African research has concluded that international trade has been neutral to positive with respect to employment generation. However, the costs and benefits have not been shared equally between regions or households. If there is a policy case to be made, it is to alleviate the suffering of hard hit areas through public works programs and compensating welfare transfers (where feasible).

4 Conclusion

The impact of the new (global) economy on South Africa has reflected the character of South Africa's particular experience of globalization and the effects of other, coincident processes or trends. For South Africa, 'globalization' – in terms of falling rates of effective protection and rising levels of trade and capital flows – is of recent origin, really only kicking in during the 1990s. This was in part because of the political context: opportunities to expand exports (or to negotiate trade agreements) were limited in the 1980s. The end of apartheid exposed South Africa anew to the opportunities entailed in globalization.

But South Africa's belated opening was also due to economic changes. Until the 1980s, the gold industry insulated South Africa from the need for major trade liberalization. The crisis of the gold industry, with falling international demand and rising production costs, left policy makers with little choice but to expand other exports. South Africa's engagement with the global economy reflected these specific political and economic factors.

The effects of globalization on inequality in South Africa have also been shaped by the nature of the South African economy and social structure. By the end of the twentieth century South African households had for some time been overwhelmingly dependent on paid employment (or on transfers of wage income through remittances). There was negligible subsistence or peasant agricultural production, and the informal sector was small in comparison with (for example) most of Latin America. Globalization thus affected inequality almost entirely through its effects on the labour market.

Methodological problems beset any attempt at identifying precisely the effect of globalization on the labour market. The decline in effective rates of protection has induced, or at least accelerated, structural adjustment in the economy. Previously protected sectors have taken strain but other sectors have taken advantage of new export opportunities. Trade liberalization has resulted in import penetration in labour-intensive sectors and growth in capital-intensive export sectors. But the overall impact (i.e., including indirect effects) of increased international trade has been estimated to have been neutral to mildly positive (although the impact of trade on technology is almost certainly underestimated by such calculations). Net capital flows probably remain too small to have had a major effect on employment trends.

These employment trends affect inequality primarily through the increased demand for skilled labour and declining demand for unskilled labour. The declining demand for unskilled labour, despite the existence of a massive surplus of the latter, clearly demands analysis. We suggest that contributory factors include labour market regulation, which serves to inhibit job creation in the unskilled labour market.

Globalization is often said to reduce the scope for domestic policy choices. The South African case suggests that there are at least three major areas where the government continues to make real choices that have major effects on distribution. The first of these is the labour market (discussed above). The second is the budget. South Africa redistributes a remarkable amount through the budget, including through welfare transfers (McGrath *et al.*, 1997). An official committee of inquiry is currently considering reforms of welfare policy, including the possible introduction of some kind of financial support for the unemployed. Government spending on health care, education and welfare peaked in 1996–97, but the planned decline is tiny, from just over 44 per cent of the budget in 1996/97 to less than 43 per cent by 2002/03.

The third area in which the government makes clear choices is education. Education mediates the effects of globalization on inequality, and changes in the education system can therefore have significant effects on inequality. Education is the largest area of expenditure, comprising about a fifth of the South African budget. Education is also remarkably egalitarian, at least in comparison with the level of inequality in the distribution of income. The variation in terms of educational attainment by age is much less in South Africa than in Brazil. Yet the quality of schooling is not believed to be commensurate with the amounts spent. South African children appear to share fairly equally in a low-quality but expensive schooling system. Pass rates for the matriculation exams are alarmingly low – especially in comparison to the numbers of pupils entering the secondary school system. Fifteen years of expanding expenditure led to big gains in the number of school grades supposedly completed, but without major improvements in actual literacy or numeracy (Fuller *et al.*, 1995). Under these conditions it is not clear that extra spending would improve the quality of education.

Policy reform is, of course, the result of political processes. The choices made by the South African government reflect the power of important constituencies: the trade unions, with respect to labour policies, and the teaching union in particular with respect to educational reform (or the lack thereof). South Africa's overall policy framework and associated growth strategy thus entails an uneasy combination of political and economic pressures.

4.1 Distributional dilemmas of South Africa's growth strategy

Improved education and training is desirable, and probably will have positive consequences for distribution. However, unless there is a significant expansion of employment (particularly for the many relatively unskilled unemployed people), South Africa's overall growth path is unlikely to reduce inequality. As argued above, South Africa's combination of labour market and trade policies is not conducive to the expansion of labour-intensive firms and sectors. Increasing the skills of the workforce will help reduce wage inequality and will (hopefully) improve the employment prospects of the unemployed. But on its own, it will do little (at least in the short or even medium term) to improve the access of the vast numbers of unemployed people to jobs.

This is why we favour strategies which improve education and skills – but which also allow for the simultaneous expansion of unskilled employment. Labour market reforms are, in our view, a central plank of any egalitarian strategy. Given that unemployment is a major determinant of poverty and inequality, only a significant expansion of jobs (even at relatively low wages) will reduce society-wide inequality (see, Nattrass, 2000b). Such job creation will only occur in the current context of increased international competition if greater wage-flexibility is injected into labour market policy.

Some people object to such labour market reforms on the grounds that South Africa should follow an exclusively 'high-wage, high-productivity' strategy – even when this means no jobs for the unemployed in the foreseeable future. Their argument assumes that even in the context of high unemployment, it is necessary to focus exclusively on increasing labour productivity today in order to project the economy onto a more dynamic ('new economy') growth path. The message is attractive: invest in people, technology, infrastructure, workplace reorganization, inter-firm co-operation etc., and achieve the win-win scenario of greater competitiveness, a better-paid workforce, and faster, sustainable growth. This 'high-productivity now' (HPN) strategy is evident in South African labour market policies, and (to a lesser extent) trade and industrial policy.

The HPN strategy may well deliver benefits in terms of income growth in the longer term. The underlying assumption behind the HPN strategy is that South Africa has to adopt 'best practice techniques' and 'new heartland technologies' or die. In this regard, South Africa's policy makers have bought into the 'new economy' rhetoric of absolute rather than comparative advantage. The argument is that South Africa has no choice but to go the route of skill-intensive production using 'new economy' technologies and other sophisticated techniques – rather than exploit the vast unemployed reserves of unskilled labour through relatively low-wage, low-productivity, labour-intensive production. The gamble being taken is that the skill-intensive route, while doing little to improve labour absorption in the short term, will prove the most effective job-creating strategy in the medium to long term (see discussion in Nattrass, 2001).

However, the success of the strategy will depend in large part on skills development and sustained investment. Unfortunately, skills shortages (which are currently driving up the price of skilled labour relative to unskilled labour) will continue to act as a constraint on growth – and the brain-drain of young white professionals will exacerbate the situation for some time. The AIDS pandemic (which has affected predominantly unskilled labour) is already exercising a dampening impact on growth (Arndt and Lewis, 2002). As it takes more of a hold on skilled labour, the burden on South Africa's growth path will increase exponentially (Nattrass, 2003)

Trends in employment and productivity growth in the 1990s are consistent with the HPN growth strategy. As shown in Figure 9.2, real earnings per worker increased over the decade. This was the result of trade union pressure (especially in the public sector) and the changing skill composition of the employed workforce (as relatively unskilled workers bore the brunt of retrenchments). It is thus unsurprising that labour productivity and average earnings rose as employment fell.

Notice that the growth in labour productivity exceeded that of average wages for most of the period – thus facilitating a slight growth in the profit

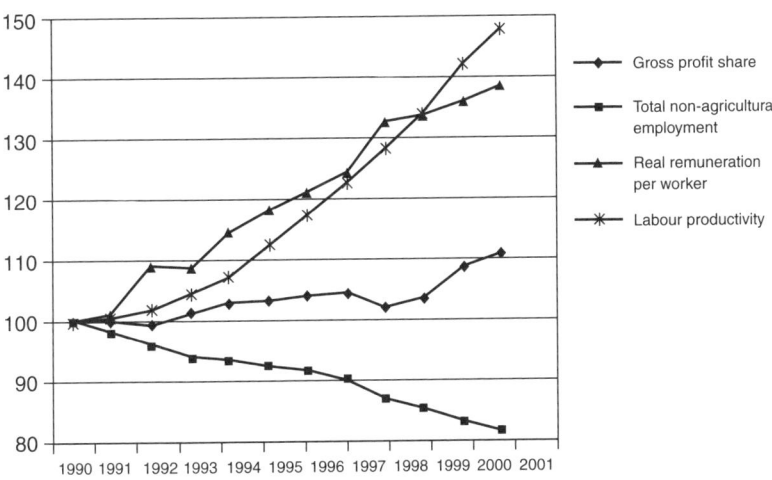

Figure 9.2 Index of labour productivity, employment, average wages and the profit share (data from the South African Reserve Bank).

share. This suggests that in this regard, the post-apartheid HPN growth path has been relatively kind to employed (especially skilled) labour and capital, and unkind to unskilled labour and the unemployed.

This is the cost that lurks behind the glamour of HPN rhetoric: significant employment creation is relegated to second- or third-round effects. The HPN strategy is, in other words, a reincarnation of the old 'trickle-down' story: increases in productivity drive the rising tide of growth; the unemployed must go to night school and training programmes whilst waiting for the employment waters to rise. Labour market reforms which may provide jobs for the unemployed today are rejected by proponents of HPN on the grounds that the expansion of low-wage employment would undermine productivity growth – and thus reduce the capacity of the economy to create jobs tomorrow.

We find such arguments unconvincing. First, how is productivity growth in existing firms harmed if average labour productivity is reduced through the expansion of new jobs? The expansion of low-productivity sectors does not – in and of itself – reduce the capacity of high productivity sectors to develop and grow. Second, there is no reason why firms paying lower wages will necessarily undermine the growth of high-wage firms and sectors. HPN arguments often implicitly assume that capital will necessarily flow to low-wage activities, thereby undermining the high-productivity sector of the economy and bringing about a 'race to the bottom'. But as long as higher-wage firms have a correspondingly higher level of productivity, there will be no threat to their profit margins. Furthermore, as lower-wage, lower-productivity firms tend to produce very different products to higher-wage, higher-productivity firms, it is unlikely that they will often be competing in the same niche markets. Third, we believe there are ethical problems with a strategy that boosts average productivity in a middle-income labour-surplus economy by destroying low-wage jobs. Increasing the costs of employing labour is certainly one way of raising average productivity – but it comes at the cost of job losses (or at least no job increases) in low-productivity sectors. Such a strategy is acceptable where unemployment is relatively low, and where welfare and training is provided for the unemployed. This was the case with regard to the post-war 'Scandinavian model'. Centralized wage bargaining set wages across all firms, regardless of productivity performance, thus putting pressure on low-productivity firms and sectors (Henley and Tsakalotos, 1993). Workers who lost their jobs as a result of such restructuring received generous welfare benefits whilst being retrained for employment.

However, in the case of South Africa – where unemployment is high and there is no adequate welfare provision for the unemployed – such a strategy is ethically questionable. It asks the currently unemployed generation to make a sacrifice for the sake of the employed and better skilled among them, and for the next generation that will (supposedly) enjoy the fruits of a more dynamic ('new') economy. Given the strong relationship between unemployment and poverty, these are serious sacrifices indeed.

One way of addressing this distributional dilemma would be if those who gained from the HPN 'new-economy' growth path (i.e., high-tech industry and the better educated, skilled and currently employed workforce) were taxed sufficiently to finance adequate welfare grants and training programmes for the unemployed. This was the implicit 'social contract' behind the Scandinavian model – but it only held together while growth was rapid and unemployment relatively low. In a labour-surplus middle-income country like South Africa, such a scenario seems highly unlikely.

Given the above fiscal and political realities, there is little hope of an exclusive HPN strategy delivering many benefits to the unskilled unemployed in the foreseeable future. For this reason, it is important that South Africa's growth strategy encourage productivity growth in some sectors and facilitate the expansion of relatively low-wage, low-productivity jobs for the unemployed. 'New economy' sectors and product niches must be encouraged – but not at the cost of the destruction of lower-tech, labour-absorbing sectors and activities.

Notes

1 Schultz and Mwabu estimate that reducing the impact of unions on wages by half would result in a 2 per cent increase in employment, and in a 'redistribution of wage payments from the upper-middle-class African union workers to lower-wage non-union workers and the marginalized poor who are often now not actively participating in the labour market' (1998b).
2 The concern raised by Stiglitz in his chapter about VAT harming the formal sector (relative to the informal sector) does not have direct relevance to South Africa.
3 The Basic Condition of Employment Act provided for longer annual and family leave (thus increasing the direct cost of employing labour) and reducing hours of work (thus increasing hourly fixed costs). The overtime premium was also increased; with that, overtime labour pay is now over two and a half times that of workers in comparable middle-income countries (Barker, 1999).
4 Both the Ministry of Finance's GEAR strategy (RSA, 1996) and the Ministry of Labour's Employment Strategy Framework (RSA, 1998) recommended that amendments be made to the extension of collectively bargained wage agreements to non-parities. Soon after the Labour Market Commission (LMC, 1996) presented its report, the Minister of Labour announced that changes to the mandatory extension provision were imminent – yet nothing came of it. The State President made a similar announcement in early 2000, but this too appears to have been empty.
5 Some 'revisionist' economists have used cross-country growth regressions to question the assumed links between openness and growth (e.g., Rodriguez and Rodrik, 1999). However, such methodology has been questioned by others who argue that case studies are more meaningful and that they show a clear correlation between openness and growth (Srinivasan and Bhagwati, 1999).

References

Arndt, C. and J.D. Lewis (2002). The macro implications of HIV/Aids in South Africa: a preliminary assessment, *South African Journal of Economics*, 68(5): 856–887.

Barker, F. (1999). On South Africa's labour policies, *South African Journal of Economics*, 67(1): 1–33.

Bell, T. and N. Cattaneo (1997). *Foreign Trade and Employment in South African Manufacturing Industry*, Occasional report No. 4, Geneva: Employment and Training Department, International Labour Office.

Bhorat, H. and J. Hodge (1999). Decomposing shifts in labour demand in South Africa, *South African Journal of Economics*, 67(3): 348–380.

Dirwan, I. and M. Walton (1997). How international exchange, technology and institutions affect workers: an introduction, *The World Bank Economic Review*, 11(1): 1–15.

DTI (1995). *Support Measures for the Enhancement of the International Competitiveness of South Africa's Industrial Sector*, Pretoria: Submission by Government to the Trade and Industry Chamber of NEDLAC.

DTI (1998). *Industrial Policy and Programmes in South Africa*, Discussion Document, April.

Edwards, L. (1999). Trade liberalisation, structural change and occupational employment in South Africa, Paper presented at Trade and Industrial Policy Secretariat (TIPS) Annual Forum, South Africa, September.

Edwards, L. (2000). Globalisation and the skill bias of occupational employment in South Africa. Unpublished paper, School of Economics, University of Cape Town.

Fedderke, J., Y. Shin and P. Vaze (2000). Trade and labour usage: an examination of the South African manufacturing industry, ERSA Working Paper No. 15. Department of Economics, University of the Witwatersrand, Johannesburg.

Fleming Martin (2000). *South Africa's Monetary Policy: A Capital Crime?*, Johannesburg: Fleming Martin Securities.

Fuller, B., P. Pillay and N. Sirur (1995). *Literacy Trends in South Africa: Expanding Education Whilst Reinforcing Unequal Achievement*, Cape Town: University of Cape Town (SALDRU Report).

Gibson, B. and D. Van Seventer (1995). Restructuring public sector expenditure in the South African economy, Unpublished paper, Development Bank of Southern Africa.

Gordon, R. (2000). Does the new economy measure up to the great inventions of the past? *Journal of Economic Perspectives*, 14(4): 49–74.

Heese, K. (2000). Foreign direct investment in South Africa (1994–9) – confronting globalisation, *Development Southern Africa*, 17(3): 389–400.

Henley, A. and E. Tsakalotos (1993) *Corporatism and Economic Performance: A Comparative Analysis of Market Economies*, Vermont: Edward Elgar.

ILO (1999). *South Africa: Studies on the Social Dimensions of Globalisation* (drafted by S. Hayter, G. Reinecke and R. Torres), Geneva: Task Force on Country Studies on Globalisation, International Labour Office.

Kaplan, D. (2003). Manufacturing performance and policy in South Africa, Paper presented at Trade and Industry Policy Secretariat and Development Policy Research Unit Forum, Johannesburg.

Labour Market Commission (LMC) (1996). Report of the South African Presidential Comprehensive Labour Market Commission, Cape Town.
Lam, D. (1999). *Generating Extreme Inequality: Schooling, Earnings, and Intergenerational Transmission of Human Capital in South Africa and Brazil*, South Africa: Population Studies Center at the Institute for Social Research (Research Report), 99–439.
Leibbrandt, M., H. Bhorat and I. Woolard (2000). Understanding contemporary household inequality in South Africa, *Studies in Economics and Econometrics*, 24(4): 31–52.
McGrath, M., C. Janisch and C. Horner (1997). Redistribution through the fiscal system in the South African economy, Paper presented at Economics Society of South Africa Conference, Potchefstroom.
Moll, P. (1996). Compulsory centralisation of collective bargaining in South Africa, *American Economic Review: Papers and Proceeding*, 82(2): 326–329.
Moll, P. (2000). Discrimination is declining in South Africa but inequality is not, *Studies in Economics and Econometrics*, 24(4): 91–108.
Morley, S. (1995). *Poverty and Inequality in Latin America: The Impact of Adjustment and Recovery in the 1980s*, London: Johns Hopkins University Press.
Morley, S. (2000). Distribution and growth in Latin America in an era of structural reform, Paper presented at Poverty and Income Inequality in Developing Countries: A Policy Dialogue on the Effects of Globalisation, OECD. Paris.
Nattrass, N. (1996). Gambling on investment: competing economic strategies in South Africa, *Transformation*, 31: 25–42.
Nattrass, N. (1998a). Globalisation and the South African labour market, *Studies in Economics and Econometrics*, 22(3): 71–90.
Nattrass, N. (1998b). Growth, employment and economic policy in South Africa: a critical review. Paper Published by the Centre for Development and Enterprise, September.
Nattrass, N. (2000a). The debate about unemployment in the 1990s, *Studies in Economics and Econometrics*, 24(3): 73–90.
Nattrass, N. (2000b). Inequality, unemployment and wage-setting institutions in South Africa, *Studies in Economics and Econometrics*, 24(3): 129–142.
Nattrass, N. (2001). High productivity now: a critique of South Africa's growth strategy, *Transformation*, 45: 1–24.
Nattrass, N. (2003). IDS, economic growth and income distribution in South Africa, *South African Journal of Economics*, 71(4): 428–454.
Nattrass, N. and J. Seekings (1997). Citizenship and welfare in South Africa: deracialisation and inequality in a labour-surplus economy, *Canadian Journal of African Studies*, 31(3): 452–481.
Nattrass, N. and J. Seekings (2001). Two nations? Race and economic inequality in South Africa today, *Daedalus*, 130(1): 45–70.
NIEP (1996). *From the RDP to GEAR: The Gradual Embracing of Neo-Liberalism in Economic Policy*, Johannesberg: National Institute for Economic Policy.
NLC (1996). *Social Equity and Job Creation*, Johannesberg: NEDLAC Labour Caucus.
OECD (1997). Trade, earnings and employment: assessing the impact of trade with emerging economies on OECD labour markets, Paper presented at *OECD Employment Outlook*, July.

OECD (1999). Labour market performance and the OECD jobs strategy, *Economic Outlook*, 65(June): 142–161.
Oliner, S. and D. Sichel (2000). The resurgences of growth in the late 1990s: is information technology the story?, *Journal of Economic Perspectives*, 14(4): 3–22.
Perry, L. (1995). Asian labour markets: some comparisons, *Labour and Industry*, 6(2): 103–109.
Rodriguez, F. and D. Rodrik (1999). Trade policy and economic growth: a skeptic's guide to cross-national evidence, NBER Working Paper No. W7081.
RSA (1996). *Growth, Employment and Redistribution: A Macroeconomic Strategy*, South Africa: Department of Finance.
RSA (1998). *Creating Jobs, Fighting Poverty: An Employment Strategy Framework*, Department of Labour, Government Gazette, 397(19040).
Samson, M. (1997). *Fiscal Policy for Job Creating Growth: A NIEP Report Prepared for COSATU*, Johannesburg: National Institute for Economic Policy.
Schultz, T.P. and G. Mwabu (1998a). Wage Premia for Education and Location, by Gender and Race in South Africa, Discussion Paper No. 78, Economic Growth Center, Yale University.
Schultz, T.P. and G. Mwabu (1998b). Labor unions and the distribution of wages and employment in South Africa, *Industrial and Labour Relations Review*, 51(4): 680–703.
Seekings, J. (2000). Visions of society: peasant workers and the unemployed in a changing South Africa, *Studies in Economics and Econometrics*, 24(4): 53–72.
Srinivasan, T. and J. Bhagwati (1999). Outward Orientation and Development: Are Revisionists Right?, Discussion Paper No. 806, Economic Growth Center, Yale University.
Standing, G. (1997). Labour market dynamics in South African industrial firms: the South African labour flexibility survey, Paper presented at the Workshop on Labour Markets and Enterprise Performance in South Africa, Johannesburg: 30 January.
Standing, G., J. Sender and J. Weeks (1996). *The South African Challenge: Restructuring the South African Labour Market*, Geneva: International Labour Organisation.
Stiglitz, J. (1998). More instruments and broader goals: moving towards the post-Washington consensus, *WIDER Annual Lectures 2*, UNU World Institute for Development Economics Research, Helsinki.
Stiglitz, J. (2002). *Globalisation and its Discontents*, London: Penguin.
Tsikata, Y. (1998). Liberalisation and Trade Performance in South Africa, Informal draft, Macroeconomics Division Southern Africa Department, World Bank.
Weeks, J. (1999). Stuck in low GEAR? Macroeconomic policy in South Africa, 1996–98, *Cambridge Journal of Economics*, 23(4): 795–811.
Weiss, L. (1998). *The Myth of the Powerless State: Governing the Economy in a Global Era*, Cambridge: Polity Press.
Whiteford, A. and D. Van Seventer (2000). South Africa's changing income distribution in the 1990s, *Studies in Economics and Econometrics*, 24(3): 7–30.
Wood, A. (1994). *North South Trade, Employment and Inequality*, Oxford: Oxford University Press.
Wood, A. (1995). How trade hurt unskilled workers, *Journal of Economic Perspectives*, 9(3): 57–80.

Wood, A. (1997). Openness and wage inequality in developing countries: the Latin American challenge to East Asian conventional wisdom, *World Bank Economic Review*, 11(1): 33–57.

World Bank (1993). *The East Asian Miracle: Economic Growth and Public Policy*, New York: Oxford University Press.

Part III
New critical perspectives

10 The political philosophy of needs and weak states

Lawrence Hamilton

1 Introduction

'Globalization' is more than an essentially contested concept. It is an amorphous notion that has been used to capture a whole myriad of allegedly new economic and political developments and aspirations. Like a few other contributors to this book, for example Bates and Nattrass and Seekings, I question two common assumptions: that 'globalization' now is a completely new phenomenon; and that the 'new economy' demands a complete rethink of how to proceed in economic and political terms. Globalization is characterized by a few new developments, but all of these are simply the logical extension of a much older set of economic and political institutions. And these institutions owe their existence to a history of political decisions, or the lack thereof, and subsequent conceptual and institutional developments, many of which have palpable negative effects on weak states. It follows from this that globalization and its effects can where necessary be remedied by political action. In particular it can be remedied by prudent and determined political decision making. However, all of these past and possible decisions are constrained by the current political and economic context and the concepts that determine that context. Thus, the first goal is to provide an understanding of this conceptual and institutional context.

For at least the last fifty years, if not much longer, the conceptual and institutional context has been dominated by what I call the rights-preferences couple. The rights-preferences couple is a way of understanding and practising politics common to liberal political and economic theory and liberal democratic practice that *reduces* politics to the security of individual human rights, the aggregation of individual preferences, or a contrived combination of both. This reduction excludes the two main components of politics: collective decision determined by the need to act and collective evaluation determined by the requirement to control and enhance the development and satisfaction of individual human needs. As a consequence the rights-preferences couple impoverishes practical and theoretical understanding of the nature of human needs and how to satisfy them. In the first part of this chapter I discuss these problems. Then in the rest of the chapter I use an alternative conceptual framework based on the concept of human needs to develop a couple of suggestions for tackling the problem of the development of weak states. I begin by developing an account of the normative, historical and political nature of needs. This involves an account of how needs simultaneously can be distinct from and related to wants, a definition of needs in terms of human functioning, and a causal understanding of the formation, evaluation and satisfaction of needs. I then provide suggestions for how to obtain democratic, sovereign evaluation of needs and institutions, and why this would require radically new kinds of political participation and coercive authority. The chapter ends with an application of these ideas to the realities of the development of weak states such as African states within the new economy, which includes an analysis of markets and the power of these states.

2 Rights and preferences

Within the contemporary legal, political and economic framework, rights are legally, coercively enforceable entitlements that are conceived as being objective, abstract and universal. Preferences, on the other hand, are construed as avowed human wants that are subjective and particular to context, agent and time. The main assumption in the practice and theory of the rights-preferences couple is that a properly instituted and enforced rights framework guarantees human life and liberty, and freedom over preferences and choices. This is not only untrue in practice but it is a consequence of an historically contingent, practical combination of three *meta*-political theories: neo-Kantian moral theory, natural rights theories (and related legal frameworks) and welfare utilitarianism. Given their foundational differences, this combination is an odd *ménage à trois*. Nevertheless, together these theories defend in terms of rights and preferences the alleged virtues of justice and welfare at the expense of political participation, democratic sovereignty and the satisfaction of human needs. This imbalance is a result of the fact that these theories either focus exclusively on normative questions discussed in purely moral terms, or they concentrate on technical issues alone. In contemporary political and economic theory the moral and the technical are understood and developed in artificial isolation from one another. For example, natural rights theory ostensibly has little or nothing to do with governance and market equilibrium, while in practice they form a conceptual and institutional union. The result is an unhelpful theoretical bifurcation of the main concerns of politics: normative political questions are reduced to moral philosophical evaluation of *individual* action, and questions about collective choice are reduced to technical, administrative questions.[1]

The dominant technical approach is characterized by a reliance on rational social choice, which antecedently excludes any reference to human goods. It is argued or assumed that only individuals are concerned with their goods and thus social policy should confine itself to the mechanical aggregation of revealed *individual* preferences.[2] This curtails the evaluation of preferences and their transformation – how they are and ought to be transformed – which deprives us of an understanding of the institutions and practices that do in fact determine, influence and transform our preferences, for example, those related to markets. And this in turn usually condones the common assumption that it is best to allow free reign to these institutions and practices. See, for example, the dominant discourse of free trade and trade liberalization within the theory and practice of development: the need to protect weak, developing markets is derided in the face of allegedly neutral free markets, even as 'developed' states maintain tried and tested forms of protecting their own national markets.

In the main moral approach, which has natural law and Kantian roots, the normativity of a claim or theory is determined by whether or not it incorporates a claim that there is an absolute moral obligation on some *particular* agent that X should come about. This conceptual frame removes from consideration the wider normative concerns that relate, for example, to individual and collective ends and values and choice over the possible paths and political means to reach these ends. The common political application of this narrow normative conception understands political problems and the means to their resolution in terms of imprescriptible, individual, natural, human rights. The most important example of this is the Universal Declaration of Human Rights. In the last thirty years political philosophy has mirrored this practical dependence on rights. It is dominated by a number of rights-based political philosophies, all of which use different means of justifying from first principles the imprescriptibility of certain natural, human rights.[3] These are advanced as *meta*-political means of assessing the rights guaranteed by the civil law of states, or 'legal rights'. Developed in this way, rights act as moral claims about what ought to come about, but in most cases there do not exist the institutions, means or resources to actually bring them about.

More importantly for my concern here, these kinds of rights create the illusion of political power while actually undermining real individual political agency. Individual rights that can be upheld in a court of law make citizens feel relatively powerful within the existing political framework, but they do so at the expense of furnishing us with real power over the large evaluative questions that concern the framework itself. This is no accident. The rights we have are granted by states and state formations that have their origins in rapid attempts to take advantage of hard won and fragile periods of peace by constitutionalizing the existing state of order and security. Subsequently they have given ground to some of the demands of increased citizen participation in the affairs of government, for example the extension of the franchise and the more equitable representation of all groups. But the fear of 'mass democracy' has remained an efficient antidote against the idea of political participation in the really fundamental questions of political order: of who is governing whom and how; and of how we might evaluate the institutions that determine our needs. This lack of real political power is reinforced by the fact that rights create and legitimize a legalistic framework for politics, in which political evaluation is reduced to legally adjudicated conflicts over individual rights. That is, the only evaluation that occurs is neither political nor democratic, for these claims and conflicts are adjudicated within the plethora of non-elected courts and administrative institutions of the judiciary. This makes a mockery of the idea of democratic sovereignty and its requisite kind of political participation as well as the real need for it (about which, see more below). Rights create these problems not because of their individualistic character so much as their jural character. They conceive of persons as primarily legal agents and then secondarily as social and political agents rather than *vice versa*.

This *meta*-political rights-discourse is given extra impetus by the now dominant globalization debate. The argument (which is normally more like an assumption) runs as follows: now that markets and capital are global and state politics seemingly ineffectual, we need to think about these issues as if we were all isolated sovereign moral agents having trouble working out how best to treat one another in this global space. The predominance of the discourse of rights is no coincidence. If we are isolated individuals in a global space requiring safeguards against the vagaries of wayward governments, the best way to achieve this is to argue that we possess (have or own) certain imprescriptible rights to life and liberty. This is strongly reminiscent of a much older natural law discourse developed by Grotius, Hobbes and Locke that, among other things, was intended to guide imperial powers and sovereign individual *conquistadores* in their colonial land grab. The similarity is haunting: the only thing new about globalization is its new free-trade imperialism.[4]

The dominant technical approach too is reinforced by the current trend of arguments concerning 'global transformations', for now analysts and proponents of 'free' markets can focus their attention on the technical questions of how to retain or improve upon this alleged global freedom and its positive effects. That is, there is a dominant belief that the global conditions combined with the fall of Soviet Communism have changed the question from 'what are the determinants of the current arrangement and how might they be transformed to improve how we meet and develop needs'? to 'how might we secure or reform the conditions of the current successful natural order to improve its responsiveness to preferences'? If you assume that the conditions today are new, natural, and freedom-enhancing, it is easy to argue that they are consequently of purely technical as opposed to political concern.

Thus, in reducing politics to either the moral or the technical, the rights-preferences couple undermines the imperative for real *political* evaluation. If nothing else, politics is an activity defined by some notion of collective choice among differentially assessed paths where the assessment is in terms of the evaluated individual and public goods and interests, and any significant action in the light of the choice will ultimately involve coercion.[5] These aspects of politics are foreign to the rights-preferences couple. It cannot comfortably accommodate coercion, collective decision, and the evaluation of short- and long-term individual and public interests and goods. In short it excludes two parts of the reality of politics. The first part involves the goods under evaluative consideration. The second part concerns the locus and purpose of political authority and coercion. I cover each in turn. I maintain that the main goods under evaluative consideration are those constitutive of full human functioning. This is the basic definitional underpinning to the idea of human needs, but needs also include a myriad of particular means and ends. What are human needs and how are they related to wants, collective decisions, coercion and markets?

3 Wants and needs

Modern need theory understands needs either as universal, natural, material human requirements or as universal conditions for human morality and freedom. In other words, on the one hand, needs tend to be understood in terms of minimum thresholds that constitute the 'objective' conditions for physical survival, while on the other this idea is broadened and needs are conceived as objectively required conditions for agency. For ease of reference, I will call the former the 'threshold thesis' and the latter the 'agency thesis'.[6] In the threshold thesis needs are understood as three or four universal, unchanging 'basic needs' that come into consideration *in extremis*, under conditions of famine or general scarcity. In these terms the concept of needs is removed from the normal political and economic lexicon and confined to the analysis of special cases. For example, in welfare economics the analysis of needs has been relegated to the increasingly technical sub-discipline of development economics.[7] And, since political theory has become dominated by moral philosophy, the subject of 'basic needs' is deemed not to be part of the subject matter of political analysis and proposal.

In the agency thesis, needs are *not* restricted to three or four material requirements. Needs are defined as normative goals whose lack creates objective harm and whose satisfaction constitutes the objective conditions for human agency (Doyal and Gough, 1991; Brock, 1998).[8] More exactly, needs are proposed as *universal* conditions for individual freedom over choices and life plans; in other words, the meeting of these needs is conceived as a necessary condition for the realization of rights that secure free preference formation and satisfaction. This is most clearly articulated within the 'capability' approach developed by Martha Nussbaum, although of course she does not use the language of needs.[9] The agency thesis constitutes a significant advance on the threshold thesis because biological survival is, of course, not sufficient for agency. However, despite the evident differences between the threshold thesis and the agency thesis, they are similar in one very important manner. I argue that in an attempt to forge a strict, universal distinction between needs and wants, they both rely on static conceptions of human nature and human needs and thus artificially exclude some needs and fail to understand the relationship between needs and wants.

First, in both theses, needs are understood in purely instrumental terms, as the means to other goods or ends, and this excludes a wide spectrum of needs. It is true that many needs are purely mundane instrumental means to larger ends, for example my need as a tourist for camera film to photograph Cape Town. But other needs are ends in themselves, such as my need for water or autonomy or creative expression, which I discuss in the next section. Second, both theses provide little room for a causal understanding of how needs are formed, in particular how they are affected by our wants and preferences (or the avowal of wants) and the determinants and satisfiers of these wants. A quick glance into history shows that many needs are formed over time, and that many contemporary needs used to be wants. Think of the history of the need for refrigerators and televisions: not very long ago they were luxury wants and now they are 'basic' needs, even in the poorest parts of the developing world. Moreover, wants affect how we interpret our needs because they influence collective decisions, plans and institutional forms. For example, the demand for cars has generated large road-building projects normally funded by the state. This involved *political* decisions about resource-allocation and the trajectory of development that over time justified the degeneration of public transport. This is most manifest in developing countries, but it is also true of 'developed' countries: the degenerated state of public transport in the UK and USA are prime examples. As a consequence of these political decisions, in order to meet my need for mobility I need a car. Thus, a want for a car soon became a justified need for a car. For example, whether I live in Durban or Los Angeles, the fact that I need a car in order to get to work or to get to the beach to surf, both of which are important parts of my life, and, in more general terms, a good life, is contingent upon the present, poor state of public transport. My car provides the best means of meeting this need for mobility, and it is therefore a justified need. However, the rise of the car as an efficient means of transport was the result not only of the fact that it meets a need for mobility, but also of the less acknowledged fact that as a luxury item it satisfies a preference for a distorted kind of social esteem. Moreover, this development may have actually depleted our means of meeting our needs. This is arguably the case with regard to our need for mobility, for an efficient and public train service may be a better means of meeting this need. But it is beyond dispute with regard to other needs that relate, for example, to the environment: cars are a major cause in the degradation of the planetary environment. Thus, a particular car may satisfy my felt need for a combination of mobility and social esteem, but be part of a history of political, institutional arrangements that fail to satisfy my need for mobility as well as other needs of mine, not to mention the needs of others.

How is this possible? How can a felt need of mine not be a human need? How can I need something that acts against me meeting my needs as a human being? The answer to these questions depends on the kind of understanding that both the threshold thesis and the agency thesis fail to provide: the historical relationship between wants and needs and how extant institutions determine that relationship. Over time the satisfaction of human wants has an affect on human nature and thus human needs. Humans often want things that they do not need and these can become interpreted as legitimate needs; but these wants do not drop out of the sky. They have an origin and a determinate causal history, normally dependent on the prior existence of the satisfier of the want. I cannot want a car until cars are produced and thus exist.[10] Thus my need for a car has a history that goes beyond the mental or physical state that produced in me the desire to drive a car, primarily a political and economic history of the power of capitalist production and advertising. This history can be evaluated and the outcome of this evaluation can be used in the evaluation of my avowed need to drive a car and my associated avowed need for more motorways. Whether my need for a car is understood as a legitimate need is therefore a practical political question that will depend on the evaluation of needs in context (about which, see more below).

Moreover, this fact about the relationship between needs and wants is one that flows from the fact that human nature is not static. As human nature changes over time, changes that are often determined by wants and the innovations and production cycles that give rise to them, so do human needs. However, at any point in time and at a relatively abstracted level there exist material and ethical means and ends that constitute the elements of a fully functioning human life against which we can judge the lives, needs and wants of individual humans and groups. It is this general conception of human needs that I develop and discuss in the next section. Unlike the threshold thesis and the agency thesis it is a *general* account of a fully functioning human life, or at least those elements of existing conceptions of a fully functioning life that can be enabled by a political authority. Thus it goes well beyond even the 'minimum' conditions of agency developed in the agency thesis. However, unlike the agency thesis, it allows for the possibility of change in human nature and the freedom of individual choice and satisfaction of *particular* wants and needs within this framework. It achieves this as a consequence of its level of abstraction in discussing the material and ethical elements of a fully functioning human life. These general needs have identifiable links to particular needs and wants, but these can only be determined in context. Needs are distinguished from wants in that the former constitute the set of means and ends that constitute a fully functioning human life in a particular context. These can only be determined under specific conditions of political participation and coercion, which are discussed in the following two sections. However, the general needs provide heuristic guidelines both for understanding needs and their relationship to wants and for the process of distinguishing legitimate needs from mere wants or wants paraded as needs. Although humans often want what they need, needs are not reducible to wants.

This emphasis on context is not only a consequence of an attempt to take seriously the distinction between needs and wants and to provide a means of evaluating the political economic history of the relationship between needs and wants, it is also part and parcel of a conception of human needs that gives due weight to individual preferences over needs. This is important because, depending on circumstances, I may never want some of the things I know I need. For example, for health reasons I may need to stop writing about needs and take a holiday or I may need to stop smoking, but I may want the opposite. According to any version of the threshold thesis or the agency thesis you might want to choose, the smoking of cigarettes could not be classified as a need, nor could the way I go on about needs (but I'll spare you the details). Moreover, there is now substantial and clear medical evidence to show that smoking is at least detrimental to human health. Nevertheless, my want or desire to keep smoking may be the result of a number of factors, none of which are the result of distortion, illusion or addiction. I may know all too well that my obsessive desire to smoke will leave me more unhealthy than I might otherwise have been, and I may have the proven ability to put a stop to it, but I may have decided that without it I am not the person I want to be and that a part of my health is worth sacrificing in order for me to be myself. In other words, obsessive smoking is not a human need but it has become a considered need of mine. Obviously, nothing follows from this with regard to smoking legislation. All that follows from this is that my need to smoke and preferences with regard to this legislation be accepted as a legitimate part of the political evaluation of needs.

Besides the effect of the rights-preferences couple, the misconstrual of needs in both the threshold thesis and the agency thesis is a consequence of the related fact that, when modern theorists think of needs, they tend to have in mind the welfare state. Yet, the welfare state is only one contingent, flawed means of meeting needs: it dictates a set of needs as basic requirements for adequate survival without reference to the individuals whose needs are allegedly being satisfied. In contrast, conceptualizing needs in terms of human functioning, and the formation and evaluation of needs and wants, moves the political philosophy of needs out of the shadow of the rights-preferences couple and the dictates of the welfare state.

4 Needs and the evaluation of institutions

4.1 The nature of needs

Human needs are the necessary conditions and aspirations of full human functioning. Needs are not reducible to wants or preferences, but their formation and perception is causally influenced by wants and preferences. Needs manifest themselves in two forms: *particular* and *general* needs. Particular needs are felt motivational forces that take the form of drives or goals. General needs exist whether they are felt or not, and include material requirements and ethical and political objectives, which together constitute the constraints, preconditions and goals for both political agency and the everyday control over needs and choices. I call the general material requirements 'vital needs' as they are the necessary conditions for minimal human functioning. These include, for example, the need for water, shelter, adequate nutrition and mobility. The ethical and political objectives I call 'agency needs'. They are the necessary conditions and aspirations for individual and political agency that is characteristic of full human functioning; or at least this is true of the main agency needs, 'intersubjective recognition', 'active and creative expression', and 'autonomy as goal'.[11] These are *agency* needs because they are ongoing aspirations whose *development* increases an agent's causal power to carry out intended actions, and meet and evaluate needs. And met agency needs provide the feelings of safety, self-esteem and confidence that provide individuals with the ability to function fully, individually and politically. For example, meaningful employment not only allows individuals, to develop their creative capacities, it is one means through which an individual's skills and powers are recognized, which provides individual's with the confidence to further develop these skills and powers. However, met vital and agency needs do not exhaustively constitute full human functioning. There exist other needs that are fundamental for full human functioning but whose evaluation and satisfaction cannot be fully enabled by a political authority. A good example is the need for intimacy.

4.2 The formation and distortion of needs

Although general vital and agency needs do exist in theory and practice, they are *normally* formed, experienced and satisfied as particular needs, as particular drives and goals, and often as wants. Thus the everyday satisfiers of needs can be indistinguishable from the everyday satisfiers of wants; in fact under contemporary conditions often they have the same form – commodities. And as a consequence particular felt needs and wants affect how we interpret our general vital and agency needs. New satisfiers or commodities generate new wants and needs, and this is the case irrespective of whether these satisfiers are inspired by technological advances, scientific insights, or the manipulation of everyday consumption needs. This causal process is obvious in the way the car produces the need for a car and for more motorways. Need formation of this kind is an example of how needs can be generated and satisfied by commodities that are directed specifically at satisfying allegedly *'private' needs*. But even luxury commodities that are not intended to generate and satisfy needs in any sense have unintended consequences that do generate, satisfy and distort new needs. For example, a new video game might generate a new kind of addiction that creates a need for specially trained child therapists. It is a characteristic of liberal capitalist societies that all commodities are *determined by the logic of profit to an equal degree*. That is, despite their different relationship to vital and agency needs, there is no means of distinguishing between kinds of commodities since commodities owe their existence and value to whether they are consumed or not. Most contemporary political and economic theory simply avoids the significance of this fact – that under present conditions the main determinants and satisfiers of our needs are determined by profit alone and not in relation to vital or agency needs.

4.3 The evaluation of needs and institutions

As is the case in the formation of all needs, the various processes of need formation I have outlined are dependent on existing institutional structures. Most economic, political and ideological institutions and practices have some causal relation to needs and wants. Together, they determine (or at least legitimize) how needs are formed, evaluated and satisfied. Indeed, not only are institutions central components in the formation of our felt needs, they can be evaluated in relation to the more general vital and agency needs.

Institutions can be evaluated in terms of their causal role within four different mechanisms. First, at the most basic, direct level, institutions can be evaluated in terms of whether they inhibit or enhance the meeting of vital and agency needs. This is especially relevant for those institutions that react to, or are designed to react to, need-claims. Classic examples of this category are market-related institutions and various state institutions and educational arrangements that function either to meet or to develop needs. Second, institutions can be evaluated for the manner in which they affect the want-need dynamic, the articulation of needs and the recognition of needs. Institutions of production such as those of the automobile industry are important in these contexts. Third, institutions can be evaluated in the light of their causal role in the legitimation of norms that tend to govern practices. If the practices in question act counter to the perception and meeting of vital and agency needs and they are underpinned or legitimized by identifiable institutions, the institutions are suspect. For example, this is the case with the institution of rights since, for example, it legitimizes the practice of inviolable legal safeguards for the inheritance of property and the patenting of medical drugs in the face of ineluctable need. There is much evidence to show that without these two practices many more vital and agency needs could be met than are met at present, not least of all the basic health needs of large swathes of the earth's human population. Fourth, institutions can be evaluated in terms of how they affect the balance of normative power in the everyday analysis of needs. This is the case because institutions, or configurations thereof, or the combined arrangement of institutions and practices, are significant determinants of the distribution of normative power within a society. For example, unless they are otherwise regulated, large business corporations accumulate massive normative power through the control and ownership of media institutions.

5 Political participation

This kind of institutional evaluation requires a number of different forms of information. Some of this information can be gleaned from objective analyses of institutions and policies or via mechanisms such as a more elaborate census, but a large proportion of it must come directly from the individuals concerned. Felt needs are first and foremost experienced by individuals. Moreover, the evaluation of needs and institutions remains incomplete without as much information as possible about existing preferences concerning these needs and institutions. To ensure that this kind of evaluative process includes the relevant kind of subjective information, individuals must have parity of influence or power over the evaluation. In short, the participative power of individuals over these evaluative mechanisms is of paramount political importance.

I propose the following speculative procedural proposals for safeguarding this kind of participative power. The first is the institution of an annual need evaluation at local level. Rotating local level representatives would undertake this evaluation under the leadership of the local state authority. The evaluation would make use of objective and subjective information. The objective information would be derived from a more elaborate and frequent census than is usually undertaken.[12] The subjective information could be obtained via avowed preferences gathered in focus groups, at local meetings, and through representatives from local business, labour and consumer groups. The result of this evaluation would not affect the standing of the existing government. Its aim would be to reach a decision, a majority decision if necessary, over local needs in order that the extant local government can ensure that the state and the various markets and market-related institutions respond to post-evaluation needs. In sum, this is quite unlike the aggregation of individual preferences for the creation of policy; rather it constitutes an assessment of local needs, preferences and interests that relate to political and economic goods.

The second requirement is the institution of a periodic process of need trajectory evaluation and choice. Need trajectories are the various different actual and possible paths or trajectories of need development. In contrast to the short-term concerns of the annual evaluation of needs, the evaluation and choice of need trajectories would involve a relatively protracted communication and evaluation of ideas and possibilities, say over a period of one month once every ten years, that relate to long-term choices – choices that involve broad questions of public policy, for example, environmental policy, transport policy, fiscal policy and even longer-term proposals and ideas concerning very large structural issues, such as possibilities for the institutional rearrangement or transformation of production and distribution and kinds of property ownership and inheritance. This might encourage a number of things that are discouraged within liberal constitutional frameworks. First, it would provide citizens with some control over the long term and therefore might persuade them to think beyond their immediate, short-term interests. Second, it might dissociate historically specific events, successes or failures from specific parties, governments or groups. Third, it might encourage citizen groups to take risks, to put forward untried and untested novel proposals for how to evaluate and meet needs more efficiently, safe in the knowledge that a system could be tested for a ten-year period and then, if necessary, discarded. Fourth, it could react to changes in the nature and form of human needs and how they are met. It would be a great deal more flexible than a reified code of rights both because it could be adjusted more easily and because it dissociates the human goods and means under analysis from a notion of individual ownership or entitlement. Needs and trajectories are not things humans could come to think they own or deserve. And, fifth, as a consequence especially of the last two points, it would encourage consequentialist rather than deontological practical reasoning. By testing a number of variants humans could achieve a greater causal understanding of the effects of institutional arrangements on perceiving, articulating, recognizing and meeting needs. This enhanced understanding may generate the desire to experiment beyond the status quo.

In both the need and need trajectory evaluative procedures there is *no* assumption or requirement that either the process be deliberative or that the outcome be consensual. Given my understanding of needs under modern conditions, both deliberation and consensus are highly unlikely and, depending on the extant normative power relations, often undesirable. This does not mean that the process is not participative; it is highly participative. These procedures broaden and focus the normal notion of 'political participation': it is understood here as participation in the evaluation of human needs, in the sense of having the means and resources to cognize, meet and criticize needs in everyday contexts and within the two formal procedures outlined above. Hence, this approach to participation does not make the normal mistake of conflating participation with deliberation. Ultimately, because consensus is the exception within both procedures, after the process of collecting information and preference and need avowal is complete, decisions must be made dependent on a majority vote. However, the local arm of the state must be able to adjust the outcome of the final decisions dependent on its appraisal of normative power balances and publicly available evidence of justified need. And it must then justify publicly its decisions in terms of these objective conditions. More exactly, it must decide and justify based on material from the elaborate census – objective conditions of the local populace, their avowed needs and the possible means to increasing future participation. This is especially important when and where there is a split vote, distortions in turnout, or very low turnout. Moreover, once it becomes obvious that an avowed need is never simply accepted as a legitimate need, the possibility that individuals will attempt to create situations in which their (mere) wants plausibly look like needs would be reduced.

The main role of central government would then be to evaluate three institutional configurations using the outcomes of the two procedures discussed above as well as macro-economic and political analysis of regional and global institutions and practices: state security, citizen security and international markets and their effects on meeting needs. Central government could then be evaluated in terms of how efficiently it carries out these functions, how well it reacts to local evaluation and transforms suspect institutions, and how well it enables the two main procedures stipulated above.

This model of participation reduces the chance and significance of rent-seeking by powerful corporations or unions in society. It does this because it simultaneously decentralizes evaluation and centralizes the coercive capacity to make ultimate decisions. If the local evaluative process fails to remove the disproportionate influence of powerful stakeholders, there exists a second, more removed process that will. Thus this type of proposal is developed exactly in order to resolve the kind of problems discussed in Chapter 9 by Nattrass and Seekings with respect to the consequences of current labour market policy in South Africa and the power of unions to influence the formation of that policy.

The procedures I have outlined must be safeguarded as legally, constitutionally enshrined guarantees. But rather than make these a set of individual legal guarantees or trumps that are the inalienable property of individuals, they should be legally enshrined procedural guarantees. These must include: the priority to meet vital needs; the frequent local (and less frequent state-level) evaluation of everyday needs and institutions; and the periodic evaluation of vital and agency needs, need trajectories and government itself. Thus this kind of procedural needs-based constitution is not understood as some kind of *meta*-political *social* contract that exists prior to the state. Rather, it is a constitution in the sense of an established, periodically reassessed and dynamic institution whose procedures are directed at responding to needs. These procedural guarantees would ensure that individual preferences would become indispensable both as evidence in the evaluation of needs, institutions and trajectories and also as claims. They would also guarantee against the all too frequent tendency amongst political leaders and regimes to legitimize their position by adopting limited, narcissistic and self-serving conceptions of the needs of the citizenry. Together these procedures and guarantees would ensure the constant criticism and transformation of institutions and practices in line with needs rather than the relegation of need to either a moral or technical domain, which reduces them either to the individual, moral concerns of charity or to the uniform dictatorship by a central administrative authority such as the welfare state.

6 Democratic sovereignty within states of needs

As the predominant state-form in the developed world that many parts of the developing world aspire to emulate, the welfare state is an inadequate response to the requirement for parity of individual power over the evaluation of needs and institutions. However, as kinds of localized coercive authorities, actually existing modern states have the *potential* to be the kind of coercive authority that might instantiate the sorts of need-disclosing procedures outlined here. In other words, they have the *potential* to become coercive authorities that would instantiate individual evaluation in line with needs *and* act as legitimate ultimate evaluators of needs and institutions. If they were to realize this potential, modern states would become radically new kinds of political authorities, in fact they would no longer be modern states in any recognizable sense, but the state *per se* would *not* become redundant. I will distinguish this radically new kind of coercive authority from actually existing states by calling it a state of needs.

The state of needs is the kind of responsive and coercive political authority that constitutes the main precondition for democratic sovereign control over the development and satisfaction of needs, or, in other words, the main precondition for democratic sovereignty. This is the case for the following reasons. Everyday needs are normally particular needs with relations to existing wants, practices and institutions. Consequently, in order for the state of needs to become the required ultimate evaluator of needs and institutions, it would have to be in responsive contact with individuals' needs *and* preferences, as outlined in the previous section. At the same time the state of needs must have the coercive power to conclude any single evaluative exercise when it has run its course and make the ultimate decision over remaining conflicts over needs. It requires this power because agreement over needs is the exception rather than the rule. Moreover, some people's needs can and do retard the satisfaction and development of other people's needs. Once it has brought any single evaluation to completion, an ultimate coercive authority is required to weigh the objective conditions of met vital and agency needs and subjective avowals of need and preference and decide which institutions require change. Here again, the coercive element of its authority is a pre-requisite in the face of the inevitable fact that individuals, groups and classes defend criticized institutions. This is the case because most institutions legitimize highly cherished beliefs, attitudes and needs.

Moreover the decisions over need trajectories are collective, public choices that governments uniquely must make, and they can do so with varying degrees of reference to citizens' needs. In a state of needs a government's choice over need trajectories would be legitimate only when the choice is made in line with the procedures sketched in the previous section. In order to achieve this, the state of needs requires ultimate coercive control over the evaluation of needs and institutions coupled with the full democratic sovereignty of the citizenry.

Thus the state of needs is not a separate institution designed to dictate citizens' needs. Rather, it is the citizens evaluating and deciding upon their own needs under the necessary conditions of coercion, thus enhancing democratic sovereignty through simultaneously increasing citizen participation and coercive control. The constitutionally enshrined safeguards would entail the kind of political representation and universal suffrage common to modern representative democracies, but they would also require new and innovative institutions of participation and evaluation. It is counterproductive for political philosophy to provide a blueprint for these institutions. Their form and content can be decided only in the practical process of evaluating needs. But political philosophy can enable this process by helping to undermine the hegemony of the rights-preferences couple, or particular rights and rights-based constitutions, and by proposing conceptual alternatives to it. The political philosophy of needs proposed here is one such conceptual alternative. But what follows from this political philosophy in the case of weak states, in particular African states?

7 Markets and African states

I have argued for an understanding of the state of needs as final evaluator and guarantor for the meeting of needs. But it does not follow from this argument that the state is or ought to be the actual provider of the valued needs. Under certain conditions, markets do a more efficient job and might continue to do so within and between states of needs – but only in meeting needs, not in the generation and evaluation of needs. As things stand, markets and their related institutions are the central institutional generators of felt need *and* they are the main means humans have of satisfying needs. What are markets and how can states, in particular weak states such as African states, regain some control over them and how they meet the needs of their citizens? That is, how can weak states become states of needs with greater control over markets of needs?

In contrast to a marketplace, a fair, or 'the market', a market is a collection of homogeneous transactions, and is created whenever potential sellers of a good or service are brought into contact with potential buyers and a means of exchange is available. The medium of exchange may be money or barter. Today markets are constituted by commodity, service and money exchange to meet needs or generate money capital within related relations of production, consumption and distribution. The most informative debate on the nature of markets emerged within a discussion of the possibility of organizing an economy without markets – in the context of Hayek's and Mises' criticisms of the possibility of rationally organizing an economy using a centrally planned scheme. It is the most informative debate because it hits to the heart of the main political economic problems: value, evaluation and the institutional arrangement that will most effectively satisfy human needs. The most interesting thing that can be gleaned from that debate and later responses (for example the Lange–Lerner solution) is that both sides of the debate are driven by the same quest: how to reduce the separation between production and consumption in order that needs are met more responsively and efficiently. The defenders of the free market suggest that a price mechanism in an unregulated market will react rationally to all the countless individual evaluations and calculations of value, thereby in essence reducing the actual distance between production and consumption. The proponents of central, socialist planning assumed that the most rational means was to determine *ex ante* consumption demand and regulate production accordingly. The disastrous results of attempting the latter were plain for all to see, and a large number of people to experience first hand. But more than anything else they were the consequence of the fact that in never actually providing an institutional means through which citizens could state and satisfy their needs, the central planners increased rather than decreased the effective distance between consumption and production (Hayek, 1975; Lange, 1948; Lerner, 1934, 1936).

There is another similarity between the two sides, between the defenders of the free market and the central planners. They had the same all-or-nothing, ahistorical attitude to rights and needs. The defenders of the free market took existing rights to be natural and sacrosanct and argued that the free reign of preferences within that structure is the most efficient means of meeting wants and needs. The collective planners abolished rights and took needs as they were, or as the planners decided they were. The trick that can be learned, then, is that in order to reduce the separation between consumption and production we need to be flexible and historically sensitive about actually existing needs and rights. What might this entail in the context of African states?

The more markets (transactions and capital) globalize without political control, the more this separation between consumption and production grows and the more rights become entrenched and naturalized. Thus we lose more and more control over the generation and satisfaction of our needs. But things are very different in different parts of the world. As citizens of relatively powerful North Atlantic States, in which rights are well developed and supported by an efficient legal system, individuals can at least have the sense that they can affect the generation and satisfaction of their needs by making rights-claims. But this is not true of the citizens of weak, poor states with restricted national production bases, few resources (in capital goods or otherwise), and a state that does not have the legal or economic means to respond to rights-claims. The separation between production and consumption is absolute, or at least greatly increased, and this is supported by the complete asymmetry between needs and rights. Moreover, as things stand these states do not even get close to the requirements I discussed in the previous section. Some African states in particular do not enjoy coercive control over all their territories; the Democratic Republic of Congo is only one conspicuous example. And many African states do not have the resources and means to create the requisite institutional arrangements that would allow them to be responsive, accountable and legitimate ultimate evaluators of needs, or in other words, states of needs. Thus the main question for African states that have the political will to improve the power of their citizens must take this form. Given this growing separation of production and consumption and rights and needs, and given the coercive and structural weaknesses of African states, especially their general lack of resources and weakness in the face of large multi-national corporations (MNCs) and donor states, what can African states do to improve their citizens' control over how their needs are developed and met? Or, put differently, how can they regain coercive control, institute responsive and accountable states of needs and reduce this gap between production and consumption?

There are a number of things that African states could do as separate states. First, they could focus on developing innovative and local centres and forms of evaluation of needs and institutions. Second, they could enable new forms of production to meet all their citizens' vital and agency needs. Third, they could focus on training their own human resources that would be required to meet this goal. Fourth, they could spend more time and energy thinking about new ways of attracting the resources to achieve these goals. Fifth, they could de-naturalize or de-entrench rights, such as the right to private property (especially in land) and patent rights, in order that they might direct resources and technologies (i.e. production) to directly satisfy needs. The urgent need for land reform in Africa, the urgent need for African states to take control of their local MNCs (such as Anglo-American in the case of South Africa), and the urgent need for local, cheap production of vital need satisfiers (such as HIV/AIDS retrovirals) will remain unmet until the legal, constitutional restrictions on achieving these goals are removed. These urgent needs will only be satisfied if African states reform their own national constitutions and act against international 'constitutions' and norms.

It is no easy task to follow these suggestions. Most of them have been attempted with little success; bar the first and the fifth, which have not been attempted anywhere. They will continue to be attempted and bear scant fruit unless the state concerned gains sufficient power and resources to retain control over, or at least affect, the global legal and economic powers – the international courts and major production centres – that affect all the above-listed goals. African states do not possess this power. In fact, independent action by African states (even relatively strong states such as South Africa) is unusual, and this is because it faces very real obstacles. For example, all states borrow capital in order to stimulate growth and provide for basic needs, but weak states do so from weak bargaining positions. In comparative terms they have little collateral – limited capital reserves and infrastructure – and (normally) reduced 'democratic' credentials. Under these conditions, it is comparatively easy for the lender to set the terms for loans, investment, state action and scope, and development in general. Given these existing power relations and the general form of the new free-trade imperialism, the interests of powerful states, banks and other lenders tend to trump those of weak states. Internal changes that weak states would like to affect are determined by the terms and reactions of powerful external agents. These changes, such as the ones suggested above, are changes that under conditions of democratic sovereignty would be the sovereign concern of those whose needs and lives would be affected by the changes. In contrast, as things stand, powerful states and lenders can isolate and punish weak states for actions that may be in the interest of the citizens of the weak state concerned but are not in the interest of the powerful states and lenders.

Given these conditions, changes attempted by weak states will have little effect or sometimes even the opposite effect. This is an all too common occurrence. However, there remain a few avenues of escape from this cycle of depleted sovereignty and dependence, and they lie in regional and hemispherical (non-global) inter-state cooperation. Cooperation of this kind will work best when it is forged and cemented by common interests. Combined action in line with these common interests enhances individual state power. Thus African states must attempt to create regional and hemispherical trading blocks with countries with similar needs, interests, powers and problems, and from which they can withstand the reactions of powerful states. Relatively large and powerful states such as South Africa could forge closer links with the rest of Africa and other large and powerful southern states, such as Brazil, India and China. This may give them the power and ability, for example, to impose control over money markets that adversely affect smaller currencies and thus the capital reserves of weaker states, and thereby develop the resources and means of linking their citizens' needs to the production sites that will meet these needs efficiently. If this means acting against WTO free-trade imperialism and the moral discourse of natural, human rights, at least they will have the support of one another. There is no equally effective other alternative for African states, for at present the satisfaction of wants and basic needs is determined by large production sites whose main focus is the profit gained as a consequence of the demand and consumption in northern states. And the existing structure of rights (however universal in rhetoric) is designed for those conditions. It is not designed very well, but that is a separate problem. Thus African countries are alienated from production and consumption opportunities and the modicum of protection provided by rights, and thus starved of these goods. They have no option but to attempt to find ways of taking *political* control of this dire situation.

8 Concluding remarks

If your focus is markets alone, the notion that globalization and the new economy constitute a completely new, natural phase may not be too detrimental to your understanding, although I have my doubts. However, if your focus is development understood in terms of increased local power over the determination and satisfaction of needs, this kind of technical approach to the question of globalization and the new economy will severely hamper political understanding and action. In this chapter I have proposed a different conceptual framework for understanding and practising the politics of development based on an account of human needs, participant evaluation of needs and institutions in context, and the requirement of a strong, local coercive authority. Even if some of the determinants of needs may lie beyond the locale over which the state has authority, there exists a premium on evaluation in context, and thus a premium on the state and local administrative arms of the state regaining control over the means to meeting needs: markets, resources and their own state sovereignty. However meagre, African states do have certain political means at their disposal to provide their citizens with some modicum of participative control over their needs; that is, to become states of needs. But the means will only become apparent if these states improve their responsiveness to their citizens' needs and their cooperation with other states in similar predicaments. This involves acting against global economic and ideological forces that act to weaken rather than strengthen these already weak states. And this move entails the repudiation of the current globalization mantra of universal rights and free preferences, a mantra that (inadvertently) makes an end out of the allegedly most

212 *Lawrence Hamilton*

favourable means – responsive reaction to markets – and in doing so reinforces the common mistaken belief that markets are natural, wild beasts that ought to be left free to roam the global plains.

Notes

1 In criticizing the rights-preferences couple, I am not claiming that rights or preferences are useless or that they be completely scrapped. The evaluation of preferences is a central component in my alternative political philosophy of needs. And rights retain a role, especially with regard to issues of personal property ownership and exchange, and as means of safeguarding civil liberties and empowering historically unrepresented and disenfranchised classes and groups. All I argue is that it would be better to understand the components of the rights-preferences couple in a theoretical conception that captures and articulates fully the politics (see Hamilton, 2003a).

2 This modern state of theoretical affairs has strong and deep roots. In economics theses roots are the utilitarian-inspired philosophies of economics, like those developed by L. Walras and V. Pareto, which turned on the impossibility of making interpersonal comparisons of manifest preferences. This rests on scepticism about whether anything worthwhile can be said about the mental processes that might underlie manifest preferences, a scepticism with its origins in the work of Hobbes. The notion of 'revealed preferences' simply systematized this basic thought (Tuck, 1986). For more on this point, see Hamilton, 2003a.

3 For 'will' or 'choice' theories of rights, see Horfeld, 1978; Hart, 1995. For 'interest' or 'welfare' theories, see Raz, 1986; Feinberg, 1980. And for more proceduralist theories, see Dworkin, 1975; Nozick, 1975.

4 The main difference between natural rights and human rights is that in natural law theorists can draw on the idea of a single (Christian) deity that can 'enforce' these natural pre- or meta-political rights. Without recourse to god (or at least without the assumption of one Christian god) human rights has to create its own secular (human) version – we have rights by virtue of being human and once we institute a global, legal order we have a kind of global god. Monotheistic colonialism is alive and well. For the significance of colonial conquest in the political theories of Grotius, Hobbes and Locke, see Tuck, 1999; Armitage, 2000. For more on these points in general see Hamilton, 2003c.

5 Although moral beliefs do matter in politics, consensus over them is unusual and even where we do have moral agreement, such moral agreement in itself will not guarantee effective action (Olson, 1965). Thus *pace* some of Stiglitz's assumptions, the current faith in the creation of consensus within a global 'civil society' is misplaced. Even when consensus is secured, which is extremely rare, it is not sufficient to guarantee effective political action. For more on the shortcomings of the 'civil society' debate, see Hamilton, 2003b.

6 I would like to thank Don Ross for his comments on some of the issues in this section.

7 For example, Stewart, 1985; Dasgupta, 1993.

8 Besides what else I go on to say, it is simply mistaken to define need in terms of lack. It is not the case that I lack whatever I need; many things that I already have are things that I need. Or, in other words, I still need something that I no longer lack – I still need shelter even though I have a house and so do not lack shelter (Wiggins, 1998).

9 Martha Nussbaum's 'capability approach' is developed out of Amartya Sen's

original account of capabilities and functions plus a number of Aristotelian additions. For full references, an account of the differences between their two approaches and why Sen's account escapes some of the problems I discuss here, as well as a critique of the fact that Sen steers clear of the concepts of needs and interest (see Hamilton, 1999).
10 I can, of course, want to invent a car, but that is not the same as wanting to satisfy my need for mobility by means of a particular satisfier that already exists on the market.
11 For a chapter length discussion of these various vital and agency needs, see Hamilton, 2003a.
12 I discuss what this kind of census would entail in Hamilton (2003a).

References

Armitage, D. (2000). *The Ideological Origins of the British Empire*, Cambridge: Cambridge University Press.
Brock, G. (eds) (1998). *Necessary Goods: Our Responsibilities to Meet Other's Needs*, Oxford: Rowman & Littlefield.
Dasgupta, P. (1993*). An Inquiry into Well-Being and Destitution*, Oxford: Clarendon Press.
Doyal, L. and I. Gough (1991). *A Theory of Human Need*, London: Macmillan.
Dworkin, R. (1975). *Taking Rights Seriously*, London: Duckworth.
Feinberg, J. (1980). *Rights, Justice and the Bounds of Liberty*, Princeton, NJ: Princeton University Press.
Hamilton, L. (1999). A theory of true interests in the work of Amartya Sen, *Government and Opposition*, 14(4): 235–251.
Hamilton, L. (2003a). *The Political Philosophy of Needs*, Cambridge: Cambridge University Press.
Hamilton, L. (2003b). Civil society: critique and alternative, in S. Halpern and G. Laxer (eds), *Global Civil Society and Its Limits*, London: Palgrave.
Hamilton, L. (2003c). Needs, states and markets: democratic sovereignty against imperialism, *Theoria.* Online, available at: http://www.berghahnbooksonline.com
Hart, H.L.A. (1995). Are there any natural rights? *The Philosophical Review*, 64(2): 175–179.
Hayek, F.A. (ed.) (1975). *Collectivist Economic Planning: Critical Studies on the Possibility of Socialism*, Clifton, NJ: Augustus M. Kelley.
Horfeld, W. (1978). *Fundamental Legal Conceptions as Applied in Judicial Reasoning*, Westport, CT: Greenwood Press.
Lange, O. (1948). On the economic theory of socialism, in O. Lange and F. Taylor (eds), *On the Economic Theory of Socialism*, Minneapolis, MN: University of Minnesota Press.
Lerner, A.P. (1934). Economic theory and socialist economy, *Review of Economic Studies*, 2(1): 51–61.
Lerner, A.P. (1936). A note on socialist economies, *Review of Economic Studies*, 4(1): 72–76.
Nozick, R. (1975). *Anarchy, State and Utopia*, Oxford: Basil Blackwell.
Olson, M. (1965). *The Logic of Collectivist Action*, Cambridge, MA: Harvard University Press.
Raz, J. (1986). *The Morality of Freedom*, Oxford: Oxford University Press.

Stewart, F. (1985). *Basic Needs in Developing Countries*, Baltimore, MA: Johns Hopkins University Press.
Tuck, R.C. (1986). The Danger of Natural Rights, in J. Elster and A. Hylland (eds), *Foundations of Social Choice Theory*, Cambridge: Cambridge University Press.
Tuck, R.C. (1999). *The Rights of War and Peace*, Oxford: Oxford University Press.
Wiggins, D. (1998). *Needs, Values, Truth*, Oxford: Clarendon Press.

11 Modelling human behaviour

A biological perspective on the African prospect

Mike Berger

1 Introduction

Recent pioneering work has opened paths between the disparate disciplines concerned with the collective behaviour of our species. Economists, in particular, have turned to the work of their biological colleagues for insights into the systematic deviations of human behaviour from the assumptions of 'rationality', though this has not been entirely a one-way street.[1]

In the spirit of consilience,[2] this chapter will offer a view of the African prospect informed by a personal interest in the potential contribution of evolutionary and biological sciences to our understanding of human social, political and economic behaviour. More specifically it will address the ways in which biology, history, sociology, culture, material and economic realities and politics come to impact on the prospects for an 'African Renaissance', as current political rhetoric in Africa likes to refer to its latest development initiative, and on the capacity of South Africa to contribute to that objective.

Though a number of authors have taken up the challenge of relating psychological motivations to political behaviour in the real world,[3] this chapter has no overly ambitious scientific pretensions. If it intrigues and stimulates the reader to further thought on at least some of the issues raised, its purpose will have been served.

The context of this project is Africa. The minds of many South Africans, most vocally from the minority communities, are exercised by the question: 'Has South Africa a happy future?' The question is often raised in the context of a perception of Africa as a continent uniquely doomed to chronic violence, anarchy and oppression. The rejoinder that other regions of the world, including Europe, have seen equivalent bloodshed and disruption and that African chaos is, in part, a consequence of colonial exploitation is more often than not rejected, at least by non-Africans and by white South Africans. In the minds of many, Africa reflects a unique vulnerability to corruption, clannishness, violence and nepotism. Such openly racist comment is rarely expressed in polite, or even academic, company but is not uncommon in the white sector of the South African street.

The knowledge that baleful notions can lurk below the surface of even the most committed liberal is a commonplace in psychology. The accusation of 'subliminal racism' elicited a violent emotional response from leftist and liberal media in South Africa some years ago. The term 'race card' is widely employed to counter any suggestion that criticism may in part be motivated by unacknowledged prejudice. (Similar dynamics are apparent in the controversy around accusations of anti-Semitism levelled at certain vehement critics of Israeli actions in the Middle East). Yet any even casual observer of talk shows on South African radio, for example, will speedily pick up on ethnicity as a prime determinant of opinion on matters of public significance. The fact that 'race' can be and is used by opportunists to advance personal and group interests simply adds more emotional fuel. The complexity and subtlety of the social dynamics is enhanced by the interplay between various stereotypes and the values, beliefs, ideologies and strategic computations within the different sectors of South African society.

None of this should come as a surprise to the psychologist or, for that matter, economist. For those interested in the macro-implications of human nature it becomes important to face up to this tangled web, starting with the acknowledgement of one's own susceptibility. Empirical evidence indicates that emotion together with values, stereotypes and ideologies can affect cognition in ways that are largely inaccessible to introspection, but not necessarily to scientific investigation (Bargh and Chartrand, 1999).

The careful investigator will start by confirming the accuracy or otherwise of the popular perceptions of African failure. Unfortunately, she will find that it is more accurate than not. Whether measured in terms of economic or health indices, levels of literacy or inter-ethnic, political or simple criminal violence, Africa occupies the worst seats in the global arena (Mills, 2002; Human Rights Watch, 2001; Doxtader and Villa-Vicencio, 2003) with few and partial exceptions. Painfully, many experiments in post-colonial democracy have, after variably brief preludes of peace and stability, deteriorated into varying degrees of tyranny and incompetence or disintegrated further into anarchy and endemic violence (Doxtader and Villa-Vicencio, 2003; Diamond, 1995; Rotberg, 2000). The lasting impact of recent peace and trade initiatives remains to be seen. Even where some semblance of legality and democracy have been maintained, levels of economic development fall well short of many Asian nations with superficially similar colonial and poverty-stricken pasts. A graphic illustration of African impoverishment is a global photograph of the world at night: the interiors of Australia and Africa are equally empty of light, but the former is devoid of people, whereas the latter contains substantial patches with some of the highest per capita densities in the world.

The next questions cannot be avoided: why is this so and what, if anything, can be done to perturb the chaotic quasi-equilibrium into which much of Africa seems to have settled? Some have suggested that the answers lie in externalities including climate, geography and ecological factors like infectious disease, soil conditions and population density (Sachs, 2000). Such factors are likely to have been more significant at earlier stages of human history, as suggested by Jared Diamond (1997), but modern technology has variably diminished their relevance. Diseases like HIV/AIDS, malaria and tuberculosis are probably still significant contributors to social and economic underdevelopment.[4] Overpopulation, at least in a few countries in West Africa, combined with destructive and inefficient agricultural practices, have negative ecological impacts. Malnutrition is rife (Colletta *et al.*, 1996) and is a reflection of socio-economic failure in the first instance. Some of the shortcomings of global and Western policies vis-à-vis Africa are addressed in this book. The precise causal sequence may become irrelevant as these factors mutually reinforce dysfunctionality.

The following two sections will briefly review recent insights into human nature drawn from evolutionary, social, developmental and cognitive psychology, enriched by contributions from many directly and indirectly related disciplines. Such understanding may assist those Western nations, including South Africa, that have the power to promote or retard Africa's escape from the toxic web, and to productively rethink or sharpen current paradigms.

2 Biological psychology[5]

In recent decades the understanding of human behaviour has progressed beyond the psychoanalytic approaches espoused by Freud, Jung and their disciples and the rigorous but sterile formalism of the Watson–Skinnerian tradition, to tentatively embrace a host of biological disciplines.

Every organism represents a localized focus of entropy reversal for the period of its lifetime (Schrodinger, 1962; La Cerra and Bingham, 1998; Tooby and Cosmides, 1992). Nature, through the Darwinian sequence of genetic variation followed by natural selection acting mainly, but probably not exclusively, on the individual phenotype, ensures designs which represent the best 'current' accommodation within the vast array of ecological niches to which historical contingency has led the diversity of species constituting the biosphere of this planet (Dennett, 1995). 'Current' is measured in tens or even hundreds of thousands of years when referring to the generally slow pace of adaptive genomic change in long-lived organisms. Given the rate of cultural and, especially, technological and social change in the case of humans, such hopeful correspondence between our innate capacities and external challenges is questionable.

Evidence of design is apparent at all levels of functional analysis. Our concern in this section is with the evolved mechanisms whereby organisms, notably *Homo sapiens*, identify and respond to threats and opportunities emanating from the external environment. Threats may come in various forms: the attack of microbes, changes in climate and the distribution and availability of food, predation from other macro-species and, central to the concerns of this book, interaction of different kinds with conspecifics (Byrne and Whiten, 1988). The list is greatly extendable and can be mapped to specific design features of organisms, hence providing the notoriously teleological flavour to biological theories.

The means whereby organisms confront these challenges are well described in the conventional literature of biological science. For the most part, until the advent of humans, such design features were based upon an increasingly complex and subtle array of more-or-less automated responses to the reiterated contingencies in the evolutionary history of the species. Above all, species other than humans are incapable of accumulating complex and fluid cultures; thus individual behavioural phenotypes are minimally determined by the small differences in culture that do emerge between groups (McGrew, 1998). At least this seems to be true even of our closest relatives, the chimpanzees and bonobos, despite their rich sociality and political dynamics.

Humanity, through the evolution of the novel array of physical and mental attributes (Donald, 1993), represents a new line of diversification into evolutionary space, the full implications of which are yet to be understood and realized. A prime manifestation of this qualitative leap in cognitive complexity and other specialized features of design is the creation of distinctive human cultures and societies. It is by now commonplace, at least in certain circles, that culture represents a new and distinctive evolutionary path with elastic and convoluted links to the better-understood processes of Darwinian evolution.[6]

A salient consequence of this recent biological innovation is that humans reared in different cultures differ sufficiently from one another to reveal significant differences in collective behaviours and hence, potentially, on such outcomes as material success, longevity and life satisfaction (Edgerton, 2000; Etounga-Manguelle, 2000; Fukuyama, 2000; Landes, 2000; Porter, 2000). Cultural differences, however, are not the only paths leading to different outcomes. Chance and externalities derived from the physical, biological and extraneous human environment all contribute to Kipling's two impostors.[7] Furthermore, the causal arrows between culture on the one hand and political institutions and economic welfare on the other are bi-directional.

Those approaching politics, economics or any other discipline concerned with collective human action from a biological stance often make at least two further assumptions. First, that our universal biological inheritance ensures similarities in human behaviour which cross cultural, gender and racial boundaries (Brown, 1991) and, second, that our differentiated responses to experiential variables are also mediated by information residing mainly in the genome. From this perspective, biology, culture and all forms of individual or collective human action are in some way an intricate, recursive composite of our biology and the products of our biology.

Even if the 'massive modularity hypothesis' is rejected, there is evidence for the persistence of deep-seated, partly modularized, behaviours that promoted inclusive fitness in the long eons before and after the genus, *Homo*, emerged as part of the evolutionary deck. This relatively automated and unconscious infrastructure coexists with a recent, powerfully enhanced, general-purpose reasoning apparatus heavily linked to language, increased powers of mental abstraction and representation, specialized memory capacities allowing for self-motivated, off-line recall and a qualitatively unique capacity for the accumulation of knowledge and skills between generations leading to the generation of culture (Donald, 1993; Tomasello, 1999; Barresi and Moore, 1996). But even these new computational resources are not free of the 'quirks' arising out of our evolutionary past where they served ancient adaptive functions.

According to Donald, technological innovation arising from these cognitive novelties has created a distinct, non-biological layer of cognition inhering in the capacity for off-line storage and transfer of information in the form of writing and, more recently, electronic devices of various kinds. The uneven distribution of this cultural capacity was the basis for the primary global divisions between social systems until relatively recently,[8] the residues of which will be with us for generations. In general, the differences between peoples derive largely from the existence of different cultures and their accompanying socio-political-economic-technological matrices that have immeasurably, but unequally, amplified and shaped humanity's innate biological capacities.

To recapitulate: the different functional layers and components of the human neurological system outlined in the previous paragraphs interpenetrate each other so that 'cold', conscious cognition is profoundly guided by the operation of its unconscious infrastructure. The precise 'wiring' (to adopt an inaccurate but convenient shorthand for real electrochemical events in the brain–body of the individual) of the infrastructure is, in turn, determined partly by the life experiences of the individual and partly by innate information in the genome. This theme will be explored further below.

2.1 A map of the human emotional-cognitive apparatus

The fundamental contention of this chapter is that every aspect of human behaviour is bound up to some extent with innate, evolved properties of the human emotional-cognitive architecture or apparatus (ECA). Any serious attempt to introduce this construct into a consideration of political processes thus requires a functional taxonomy of its major components, of which Table 11.1 is a relatively arbitrary but didactically useful example.

Table 11.1

---
1 Primary and secondary sensory modules
2 Primary instinctual impulses or orientations appearing at specific stages of the life cycle
3 Basic emotional pathways reactive to external data or memories
4 ECA state or mood
5 More advanced social and moral emotions and behaviours
6 Personality structure or primary personal orientations
7 Evolved (universal) cognitive abilities, predispositions and intrinsic 'heuristics and biases'
8 Various memory systems and their contents
9 Value and belief systems, including ideologies, of varying degrees of complexity and emotional potency
10 Personal and culturally based cognitive skills, habits and resources
---

To provide some context, it is useful to outline the fate of incoming information, including that derived from memory stores. After initial processing by sensory modules and depending on content, incoming information may be directed to emotional centres.[9] The consequent interactions direct attention to other pertinent features of the environment and to additional memory contents, eventually eliciting muscular, endocrine and other somatic changes that prepare the organism for action, may signal motivationary predisposition to others and to self, and that participate in shaping further cognitive processing (Ekman, 1999; Cosmides and Tooby, 2000; Griffiths, 2002b). In the course of such processing various aspects of reality become more or less salient, thus further guiding attention.

The details of this sequence will vary both with the nature of the incoming data and the previous experiences of the individual. At one extreme, the involvement may be overwhelming, and at the other, subtle and complex. Emotions themselves are a heterogeneous category. Some are simple, relatively stereotyped and phylogenetically ancient (Panksepp, 2001). They are readily elicited by universal environmental cues like threat, reproductive opportunity or social separation. Secondary and nth order emotions are more heavily culturally conditioned, perhaps of longer duration and involve significantly more computational elements (Griffiths, 2002a, 2002b). These reflect the enhanced cognitive capacities of our species and hence serve more subtle, nuanced, adaptive and instrumental functions (Frank, 1988). Into this category fall the social emotions and others that straddle the borderline between what one may call values and emotions. Examples include kindness, generosity, courage, honour, aesthetic sensibility and pride (Elster, 1999). Cultural shaping takes place at all stages from perception to action and even includes the nature and recognition or existence of the emotion itself.

Ongoing cognitive processing in shaping responses to significant inputs will additionally call upon memories of different kinds, on internalized value and belief systems, on longer-term goals and previously established practices or strategies and will continue to sample the evolving situation to create an appropriate response (Cosmides and Tooby, 2000; Sloman, 2001; Griffiths, 2002a, 2002b). Much of the human external reality map is, of course, constituted by other people. In the course of normal monitoring of internal and external reality, the individual constantly readjusts her perceptions and responses in a recursive feedback cycle.

This picture does not exclude periods of relatively affectless thought, or 'cold' cognition, which focuses on issues remote from strategic social interaction. Such simple logical computation underlies many of the routine procedures of ordinary life and perhaps even more complex domains like chess or mathematics. The point is that emotion and the various layers and types of computation in most strategically relevant contexts are heavily intertwined in a recursive network much of which is inaccessible to consciousness. Mood and the temporal proximity of extraneous events will also affect response (Bargh and Chartrand, 1999; Hermalin and Isen, 1999; Nesse, 1991). Simply put, perception and behaviour are contingent on a variety of external and internal factors all operating through the final common pathway of the individual brain-mind. The ECA itself is not a neutral, general-purpose computer but a highly selective, instrumentally orientated collection of circuits shaped by evolution, random genetic variation, experiential inputs during the ontogeny of the individual and by other factors affecting its health and integrity. A few selected topics relevant to the thrust of this chapter will be briefly surveyed.

Primary instincts: According to Panksepp 2001, among others, a variety of adaptive and stereotyped behaviours appeared early in vertebrate phylogeny that are still significant in primates, including humans. These include the exploratory instinct, the territorial instinct, a set of reproductive behaviours, the maternal instinct and dominance–submission behaviours. These are expressed at different stages of ontogeny and vary according to gender as well as environmental features and cues.

The term 'resource holding potential' has been used to describe the readiness of an animal to pursue and defend resources. This may be experienced as a sense of 'potency' that is required for positive mood and a capacity for productive activity. It probably precedes the more subtle and complex sense of self-esteem in humans which includes a sense of personal competence, moral worth, social acceptability and significance.[10] It is likely that the significance of the different components varies between individuals and cultures (Quinn, 2003) and perhaps according to situation, age and gender.

However it is exactly understood, in virtually all psychologies a healthy self-esteem is regarded as key to effective human functioning. It comes as little surprise that perceived threats to self-esteem through any of its various aspects typically elicit vigorous responses (Baumeister *et al.*, 1996).

The punitive aggression directed at free riding or other forms of opportunistic behaviour may well have originated from instinctual responses to challenges directed at the capacity to defend resources, though other explanations are also current.

Emotions and social instincts: Most evolutionary psychologists view emotions as drivers of previously adaptive behaviours that promoted inclusive fitness in our era of evolutionary adaptedness and are thus intimately connected to cognition and action (Tooby and Cosmides, 1992; Cosmides and Tooby, 2000; Ekman, 1999).

Our prime concern in this chapter is with the social emotions and closely related phenomena which may be usefully termed the social instincts, prototypes of which can be discerned in primate behaviour (De Waal, 1996). These are generally divided into the altruistic emotions of empathy and sympathy, on the one hand, and, on the other, the negative emotions of embarrassment, shame and guilt (Caporael, 2001). In the human situation, social emotions are part of a cognitive continuum that serves instrumental, social and sometimes Machiavellian goals (Griffiths, 2002a, 2002b; Wilson *et al.*, 1996; Byrne and Whiten, 1988). Optimally, they fit humans for harmonious and cooperative social lives, in marked contradistinction to chimpanzees, for instance.

Also within this broad category falls the more complex but universal predispositions towards fairness and justice that manifest behaviourally as reciprocity or conditional altruism and more extended forms of altruism. Such predispositions, or moral instincts, have attracted the attention of behavioural economists and others as a means of explaining choices that systematically deviate from the assumptions of narrowly self-interested preferences which maximize the utility functions of rational *Homo economicus* (Rabin, 2002; Gintis *et al.*, 2003; Camerer, 2003). The results are by now well known. In a wide variety of cross-cultural contexts players in ultimatum and similar games offer more than predicted in Nash equilibria for narrowly self-interested players, and recipients reject offers which they perceive as 'unfair' (Fehr and Gachter, 2000). These results have been taken as an example of strong reciprocity or a universal fairness instinct.

But although the general tendency appears to be universal, the precise settings vary significantly across different societies, as demonstrated in a careful empirical study carried out on 15 widely separated and culturally distinct simple foraging or pastoralist societies (Henrich *et al.*, 2001b). Such experiments, useful though they are, do not reflect the full dimensions of natural situations in which various games are played simultaneously and which may be more sensitive to extraneous factors not directly related to the particular transaction: mood, history of previous interactions or current situational factors for instance. Some of these individual effects will fall out when averaged over time and a large number of players, but even whole societies are engaged in multi-dimensional transactions over time which cannot be captured in a single or even sequential game of a single type. The influence of prior experience has of course been shown in repeated games in which players alter strategies according to previous outcomes. These observations become extremely important when applying insights from experimental psychology to the cut and thrust of the real world.

Of interest in games of the Prisoner's Dilemma type is the willingness of many players to punish those who have defected even at cost to themselves. Such moralistic reactions, already referred to, have also been observed in reciprocity games and in more realistic settings. This phenomenon has been depicted as an evolved device to encourage mutual cooperation where 'free riding' is always an effective alternative strategy (Price *et al.*, 2002). This fundamental mechanism may also manifest as moralistic aggression towards perceived transgressions of partly innate moral values such as trust, loyalty and fairness. The extent of such a reaction will once again be heavily influenced by cultural, social and situational factors as well as by the personal characteristics of the individual.

Since the prototypical social emotions arose in the first place to protect inclusive fitness, to slip into convenient teleological mode for an instant, they participate in the elaboration made possible by cognitive and cultural enhancement of the human species. Thus, though cultures differ in their repertoire, envy, jealousy, malice, revenge, pride and other more 'advanced' emotions are commonalities unevenly expressed in a wide cross-section of cultures (Elster, 1999; Brown, 1991).

The coalitional or affiliative impulse may also be classified as a social behaviour. Coalitional behaviour, which includes in-group altruism and commitment coupled to out-group suspicion and derogation, or worse, is part of the tribal instincts cluster modelled by Richerson and Boyd (2001a). According to these and other theorists, coalitional behaviour and moralistic aggression towards free-riders and other disturbers of social norms and harmony arose initially as a cultural adaptation to Pleistocene environmental pressures, including inter-group competition and warfare. Such long-standing cultural adaptation was ultimately expressed in the human genome as innate mechanisms for structuring social reality. The egalitarian instinct, accompanied by the modern emotions of envy and jealousy, is a partial departure from the putatively despotic social structure of the last common ancestor prior to the chimpanzee (Boehm, 2000; Charlton, 1997). Like many distinctively human traits, such predispositions probably arose out of cultural group selective processes operative throughout the almost 2 million years of our ancestral passage through the Pleistocene.

Whatever its evolutionary dynamics, coalitional behaviour is a universal human characteristic and has been demonstrated in numerous laboratory and field studies. Elicitation of this response is both rapid and extremely sensitive to minimal cues. The normal cues to group identification are more commonly long term, arising from religious, ethnic and gender categories which are embedded in culture and acquired during socialization. Racial categorization, for instance, may not be innately specified (Kurzban, Tooby and Cosmides, 2001). It is probably elicited during socialization and, later, by social cues operating on a preformed tendency to coalesce around strategically relevant group markers which reflect social-political configurations charged with real or perceived competition over power, resources or status (Sidanus, 1993).

In summary, the affiliative impulse can provide a substrate for potentially destructive potent, fixed and exclusive group loyalties and behaviours engendered by socialization practices, cultural norms, history, propaganda, existential insecurity and competitive traps and perceived threats to identity and self-esteem. This topic is vitally relevant to understanding inter-group relationships and within group dynamics and will be dealt with further under identity.

2.2 Mood and core affect

Mood is commonly defined in relation to emotion, from which it differs in its more extended duration and its relative freedom from a single environmental cue or stimulus (Evans, 1999). In all likelihood the neurobiological basis is more global than the fairly well-defined emotional circuits (Greenfield, 2000). Some have treated mood as an adaptive mechanism to life circumstances (Nesse, 1991; Sloman, 1992). From this perspective, depression is partly a means of withdrawing from a damaging and apparently intractable situation to allow recuperation and re-assessment after grief or social exclusion or perceived loss of status for example. Possibly illness and even severe malnutrition may act in the same way. The effect of positive or negative affect on behaviour is obvious and attempts have been made to model its influence on utility construction (Hermalin and Isen, 1999).

Mood has generally been ignored in approaching political and economic behaviour, but that would appear to be premature. Given the capacity for social contagion, mood swings may spread through collectives, resulting in inappropriate responses to ongoing challenges and opportunities. The negative impact will depend upon the structural capacity for checks and balances and is likely to be enhanced in many socio-political situations characterized by centralized control and absence of popular power.

2.3 Personality and global orientation

Social psychologists have been preoccupied with constructing a coherent model that can account for persistent and significant behavioural features of a person over his lifespan. Along these lines personality has been cleaved by social psychologists into various static dimensions. The very idea of such global traits has been contested, though surely it is a staple of folk psychology.

A more biologically coherent view of personality (Mischel, 2004) envisages a relatively stable set of responses to a spectrum of strategically relevant[11] social situational cues and contexts. The resultant, more-or-less stable 'behavioural signature' is postulated to reflect the individual ECA, or 'cognitive-affective processing system' generated by innate and experiential inputs during development. Still to be explored is the question whether collectives may be said to possess similar 'behavioural signatures', though this would seem to be implicit in the very idea of culture. In this context it is worth mentioning Weber's famous linkage of Protestantism with a cluster of cultural attributes associated with distinctive political and economic developments (Landes, 2000).

The emphasis of recent theories of personality on 'strategically relevant' social contexts and situations is ripe for an evolutionary perspective. Different theorists (Fiske, n.d.; Caporael, 1995) have proposed various taxonomies of social reality. In a similar approach, but incorporating a strongly developmental perspective, Bugental (2000) envisages five distinctive mental domains (see Table 11.2) concerned with five corresponding categories of social challenge emerging from our era of evolutionary adaptedness. These brain-mind capabilities manifest at different ages in the course of individual ontogeny and are influenced by innate and experiential inputs in the course of socialization.

It is likely that the phenotypic expression of such functional domains reflects the interaction between innate (both universal and individual)

Table 11.2

Mental domain	Timing	Domain of challenge/ interaction	Some chemical mediators
Attachment	Days after birth	Parent–child, safety, security	Opioids, oxytocin
Coalitional	Middle childhood	Defending group's resources	Opioids, testosterone
Mating	Early–middle childhood	Select, protect access to mate, attractiveness, status	Opioids, oxytocin, sex steroids
Reciprocity	Infancy–adulthood	Maximize joint outcomes for equals, fairness	Serotonin
Hierarchical	Infancy	Optimize welfare and balance	Testosterone
Power	Young adult	Of control across power gradients involving individuals of groups	

Source: Bugental, 2000.

genomic features and experiential input during development and socialization. This taxonomy of social domains is introduced as a means of ordering such experiential inputs into biologically and behaviourally meaningful categories. Bearing in mind the similarities between individual and group dynamics, the pertinence of the coalitional, reciprocal and hierarchical domains to interactions between collectives should be considered.

Global factors including nutrition, exposure to exogenous substances – one thinks of lead for instance – disease and neglect or abuse at various stages of ontogenesis may have wide repercussions on Bugental's domains and on other fundamental attributes of personality and higher cognitive capacities (Masters, 2001). This chapter is especially concerned with the manner in which wider social, political, economic and cultural conditions impact on the developmental-socialization sequence to reproduce themselves in succeeding generations and will be addressed where relevant to the analysis of African prospects below.

2.4 Evolved (universal) cognitive abilities, predispositions and intrinsic 'heuristics and biases'

Given the meagreness and ambiguity of information, the pressures of time and the multiplicity of options in any given situation, humans have developed a set of affective-cognitive adaptations which make possible both choice and reasonable consistency of action (see Bargh and Chartrand, 1999; Macrae and Bodenhausen, 2000; Kahneman and Tversky, 1996; Gigerenzer and Goldstein, 1996; Simon, 1990). These include categorization and stereotyping, satisfying heuristics to curtail excessive and only marginally useful normative computation and a tendency towards cognitive closure, also known as 'freezing' (Kruglanski and Webster, 1996). To this may be added a set of other cognitive biases such as the attribution error and representativeness error which, while short on normative rationality, reduced costly misjudgements in our era of evolutionary adaptedness. Furthermore, the psychological phenomena of perseveration and denial help avoid excessive behavioural swings in the face of transient changes in preferences and circumstances. Since losses were generally more damaging to inclusive fitness than gains, loss aversion and the endowment effect may also be seen as adaptive design (see Krueger and Funder, 2003 for a review of non-normative but adaptive biases). This list can be considerably extended, especially to emotional-cognitive biases that maintain self-esteem and the illusion of control. The 'realist' posture is precariously balanced against a host of non-normative tendencies under many conceivable scenarios.

The manner in which such heuristics and biases operate in determining political and economic behaviour will be highly conditional on broadly contextual as well as immediate situational conditions (see Tetlock and Goldgeiger, 2000). It is plausible to suppose that their influence will be maximal under conditions of insecurity and stress, where educational exposure is low and expertise is deficient and where socialization emphasizes collective and traditional values over individual responsibility.

2.5 Identity

Identity is a multi-dimensional construct which serves various heuristic ends by collapsing a number of distinct but related ideas into a single term (Ashmore *et al.*, 2004). From a biological viewpoint, the origins of personal identity rest upon a primitive neuro-somatic foundation which requires the soma to be represented in the ECA of the organism (see Damasio, 2003; Turk *et al.*, 2003). As previously suggested prototypical forms probably appeared together with primitive instincts relating to somatic and reproductive resource capture and retention as expressed in territorial, dominance-submissive, maternal and reproductive behaviours and the basic emotions (Panksepp, 2001).

Following later cognitive enhancement and the extended social condition of human existence, the personal sense of self and self-esteem became 'linked' to group membership (Spencer *et al.*, 1998; Devos and Banaji, 2003; Jost *et al.*, 2003). Increasingly, the unconscious nature of the bonds between the various dimensions of identity and their impact on behaviour have been revealed empirically both in the laboratory and in the field (Bargh and Chartrand, 1999; Devos and Banaji, 2003).

As for self-esteem, the literature on identity is enormous and diverse, reflecting specific disciplinary perspectives and methodologies.[12] The affiliative impulse may be minimally evoked, transient and expedient (the minimal group paradigm) or may reflect long-standing, affectively potent and deeply entrenched identifications perhaps together with supportive mythological, moral and ideological components. Some of these will be attached to biological characteristics such as gender and race and others to more 'culturally' constructed categories like nationality, ethnicity, religion, class and political beliefs. A distinction also needs to be made between identification as an affectively charged process and the simple act of belonging by virtue of the bio-cultural constructs prevalent in a given society. The affective-moral salience of belonging will be heavily influenced by personal, contextual and situational factors.

On the other side of the personal identification coin lies the out-group. At least in theory, attitudes to out-groups are independent of in-group affiliation; that is, a powerful identification with a given group can coexist with negative, neutral or even positive orientations towards the other. But equally clearly, in-group/out-group orientations can become affectively polarized partly reflecting prevailing social norms and partly the consequence of more innate dynamics operative in such contexts. Thus, given that stereotypical beliefs about out-groups contain multiple components with differing evaluative connotations (Kunda and Thagard, 1996), the accessibility and salience of these will be determined by historical, contextual and situational factors referred to above. Equally, the behavioural response will also be conditioned by similar variables.

These issues have attracted a substantial literature. Relevant to our purposes, a distinction needs to be made between interactions between individuals or very small groups and between variably complex and extended collectives. Conflict, or its absence, between the latter will reflect the dynamics between various elites and the broader public within the collective itself. The interactions will depend, inter alia, upon the system of governance, the economic and identity interests of the various parties, and the most prevalent stereotypes as well as the moral norms operative in a given context together with the more immediate strategic considerations of the interacting groups. Various national or transnational lines of conflict may ensue, depending on the factors noted above among others.

It seems reasonable to conclude that significant ethnic and religious heterogeneity, high levels of economic and physical insecurity, vast gradients in power and wealth, potent historical memories of conflict or oppression, inadequate or distorted information, low educational attainments and absence of expertise, and a strongly collectivist, patriarchal and traditionalist culture will enhance the likelihood of inter-group conflict – as is apparent in much of Africa. In this connection it needs pointing out that inter-group warfare and conflict has been the norm throughout our pretechnological and more recent history (Keeley, 1996). The absence of violent conflict, notably the phenomenon of the 'democratic peace', and reduction in levels of discrimination in much of the developed world is a departure from historical precedent, suggesting the importance of cultural and contextual factors in determining the expression of innate predispositions.

3 Socialization, culture and democracy

The relationship of culture to political, social and economic outcomes was revisited in a recent compendium of essays edited by Harrison and Huntington (2000). Besides some controversy concerning the salience of culture versus that of exogenous factors such as location, geography, climate and other ecological factors, a striking feature was the range of socio-cultural factors implicated in shaping material prosperity and the quality of social existence (see, for example, Edgerton, 2000; Etounga-Manguelle, 2000; Fukuyama, 2000; Landes, 2000; Porter, 2000). Somewhat surprisingly, the relationship of malnutrition, physical and emotional child abuse, disease, noxious physical and chemical agents and social violence to the cycle of failure (Masters, 2001) was not seriously considered in this collection.

This chapter presupposes that democracy, sustainable economic welfare and human freedoms and rights are inseparable. The preconditions for the establishment of a sustainable democracy have attracted a large and diverse literature (see Lipset, 1998; Vanhanen, 1997). From an evolutionary perspective, the successive waves of democratization which have taken place over the past two centuries represents a remarkable cultural innovation. Following the largely egalitarian, deliberative cultures of pre-technological bands (Boehm, 2000; Richerson and Boyd, 1999, 2001b), stratification and varying degrees of oligarchy or authoritarianism became the rule in the larger social units made possible by agriculture and its subsequent technological products (Carneiro, 2000). Some evolutionary theorists have argued that decentralized, multifocal, democratic forms of social organization best fit evolved human predispositions towards egalitarianism and small-group commitment (Rubin, 2002; Richerson and Boyd, 1999, 2001a, 2001b), thus in part accounting for the higher innovative and productive potential of democracies relative to more hierarchical systems.

Be this as it may, the rhetorical commitment to democracy is almost universal, except perhaps in a few strongly theocratic states. It is legitimate to enquire whether the bio-evolutionary perspective adopted in this chapter can offer any useful insight to the preconditions for sustainable implementation? The argument takes the following form: The human psychological phenotype is partially organized into a number of domains (see previously) reflecting evolved design in response to universal strategically relevant social challenges. The impact of the relevant social, political, cultural and economic context will affect behaviour within and across these domains in ways that promote or retard democracy. Most commentators accept that democracy minimally requires adequate levels of interpersonal trust and cooperation together with the capacity, within bounds, to place longer-term and broader strategic interests ahead of short-term egoistical actions. Furthermore, sufficient self-control to overcome impulsive responses, to pursue longer-term goals and to acquire the cognitive skills necessary to evaluate political options and create economic value in a competitive global society would be important components of sustainability. Many of these attributes are acquired in the course of socialization though the contextual matrix and will continue to affect behaviour throughout adult life.

It may thus be predicted that widely prevalent malnutrition, disease, excessive stress, pollution, neglect and abuse during childhood will severely impact on the distribution and levels of intellectual, emotional and self-regulatory abilities within the population.[13] Furthermore, high levels of economic insecurity and the experience of criminal or political violence within such societies will tend to promote narrow coalitional and expedient behaviours limited to egoistical, clan or tribal identities. The same factors will enhance Machiavellian traits of patronage, corruption and outright criminality. Additionally, strong reciprocity, altruistic and fairness values are likely to be reduced by personal insecurity and by cultural factors which promote clannishness, xenophobia and intolerance. Given the low level of education prevalent in such societies, the cognitive resources required for economic growth and more broadly realistic political choices will be reduced. If depressed mood is in part an adaptive response to intractable and painful life circumstances (see previously), the prevailing apathy, fatalism and anomie commonly ascribed to Africans is understandable. Such psychological states may be volatile, alternating with heightened excitement and violence, depending on circumstance.

This depiction is quite incompatible with many of the preconditions for democracy listed by political theorists: an adequate and sufficiently equitable distribution of wealth, reasonable levels of education, and absence of on-going coalitional violence or active xenophobia between ethnic, religious or other groups, together with an active civic society, a tolerant cultural climate, the rule of law, and respect for the legitimacy of existing authority. The causal interactions between macro-political, economic and technological factors and the micro-psychological features described above will stabilize the anti-democratic network in many societies. Hence interventions designed to prepare the ground for the introduction of democracy will need to address a number of the nodes simultaneously. In particular, entrenched elites within such environments will be reluctant to concede real power and may prevent or sabotage moves towards democratization.

4 Africa in bio-cultural context

The issue to be addressed in this section is the prospect for a sustainable, pan-African, democratic transition. Even more focally, it poses the question of South Africa's longer-term political fate. The relationship of democracy to levels and distribution of national wealth, to civil institutions and to democratic aspirations are widely recognized. But equally significant is the interaction of such factors with issues of human capital, cultural attitudes, historical narratives and group dynamics. These will be the focus of this section.

It is common cause that in most African countries, perhaps with the partial exception of South Africa, the middle class is relatively small, politically insignificant and insecure. The general picture is one of a large, impoverished population leading a precarious, subsistence existence in juxtaposition to more wealthy elites whose hold on wealth is largely dependent on rent-seeking activities and is vulnerable to shifts in power and the self-interested decisions of various factions within the elites themselves (Mung'omba and Herbert, 2003; Rotberg, 2000; Doxtader and Villa-Vicencio, 2003). Thus the situation is not wholly static. Nevertheless, most African countries are characterized by wide gradients of wealth and power (see Mattes and Manning, 2003 for the Southern African region). The picture is complicated in many countries by ethnic or religious divisions, by rural and urban lifestyles or by regional loyalties and commitments that, more often than not, align with ethnic or religious affiliations, or with both (Doxtader and Villa-Vicencio, 2003). The social and cultural environments of urban and rural dwellers may also result in different perspectives, attitudes and needs.

To this can be added episodes, sometimes prolonged, of coalitional and ethnic violence as well as criminal depredations, substance abuse and random brutality often directed at women (Human Rights Watch, 2001). This is true for many South African peri-urban and even rural communities, but the incidence and severity of generalized social violence may vary considerably between countries and regions. Where coalitional conflict has occurred the brutality has been horrific.

Ignorance is rife and is probably underestimated by simple literacy figures (World Health Organization, 1999). Certainly the scientific and technological skills along with the accompanying culturally derived norms of self-regulation, independence and persistence are mostly absent or severely attenuated. Compared with Western states scientific and mathematical competence is meagre and exposure to other cultures and ideas is often entirely absent or limited to the commercial products of the entertainment industry. News may be heavily tinted by ideological, ethnic and religious orientations of an under-resourced, heavily regulated or impoverished media. While the Internet is, in theory, a universal facilitator of information transfer, observation suggests that individual disinclination and limited resources severely limits this route to wider political insights. Sheer distance from the centre impacts negatively on norms of performance and evaluation and has direct negative economic consequences (Redding and Schott, 2003). Yet the children of elites and some middle class children may receive excellent, often foreign, education, thus further alienating them from the majority of the population.

Through history and necessity African society shows strong clan and hierarchical features, especially in rural areas (Etounga-Manguelle, 2000). Informal local networks may reduce the sheer uncertainty of existence and could offer a path to wider self-help projects, thereby building social capital (Rose, 1997) – but see Mattes *et al.* (2002) for a somewhat contrary perspective. Factionalism at all levels will likely limit the capacity of social capital to build truly national identities and coherence. In South Africa a pronounced xenophobia within the black sector towards immigrants from other African countries has proven quite resistant to efforts by the government to create an encompassing and stable African identity. The instability and uncertainty is further exacerbated by HIV/AIDS and the prevalence of young people, notably young men, with a predisposition to male coalitional violence (Tiger and Fox, 1971) and criminal entrepreneurship.

Given the African experience of colonial humiliation, including the South African variant of apartheid, and bearing in mind the centrality of self-esteem to psychic functionality, it is not surprising that coalitional impulses around ethnicity can be readily evoked (Rothgerber, 1997; Ellemers *et al.*, 2002). Hierarchical predispositions are innate in people together with more recently evolved egalitarian and normatively altruistic impulses. But dominance concerns and behaviours can be readily elicited by perceptions of threat, by opportunities for gain or by suggestions of inferiority.

In general the African combination of historical, socio-cultural, economic and political factors will undermine the ability to create strong, overriding national identities and widespread social capital defined as instantiated norms of cooperation. Thus fluctuating identification with ethnic or more local tribal or clan loyalties may compete for dominance with national or universal values espoused by some ideological movements or even calculations of long-term self-interest. Impulses towards a wider national or even African identity may arise from sport or from a fraught interaction with 'European' interests derived from memories of a traumatic past. The outcome will to some extent reflect the strategic topography of the contextual matrix, which, as we have seen, is generally not conducive to sustained commitment to the broader good or to pragmatic, long-term considerations. It is hardly surprising that a variety of opportunistic activities, including corruption, rent seeking and nepotism, perpetuate the dysfunctional quasi-equilibrium state within most African countries.

From this description little reason for hope can be mined, but humans are equipped to seek solutions to difficult situations. Furthermore, this pessimistic narrative depicts the worst of the African predicament and ignores the elements within some African societies that may offer a shaky foundation for self-improvement (Mason, 2004). But even given this bias, the question remains whether the insights, motivations and resources within Africa are sufficiently close to the critical threshold for democratization and sustainable development.

The answer to this question is likely to be negative in most of the sub-Saharan states. The omnipresent political, social and economic realities largely preclude bootstrapping solely based on available indigenous resources. Any hope must lie in multifaceted outside intervention; a complex route fraught with obstacles. The continent is neither insulated from nor immune to the currents, good and bad, sweeping the rest of the world. Potentially, therefore, Africa can piggyback on centuries of social and political experience in the rest of the world, especially if funnelled through an African state powerful and insightful enough to carry such a role, namely South Africa. Such backing must be accompanied by sufficient economic development and redistribution together with conflict resolution prior to the outbreak of violence so as to overcome the pervading sense of existential insecurity that afflicts a high proportion of African society (see NEPAD, 2003). Only this can counter the short-term, 'adaptive' behaviours that result in the self-defeating political landscape of Africa.

But this route would require that South Africa can live out its own mixed heritage in a way that will serve the inclusive and long-term needs of its own population as well as that of Africa. South Africa, more than any other African country, has lived with European and Western influences for centuries. This has created certain benefits in addition to the psychological, socio-political and human ills which are chiefly remembered and referenced. Since these are well known and are implicit in my treatment of Africa as a whole, I will briefly summarize the former.

South Africa has the highest physical and human capital in Africa (Mills, 2002; Swarns, 2002). In some instances these once met or even exceeded Western norms; for instance, in medicine, some branches of science, in business infrastructure and in literature and general tertiary-level skills. Granted most of this was retained in white hands, but much did leak through to excluded groups, including blacks. With this baggage came a nominal attachment to democracy and mainly Judeo-Protestant attitudes towards work, human rights and social obligation capable of advancing nationwide social capital. Other immigrant groups from India and elsewhere also brought some economic, social and cultural traits well adapted to a modern, globalizing world. Many black activists spent much of their adult lives overseas, including in the West, where they received a good education unavailable to them in South Africa and were exposed to the currents sweeping the world in the last half of the twentieth century – some of them profoundly unhelpful. In African terms, therefore, South Africa is a wealthy country with an enormous reservoir of physical and human resources. Given its history, close ties to a mix of global cultures and ethnic composition it is ideally placed to provide just the reinforcement and example that Africa needs.

The question remains as to whether South Africa will be able to extract the value in its chequered past. A personal response to this question will constitute the final part of this chapter. But even if it does, it will continue to face the concern and resentment of its fellow Africans faced with a powerful and potentially hegemonic neighbour (Swarns, 2002).

As discussed earlier, ethnicity is the major current vector for coalitional behaviour in South Africa. The main axis is generated by black–white polarization, but other identities, religious, ideological and ethnic, derived from the Indian and coloured communities as well as from within the black–white axis, distorts and blurs the simplicity of a bipolar perspective. Despite a significant increase in the black middle class and the appearance of a small wealthy elite over the past decade, substantial inequalities in wealth, education, skills, employment levels and other indices of welfare like health persist, partly along ethnic lines. Furthermore, the vertical distance in the black community is greater and more sharply demarcated than within the white, which, together with other factors, creates more economic and status insecurities in the former group with obvious impact on levels of rent seeking, nepotism and corruption.

Such variations in material and human resources is accompanied by formal and informal ideological distinctions. The 'liberation' movement in South Africa, from which its present governing elite evolved, reflects a smorgasbord of ideologies and belief systems partly, but incompletely, reflected in the tripartite structure of the ruling alliance. These include liberal ideas of universal human rights, ethnic, religious and gender equality, and democratic governance instantiated in the South African constitution, coexisting with potent Africanist and socialist leanings and hostility towards real and perceived Western imperialism and arrogance. Actual behaviour within the alliance reveals a distinct bias towards centralized, command governance, contrary to the dictates of a more distributed, liberal democracy. But possibly the most powerful motivational impulses emerge from the vision of a victimized African identity rising from a humiliating past to assert a new dignity and strength in the community of nations. This has been explicitly, even movingly, expressed by President Mbeki in speaking to the slogan 'African Renaissance'. It is potentially heightened by the continued proximity and economic power of a smaller white community which encapsulates all that is humiliating and demeaning in African history.

Much of the convoluted politics of the ruling alliance can only be understood in terms of these conflicting identities, loyalties, normative and ideological values and strategic computations. The African National Congress under Mbeki thus pursues a multi-faceted strategy designed to simultaneously hold and extend power, to unite its disparate factions, to promote the African Renaissance within South Africa and elsewhere, to demonstrate its strategic and emotional commitment to Third World countries around the world, and to express its resistance to perceived, and real, Western hegemonic aspirations, while at the same time pragmatically maintaining a mutually rewarding relationship with critical white sectors like the big business community. At times the emotional, moral-ideological and strategic drivers of perception collide, accounting for erratic and inexplicable policies and behaviours especially, but not exclusively, apparent in health, economic and foreign policy and highly symbolic arenas like sport. The country has seen the rapid emergence of a wealthy black elite with links to the ruling alliance as well as a significant expansion of the black middle class but leaving the severely impoverished sector still relatively intact.

These motivations, values and ideological perspectives are by no means shared by all sectors of South African society. The white population, in so far as it has articulated a coherent political belief, probably falls mainly along a conservative–liberal axis, as do significant numbers within the Indian and coloured communities. Such an orientation is not surprising in view of its origin, intellectual and ideological history and present precarious superiority in terms of education and per capita wealth. As with the black community, much of white behaviour is driven by a perceived incompatibility of interests between themselves and their black fellow citizens. Just as the ANC superiority currently rests on the loyalty of the black voter, so the largest opposition party, the Democratic Alliance (DA), relies on white identity to constitute a core support base. But, unlike the ruling alliance, any hope of power for the DA demands substantial support not only from the coloured and Indian communities but also from within the black sector. This strategic reality ensures that the DA broadcasts a strong liberal, non-racial and somewhat interventionist economic ideology.

For reasons of space I have confined myself to the main ethnic-ideological protagonists. Nevertheless, it should be acknowledged that other political groupings, labour unions, associations of (white and black) business interests, and even informal religious and ideological coalitions within the white, Indian and coloured communities can play a key role in determining outcomes under various credible scenarios. These complexities render South African politics fragmented and potentially fluid.

4.1 The next 10 to 30 years

South Africa is emphasized because of its potentially central role in the African Renaissance and because of my own greater familiarity with this region. To overcome the barriers to a stable and prosperous future the following conditions will need to be met:

1. Free and effective political activity together with a vigorous and diverse media and an independent and competent judiciary. Only the existence of such institutions and ideological diversity can raise the costs of various forms of personal and coalitional opportunism sufficiently to ensure that all parties promote more inclusive policies. The longer the institutionalization of democratic norms, the more embedded they become in national consciousness.
2. Sufficient economic and personal security to reduce tendencies towards narrow altruistic and coalitional impulses and to diminish the fuel available for opportunistic politicians to exploit. This demands a reduction both in absolute poverty and the wealth gradient, a reduction in unemployment, adequate control of corruption and violent crime and an enhancement of general skills within the population, while simultaneously retaining and strengthening the high-level expertise required to exploit technological opportunity. Of course, as expectations rise, so goalposts shift.
3. A more tolerant and inclusivist culture so as to counter the tendency of South Africa and Africa to cleave along religious and ethnic lines. Optimally, such policies should come from the governing elite so as to exploit the prestige-based path of cultural transmission. Failing that, the media and other prominent social structures should reflect a moral commitment to the principles of a colour and gender-blind reward

system based on achievement as well as personal accountability. If implemented with a sensitive awareness of the psychological dynamics and historical inequalities reviewed in this chapter, these values could enhance a broader sense of social and communal responsibility while facilitating the moral imperative of transformation.

4   A functional health system with a special focus on ensuring the optimal physical, intellectual and psychological development of all children. This is a multi-dimensional problem and includes proper attention to the prevention and treatment of HIV/AIDS.

5   A sensible, stable and even-handed foreign policy which focuses on the long-term economic and political interests of South Africa and Africa as a whole.

Some, but certainly not all, of the present policies and actions of the ANC-led alliance run counter to certain important conditions listed above. To mention a few, there is an ambiguous commitment to a broader South African identity, an overly ideological and ethnic bias to foreign policy, ineffective delivery of important services in the fields of health, crime prevention and economic development, and mixed signals concerning democratic constraints. Whether the broader South African population, including the political opposition, have the insight and will to impose these conditions on themselves as well as the ruling elite through the electoral process remains to be seen.

4.2 Coda

This chapter is written to introduce a broad biological and scientific perspective to the disciplines dealing with human political and economic behaviour. Most traditional and realist approaches take 'human nature' implicitly for granted. A few in the democratization literature (see Vanhanen, 1997) make explicit reference to human nature as a foundation for their own theoretical formulations, but do not seriously explore its dimensions or specific impact on the macro-political issues being considered. More serious attempts at including psychological and even evolutionary concepts have appeared (Tetlock and Goldgeier, 2000; Goldgeier and Tetlock, 2001; Rubin, 2002; Richerson and Boyd, 2001b), but not in the present context and somewhat constrained in terms of scope and application.

Given the enormous advances and increasing sophistication of research in the broad field of neurobiology and in evolutionary, developmental, social and cognitive psychology, the time seems ripe for a more consilient research agenda, especially in the domain of political, cultural, social and economic studies. For instance, it may be asked whether and how does the coalitional impulse (or, to put it another way, group behaviour) differ systematically between cultures and societies, or between groups within a single society, or over time? If it does, what are the important mediators of such changes? Do coalitional behaviours respond predictably to contextual and situational variables and in what way does variation in these psychological processes impact upon such issues as democratization and its maintenance?

Partly, my intent was to provoke or induce scholars in the social sciences to undertake a more analytically and operationally rigorous approach to some of the many connections hinted at in this chapter. In the meantime, based on what we do know, it seems reasonable to suggest that continued experience with and internalization of democratic practices, better developmental environments, diminished existential insecurity through a reduction in poverty, crime, violence and disease, the creation of wider norms of social capital, and more realistic political attitudes within the frame of an inclusive, free-market based, liberal democracy are the best guarantors of South African and African sustainable development.

The fact that innate (genetic) factors can play a decisive but not deterministic role in determining psychological phenotype (Marcus, 2004) appears to represent a major conceptual obstacle and ideological hurdle to many commentators (see *Psychological Bulletin*, November 2003 and note 5). The important point is that the hypothetical, multi-dimensional space of all possible human psychological phenotypes is not uniformly occupied but is heavily skewed into finite and recognizable patterns determined by gene interactions with other genes and with intra-uterine and post-gestational inputs of all kinds. The nature of these interactions is a legitimate and important topic of research; the outcome is what we know as 'human nature' in its many forms.

Notes

1 In the past decades a substantial literature has emerged that explores political and economic behaviour from a broad evolutionary psychological perspective: Camerer, 2003; Frank, 1988; Rubin, 2002; Simon, 1990; Gintis, 2003; Bowles *et al.*, 2002; Boyd and Richerson, 1985; Richerson and Boyd, 2001b. Biologists too have adopted economic tools and concepts to address important evolutionary issues: Kaplan and Robson, 2002; Robson and Kaplan, 2003. Even cognitive neurobiology has recruited economic perspectives into the calculation of future reward and punishment by brain circuits; see Montague and Berns, 2002. Despite the growing extent, sophistication and depth of this literature it still remains terra incognita to most scholars in the social sciences and humanities.

2 The case for consilience has been forcefully and comprehensively articulated by E.O. Wilson (Wilson, 1998). Paul Thagard (2001) recently reviewed the contributions of five distinct disciplines to the recent advances in cognitive psychology. Panksepp (1999) makes a similar appeal for a new consilient approach to emotion, and Mischel (2004), by implication, does the same for theories of personality. A particularly good example is the review by Moss (2003) on theories of self. The penetration of the biological and natural sciences into the humanities holds enormous promise for both sides.

3 See, for example, recent reviews by Rubin, 2002; Goldgeier and Tetlock, 2001; Monroe et al., 2000; Tetlock and Goldgeier, 2000; Richerson and Boyd, 2001a.
4 The horrifying toll of HIV/AIDS, tuberculosis and malaria has been thoroughly documented (see Mattes and Manning, 2003). The death rate from disease and malnutrition significantly exceeds that of political, and probably all forms, of violence with similarly negative psychological, sociological, political and economic impacts.
5 The paradigmatic foundations of evolutionary psychology have been most systematically stated by Cosmides and Tooby in a series of publications over the past decade; see Tooby and Cosmides, 1992; Tooby et al., 2003. The popular writings of Ridley, 1996; Pinker, 2002 and others have brought the topic to a wider audience. The November 2003 issue of *Psychological Bulletin* contains a useful debate that clarifies persistent sources of misunderstanding in response to a somewhat genophobic lead article by Lickliter and Honeycutt (2003). For more of the same and further insight into the potential and limitations of evolutionary psychology see Caporael, 1995, 2001; Panksepp, 2001; Kurzban, 2002; Karmiloff-Smith, 1994, to select a few.
6 The interactions, similarities and differences between cultural evolution and Darwinian genomic-level processes have been widely explored, inter alia, by Boyd and Richerson, 1985; Laland et al., 2000; Richerson and Boyd, 2001b; Gil-White, 2004; Boehm, 2000; Dennett, 2001. Economists (see Henrich, 2001a; Gintis et al., 2003; Bowles et al., 2002) have recently been prominent in addressing the evolution of social norms using tools familiar to population geneticists.
7 The two imposters are 'Triumph and Disaster', in 'If' by Kipling (in Eliot, 1954: 273).
8 Jared Diamond (1997) in particular has laid considerable stress on the salience of geographic and ecological factors in determining the huge differentials in technological innovation and their consequences between human cultures. Others have stressed the significance of site and ecology as well (Sachs, 2000); but while not necessarily insignificant, a global survey of successful societies suggests that these no longer loom as large as in the past.
9 The linkages between emotion and cognition are the focus of an intense research programme reflected in a burgeoning literature; see Adolphs, 2003; Rolls, 2000; Cardinal et al., 2002; Miller, 2000; Montague and Berns, 2002; Eisenberger et al., 2003, for some recent reviews. Some authors (e.g., Panksepp, 2001; Damasio, 2003) lay greater emphasis on ancient brainstem and other subcortical structures in regulating mood and foundational behavioural instincts. The role of chemical mediators like oxytocin, dopamine and serotonin in mediating characteristic response patterns is as important as 'circuitry' (Knutson et al., 1998; Greenfield, 2000). Particularly interesting is developmental research linking particular brain regions to phenotypic outcomes (Davidson, 2001) which includes work on abused children (Teicher, 2002). Furthermore, holistic or gestalt approaches differ significantly from the circuit specialists. While current achievements, considerable though they are, do not add up to a comprehensive neurobiological foundation for behaviour, they do confirm the intimate ties between emotion and cognition in constructing human behavior (Moss, 2003). There remains enormous work to be done uniting the different approaches to the human emotional-cognitive system.
10 A recent meta-review puts the number of papers on self-esteem in the region of 15 000. Despite this quantitative largesse, remarkably little of substance has emerged (Scheff and Fearon, 2003). Notably, the documented relationships between the 200 measures of self-esteem and behaviour appear slight and inconsistent. This probably reflects, in part, the absence of an operationally and

biologically meaningful definition. I propose that self-esteem will ultimately be linked at the lower end with primitive feelings of social potency and sexual attractiveness and at the upper end with cognitively advanced emotions of moral worth and status. In one way or another self-esteem is bound up with strategically relevant contexts which will render more or less salient its different dimensions, as seen in the wider concept of personality (Mischel, 2004).

11 'Strategically relevant' refers to situations within a given socio-political context which have or are perceived to have implications for 'inclusive fitness' interests of the individual or for the power and status of a group. These commonly occur in many social contexts and intergroup transactions.

12 In a recent monumental review, Ashmore *et al.* (2004) have deconstructed some of the literature and clarified some of the terminology and concepts. Other reviews by Macrae and Bodenhausen (2000), Ellemers *et al.* (2002), Hewstone *et al.* (2002), together with the vast empirical literature derived from evolutionary, developmental (Bugental, 2000; Caporael, 1995), psychological (Baumeister *et al.*, 1996; Bettencourt and Hume, 1999; Moskowitz *et al.*, 1999; Verkuyten *et al.*, 1999; Hong *et al.*, 2003), sociological (Sidanus, 1993; Tiger and Fox, 1971) and neuro-cognitive (Kunda and Thagard, 1996; Moss, 2003) sources are relevant to the topic.

13 See Case *et al.* (2002) for the relationship of chronic childhood disease to future income in the USA. The cake cuts both ways: massive income disparities for example contribute to health inequalities with predictable positive-feedback effects (Deaton, 2003). The long-term effects of childhood 'stress' are now well documented (McEvan and Seeman, 1999; Teicher, 2002). These realities are only too prevalent in Africa.

References

Adolphs, R. (2003). Cognitive neuroscience of human social behaviour, *Nature Reviews: Neuroscience*, 4: 165–178.

Ashmore, R.D., K. Deaux and T. McLaughlin-Volpe (2004). An organizing framework for collective identity: articulation and significance of multidimensionality, *Psychological Bulletin*, 130(1): 80–114.

Bargh, J.A. and T.L. Chartrand (1999). The unbearable automaticity of being, *American Psychologist*, 54(7): 462–479.

Barresi, J. and C. Moore (1996). Intentional relations and social understanding, *Behavioral and Brain Sciences*, 19(1): 107–154.

Baumeister, R.F., L. Smart and J.M. Boden (1996). Relation of threatened egotism to violence and aggression: the dark side of high self esteem, *Psychological Review*, 103(1): 5–33.

Bettencourt, B.A. and D. Hume (1999). The cognitive contents of social group identity: values, emotions and relationships, *European Journal of Social Psychology*, 29: 113–121.

Boehm, C. (2000). Conflict, and the evolution of social control, in L.D. Katz (ed.), *Evolutionary Origins of Morality*, Exeter: Short Run Press.

Bowles, S., J. Choi and A. Hopfensitz (2002). The co-evolution of individual behaviors and social institutions, Working Paper No. 00-12-073, Santa Fe Institute.

Boyd, R. and P.J. Richerson (1985). *Culture and the Evolutionary Process*, Chicago: University of Chicago Press.

Brown, D.E. (1991). *Human Universals*, New York: McGraw-Hill.

Bugental, D.B. (2000). Acquisition of the algorithms of social life: a domain based approach, *Psychological Bulletin*, 126(2): 187–219.

Byrne, R. and A. Whiten (1988). *Machiavellian Intelligence: Social Expertise and the Evolution of Intellect in Monkeys, Apes and Humans*, Oxford: Clarendon Press.

Camerer, C.F. (2003). Strategizing in the brain, *Science*, 300: 1673–1675.

Caporael, L.R. (1995). Sociality: coordinating bodies, minds and groups, *Psycoloquy*, 6(1). Online, available at: http://psycprints.ecs.soton.ac.uk.

Caporael, L.R. (2001). Evolutionary psychology: toward a unifying theory and a hybrid science, *Annual Review of Psychology*, 52: 607–628.

Cardinal, R.N., J.A. Parkinson, J. Hall and B.J. Everitt (2002). Emotion and motivation: the role of the amygdala, ventral striatum and prefrontal cortex, *Neuroscience and Biobehavioral Reviews*, 26: 321–352.

Carneiro, R.L. (2000). The transition from quantity to quality: a neglected causal mechanism in accounting for social evolution, *PNAS*, 97(23): 12926–12931.

Case, A., D. Lubotsky and C. Paxson (2002). Economic status and health in childhood: the origins of the gradient, *The American Economic Review*, 92(5): 1308–1334.

Charlton, B.G. (1997). Injustice, inequality and evolutionary psychology, *Journal of Health Psychology*, 2: 413–425.

Colletta, N.J., J. Balachander and X. Liang (1996). The condition of young children in sub-Saharan Africa: the convergence of health, nutrition and early education, Technical Paper No. 326, World Bank, Washington, DC.

Cosmides, J. and J. Tooby (2000). Evolutionary psychology and the emotions, in M. Lewis and J.M. Haviland-Jones (eds), *Handbook of Emotions*, 2nd edn, New York: Guilford Press.

Damasio, A. (2003). Feelings of emotion and self, *Annals of the New York Academy of Sciences*, 1001: 253–261.

Davidson, R.J. (2001). Towards a biology of personality and emotion, *Annals of the New York Academy of Sciences*, 935: 191–207.

Deaton, A. (2003). Health, inequality and economic development, *Journal of Economic Literature*, 41: 113–158.

Dennett, D. (1995). *Darwin's Dangerous Idea: Evolution and the Meanings of Life*, New York: Simon and Schuster.

Dennett, D.C. (2001). The evolution of culture, *The Monist*, 84(3): 305–324.

De Waal, F. (1996). *Good-natured. The Origins of Right and Wrong in Humans and Other Animals*, Cambridge, MA: Harvard University Press.

Devos, T. and M.R. Banaji (2003). Implicit self and identity, *Annals of the New York Academy of Sciences*, 1001: 177–211.

Diamond, J. (1997). Why did human history unfold differently on different continents for the last 13000 years? *Edge*. Online, available at: http://www.edge.org.

Diamond, L. (1995). Africa, SubSaharan, in S.M. Lipset (ed. in chief), *The Encyclopedia of Democracy*, Washington, DC: Congressional Quarterly.

Donald, M. (1993). *Origins of the Modern Mind: Three Stages in the Evolution of Culture and Cognition*, Cambridge, MA: Harvard University Press.

Doxtader, E. and C. Villa-Vicencio (2003). *Through Fire with Water: The Roots of Division and the Potential for Reconciliation in Africa*, Claremont: New Africa Books.

Edgerton, R.B. (2000). Traditional beliefs and practices – are some better than others?, in L.E. Harrison and S.P Huntington (eds), *Culture Matters*, New York: Basic Books.

Eisenberger, N.I., M.D. Lieberman and K.D. Williams (2003). Does rejection hurt? An fMRI study of social exclusion, *Science*, 302: 290–292.

Ekman, P. (1999). Basic emotions, in T. Dalgleish and T. Power (eds), *The Handbook of Cognition and Emotion*, Chichester: John Wiley and Sons.

Eliot, T.S. (1954). *A Choice of Kipling's Verse*, London: Faber and Faber.

Ellemers, N., R. Spears and B. Doosje (2002). Self and social identity, *Annual Review of Psychology*, 53: 161–186.

Elster, J. (1999). *Alchemies of the Mind: Rationality and the Emotions*, Cambridge: Cambridge University Press.

Etounga-Manguelle, D. (2000). Does Africa need a cultural adjustment program?, in L.E. Harrison and S.P. Huntington (eds), *Culture Matters*, New York: Basic Books.

Evans, D. (1999). From moods to modules: preliminary remarks for an evolutionary theory of mood phenomena. Online, available at: http://cogprints.ecs.soton.ac.uk.

Fehr, E. and S. Gachter (2000). Cooperation and punishment in public goods experiments, *American Economic Review*, 90(4): 980–994.

Fiske, A.P. (n.d.). Human sociality: the inherent sociability of *Homo sapiens*. Online, available at: www.sscnet.ucla.edu/anthro/faculty/fiske/relmodov.htm.

Frank, R.H. (1988). *Passions Within Reason: The Strategic Role of the Emotions*, London: Norton.

Fukuyma, F. (2000). Social capital and civil society, IMP Insatiate Working Paper, April 2000.

Gigerenzer, G. and D.G. Goldstein (1996). Reasoning the fast and frugal way: models of bounded reality, *Psychological Review*, 103(4): 650–669.

Gil-White, F.J. (2004). Common misunderstandings for memes (and genes), in S. Hurley and N. Chater (eds), *Perspectives on Imitation: From Mirror Neurons to Memes*, Cambridge, MA: MIT Press.

Gintis, H., S. Bowles, R. Boyd and E. Fehr (2003). Explaining altruistic behavior in humans, *Evolution and Human Behavior*, 24: 153–172.

Goldgeier, J.M. and P.E. Tetlock (2001). Psychology and international relations theory, *Annual Review of Political Science*, 4: 67–92.

Greenfield, S. (2000). *The Private Life of the Brain*, London: Penguin Books.

Griffiths, P.E. (2002a). Basic emotions, complex emotions, Machiavellian emotions. Online, available at: http://philsci-archive.pitt.edu/archive/00000604.

Griffiths, P.E. (2002b). Toward a 'Machiavellian' theory of emotional appraisal. Emotions, evolution and rationality. Conference paper. Online, available at: philsci-archive.pitt.edu/archive/00000667/00/AppraisalMachiavellian.PDF (accessed April 2002).

Harrison, L.E. and S.P. Huntington (eds) (2000). *Culture Matters*, New York: Basic Books.

Henrich, J. (2001a). Cultural transmission and the diffusion of innovations: adoption dynamics indicate that biased cultural transmission is the predominate force in behavioral change and much of social cultural evolution, *American Anthropologist*, 103: 992–1013.

Henrich, J., R. Boyd, S. Bowles, C. Camerer, E. Fehr, H. Gintis and R. McElreath (2001b). Cooperation: reciprocity and punishment in 15 small scale societies, *American Economics Review*, 91(2): 73–78.

Hermalin, B.E. and A.M. Isen (1999). The effect of affect on economic and strategic decision making. Online, available at: http://faculty.haas.berkely.edu/hermalin/affect_v4.pdf.
Hewstone, M., M. Rubin and H. Willis (2002). Intergroup bias, *Annual Review of Psychology*, 53: 575–604.
Hong, Y., G. Chan, C. Chiu, R.Y.M. Wong, I.G. Hansen, S. Lee, Y. Tong and H. Fu (2003). How are social identities linked to self conception and intergroup orientation? The moderating effect of implicit theories, *Journal of Personality and Social Psychology*, 85(6): 1147–1160.
Human Rights Watch. (2001). Human Rights Watch World Report 2001. Online, available at: http://www.globalmarch.org.
Jost, J.T., J. Glaser, A.W. Kruglanski and F.J. Sulloway (2003). Political conservatism as motivated social cognition, *Psychological Bulletin*, 129(3): 339–375.
Kahneman, D. and A. Tversky (1996). On the reality of cognitive illusions, *Psychological Review*, 103(3): 582–591.
Kaplan, H.S. and A.J. Robson (2002). The emergence of humans: the co-evolution of intelligence and longevity with intergenerational transfers, *PNAS*, 99(15): 10221–10226.
Karmiloff-Smith, A. (1994). Precis of beyond modularity: a developmental perspective on cognitive science, *Behavioral and Brain Sciences*, 17(2): 693–745.
Keeley, L.H. (1996). *War Before Civilization*, New York: Oxford University Press.
Knutson, B., O.M. Wolkowitz, S.W. Cole, T. Chan, E.A. Moore, R.C. Johnson, J. Terpstra, R.A. Turner and V.I. Renus (1998). Selective alteration of personality and social behavior by serotonergic intervention, *American Journal of Psychiatry*, 155(3): 373–379.
Krueger, J.I. and D.C. Funder (2003). Towards a balanced social psychology: causes, consequences and cures for the problem-seeking approach to social behaviour and cognition. Online, available at: Krueger and Funder maillist.cogpsyphy.hu/pipermail/koglist/2003-March/001850.html.
Kruglanski, A.W. and D.M. Webster (1996). Motivated closing of the mind: 'seizing' and 'freezing', *Psychological Review*, 103(2): 263–283.
Kunda, Z. and P. Thagard (1996). Forming impressions from stereotypes, traits and behaviors: a parallel-constraint-satisfaction theory, *Psychological Review*, 103(2): 284–308.
Kurzban, R. (2002). Alas poor evolutionary psychology: unfairly accused, unjustly condemned, *The Human Nature Review*, 2: 99–109.
Kurzban, R., J. Tooby and L. Cosmides (2001). Can race be erased? Coalitional computation and social categorization, *PNAS*, 98(26): 15387–15392.
La Cerra, P. and R. Bingham (1998). The adaptive nature of the human neurocognitive architecture: an alternative model, *PNAS*, 95: 11290–11294.
Laland, K.N., J. Odling-Smee and M.W. Feldman (2000). Niche construction, biological evolution and cultural change, *Behavioral and Brain Sciences*, 23: 131–175.
Landes, D. (2000). Culture makes almost all the difference, in L.E. Harrison and S.P. Huntington (eds), *Culture Matters*, New York: Basic Books.
Lickliter, R. and H. Honeycutt (2003). Developmental dynamics: toward a biologically plausible evolutionary psychology, *Psychological Bulletin*, 129(6): 819–835.
Lipset, S.M. (1998). Excerpts from three lectures on democracy: The 1997 Julian J

Rothbaum Distinguished Lecture in Representative Government, *Extensions*, Carl Albert Congressional Research and Studies Center.

Macrae, C.N. and G.V. Bodenhausen (2000). Social cognition: thinking categorically about others, *Annual Review of Psychology*, 51: 93–120.

Marcus, G. (2004). Making the mind: why we've misunderstood the nature–nurture debate, *Boston Review*. Online, available at: http://bostonreview.net.

Mason, D. (2004). Africa's extremes, *The Economist: The World in 2004*, 84.

Masters, R.D. (2001). Biology and politics: linking nature and nuture, *Annual Review of Political Science*, 4: 345–369.

Mattes, R. and R. Manning (2003). The impact of HIV/AIDS on democracy in Southern Africa: What do we know, what we need to know, and why?, CSSR Working Paper No. 34, University of Cape Town.

Mattes, R., M. Bratton and Y.D. Davids (2002). Poverty, survival and democracy in Southern Africa, CSSR Working Paper No. 27, University of Cape Town.

McEvan, B.S. and T. Seeman (1999). Protective and damaging effects of mediators of stress: elaborating and testing the concepts of allostasis and allostatic load, *Annals of the New York Academy of Sciences*, 896: 30–47.

McGrew, W.C. (1998). Culture in non-human primates, *Annual Review of Anthropology*, 27: 301–328.

Miller, E.K. (2000). The prefrontal cortex and cognitive control, *Nature Reviews*, 1: 59–65.

Mills, G. (2002). *Poverty to Prosperity: Globalization, Good Governance and African Recovery*, Tafelberg: South African Institute of International Affairs.

Mischel, W. (2004). Toward an integrative science of the person, *Annual Review of Psychology*, 55: 1–22.

Monroe, K.R., J. Hankin and R.B. Van Vechten (2000). The psychological foundations of identity politics, *Annual Review of Political Science*, 3: 419–447.

Montague, P.R. and G.S. Berns (2002). Neural economics and the biological substrates of valuation, *Neuron*, 36: 265–284.

Moskowitz, G.B., P.M. Gollwitzer, W. Wasel and B. Schaal (1999). Preconscious control of stereotype activation through chronic egalitarian goals, *Journal of Personality and Social Psychology*, 77(1): 167–184.

Moss, H. (2003). Implicit selves, *Annals of the New York Academy of Sciences*, 1001: 1–30.

Mung'omba, D. and H. Herbert (2003). Wither 'of the people, by the people, for the people'?, *eAfrica*, 1: 6–7.

NEPAD (2003). Objectives, standards, criteria and indicators for the African Peer Review Mechanism ('The APRM'). Online, available at: NEPAD/HSGIC-03-2003/APRM/Guideline/OSCI.

Nesse, R.M. (1991) What is mood for?, *Psycoloquy*, 9(2). Online, available at: http://psycprints.ecs.soton.ac.uk.

Panksepp, J. (1999) Emotions as viewed by psychoanalysis and neuroscience: an exercise in consilience, *NeuroPsychoanalysis*, 1: 15–38.

Panksepp, J. (2001). The neuro-evolutionary cusp between emotions and cognition, *Evolution and Cognition*, 7(2): 141–161.

Pinker, S. (2002). *The Blank Slate*, New York: Viking.

Porter, M.E. (2000). Attitudes, values, beliefs, and the microeconomics of prosperity, in L.E. Harrison and S.P. Huntington (eds), *Culture Matters*, New York: Basic Books.

Price, M.E., L. Cosmides and J. Tooby (2002). Punitive sentiment as an anti-free rider psychological device, *Evolution and Human Behaviour*, 23: 203–231.
Quinn, N. (2003). Cultural selves, *Annals of the New York Academy of Sciences*, 1001: 145–176.
Rabin, M. (2002). A perspective on psychology and economics, Working Paper No. E02-313, University of California.
Redding, S. and P.K. Schott (2003). Distance, skill deepening and development: will peripheral countries ever get rich?, *Journal of Development Economics*, 72: 515–541.
Richerson, P.J. and R. Boyd (1999). Complex societies: the evolutionary origins of a crude superorganism, *Human Nature*, 10: 253–289.
Richerson, P. and R. Boyd (2001a) The biology of commitment to groups: a tribal instincts hypothesis, in R.M. Nesse (ed.), *Evolution and the Capacity for Commitment*, New York: Russell Sage Press.
Richerson, P.J. and R. Boyd (2001b). Built for speed, not for comfort: Darwinian theory and human culture, *History and Philosophy of the Life Sciences*, 23: 426–463.
Ridley, M. (1996). *The Origins of Virtue*, London: Penguin.
Robson, A.J. and H.S. Kaplan (2003). The evolution of human life expectancy and intelligence in hunter-gatherer economies, *American Economic Review*, 93(1): 150–169.
Rolls, E.Y. (2000). Précis of the brain and emotion, *Behavioral and Brain Sciences*, 23: 177–234.
Rose, R. (1997). Measures of social capital, in *African Surveys*, World Bank Capital Initiative. Online, available at: http://www.socialcapital.strath.ac.uk/networkindex.html.
Rotberg, R.I. (2000). Africa's mess, Mugabe's mayhem, *Foreign Affairs*, 779(5): 47–61.
Rothgerber, H. (1997). External intergroup threat as an antecedent to perceptions of in-group and out-group homogeneity, *Journal of Personality and Social Psychology*, 73(6): 1206–1212.
Rubin, P.H. (2002). *Darwinian Politics: The Evolutionary Origin of Freedom*, London: Rutgers University Press.
Sachs, J. (2000). Notes on a new sociology of economic development, in L.E. Harrison and S.P. Huntington (eds), *Culture Matters*, New York: Basic Books.
Scheff, T.J. and D. Fearon Jr. (2003). Cognition and emotion? The dead end of self esteem research. Unpublished paper.
Schrodinger, E. (1962). *What is Life?*, Cambridge: Cambridge University Press.
Sidanus, J. (1993). The psychology of group conflict and the dynamics of oppression, in S. Iyengar and W.J. McGuire (eds), *Explorations in Political Psychology*, Durham, NC: Duke University Press.
Simon, H.A. (1990). Invariants of human behavior, *Annual Review of Psychology*, 41: 1–19.
Sloman, L. (1992). How mood variation regulates aggression, *Psycoloquy*, 3(3) Mood (4). Online, available at: http://psycprints.ecs.soton.ac.uk.
Sloman, A. (2001). Beyond shallow models of emotion, *Cognitive Processing*, 2(1): 177–198.
Spencer, S.J., S. Fein, C.T. Wolfe, C. Fong and M.A. Dunn (1998). Automatic activation of stereotypes: the role of self-image threat, *Personality and Social Psychology Bulletin*, 24(11): 1139–1152.

Swarns, R.L. (2002). Awe and unease as South Africa stretches out, *New York Times*. Online, available at: http://nytimes.com (accessed 17 February).

Teicher, M.H. (2002). Scars that won't heal: the neurobiology of child abuse, *Scientific American*, 286(3): 68–75.

Tetlock, P.E. and J.M. Goldgeier (2000). Human nature and world politics: cognition, identity and influence, *International Journal of Psychology*, 35(2): 87–96.

Thagard, P. (2001). Being interdisciplinary: trading zones in cognitive science. Online, available at: philsci-archive.pitt.edu/archive/00000667/00/Appraisal Machiavellian.PDF.

Tiger, L. and R. Fox (1971). *The Imperial Animal*, New York: Holt, Reinhart and Winston.

Tomasello, M. (1999). The human adaptation for culture, *Annual Review of Anthropology*, 28: 509–529.

Tooby, J. and L. Cosmides (1992). The psychological foundations of culture, in J.H. Barkow, L. Cosmides and J. Tooby (eds), *The Adaptive Mind: Evolutionary Psychology and the Generation of Culture*, Oxford: Oxford University Press.

Tooby, J., L. Cosmides and H.C. Barrett (2003). The second law of thermodynamics is the first law of psychology: evolutionary developmental psychology and the theory of tandem, coordinated inheritances: comment on Lickliter and Honeycutt, *Psychological Bulletin*, 129(6): 858–865.

Turk, D.J., T.F. Heatherton, C.N. Macrae, W.M. Kelley and M.S. Gazzaniga (2003). Out of contact, out of mind: the distributed nature of the self, *Annals of the New York Academy of Sciences*, 1001: 65–78.

Vanhanen, T. (1997). *Prospects of Democracy: A Study of 172 Countries*, London and New York: Routledge.

Verkuyten, M., M. Drabbles and K. van den Nieuwenhuijzen (1999). Self categorization and emotional reactions to ethnic minorities, *European Journal of Social Psychology*, 29: 605–619.

Wilson, D.S., D. Near and R.R. Miller (1996). Machiavellianism: a synthesis of evolutionary and psychological literatures, *Psychological Bulletin*, 119(2): 285–299.

Wilson, E.O. (1998). *Consilience: The Unity of Knowledge*, New York: Little, Brown.

World Health Organization, World Health Report 1999. Literacy rate by country – Africa: 47–87.

Afterword

Melvin Ayogu and Don Ross

1 Reflections on measurement conventions

The chapters in this book, taken together, should be convincing evidence that understanding and assessing development policies and processes embodies both philosophical and economic dimensions. Beginning with the philosophical question of what 'development' ought to mean – contrast Hamilton and Ross, for example – it should have become clearer why economists have devoted considerable energy to studying economic *growth* – in the narrower sense that plays a role in Hausman's worries – instead of human development in the much wider sense relevant to the differing perspectives of (at least) Bates's, Hamilton's, and Berger's chapters. The choice is an escape hatch, for in focusing on a stricter construction of development defined in terms only of increase in per capita income rather than in a broader sense of the general well-being of the population, taking into account access to both social and physical infrastructure, we can measure development with data from markets. Economists do not claim to understand markets perfectly – and perhaps many should be more humble about this, for reasons Kincaid emphasizes – but they are surely more tractable objects of generalization than the whole social world. The task of grappling with the broader measurement exercises has traditionally been left to development agencies such as UNDP, which over the years has creditably championed the distinction between the narrow and the broader definitions through its now famous measure, the Human Development Index. UNDP's flagship publication, the *Human Development Report*, routinely features a section on the variation between country rankings based on measurements by the narrower definition and by UNDP's broader definition. Recent calls to incorporate non-income dimensions of poverty such as insecurity, powerlessness (lack of choice), and lack of voice or basic civil and political freedoms into the development agenda, draw attention to deep underlying ethical dimensions in development. The broader definition, which by current trends could become the future standard, does not just call into question the grouping of the least developed nations of the world, namely those in sub-Saharan Africa and

Central Asia, but reminds us of the task ahead in China, India, and Latin America. Berger's chapter reminds us that there is a tangle of still deeper issues in human identity construction we cannot ignore, even if we try to keep our attention focused on material prosperity following the advice of Rosenberg and Ross.

2 What have we learned?

We have learned that in rethinking development, we confront the tensions inherent in societies that simultaneously aim for both growth and democracy. Though these may often be correlated on some measures, there are unavoidable tensions that arise when trying to exercise policies in a context of international capitalism and local aspirations to deeper democracy. We take this to be an explicit or implicit theme in at least the chapters of Stiglitz, Bates, Rosenberg, Ross, Nattrass and Seekings, and Hamilton. As all of these chapters stress in their different ways, this tension is not the simple-minded opposition sometimes imagined by activists. Rather, it arises from the fact that what is most emphasized by democratic values, equality of access and terms of participation, need not coincide with the sorts of efficiencies that best promote poverty reduction. Yet poverty reduction is itself, surely, a key aspect of improving equality of access and participation!

These chapters draw attention to the differences across countries. Some important differences arise from varying locations in developmental space. Others lie in political values, with some countries more attentive to local voices, some more in tune to international pressures. Different countries are more or less democratic or capitalistic. All must strike particular balances in response to constraints beyond their control, as Nattrass and Seekings illustrate in the extended South African example.

We can see from the chapters that simple policy prescriptions derived from a simplistic conception of globalization are seriously problematic. Stiglitz, Hausman, Kincaid, Laffont, Rosenberg, and Nattrass and Seekings emphasize the dangers of simple policies; Bates, Kincaid, Ross, Nattrass and Seekings, Hamilton and Berger draw attention to the simplistic conceptions.

3 Global vision: melting pot or salad bowl?

The variety in the development sphere echoes a familiar adage of African folk wisdom that 'everyone can pray as he likes'. (Hamilton, especially, insists on this idea, and Bates celebrates it.) However, what implications does this hold for our vision of humanity at the global level, a vision that remains uninformed by much consensus? We raised this question in our introduction and left it to the essays to explore. Berger's pessimism about the extent to which developing countries – at least the poorest of them, in

Africa – can achieve development on their own terms is tempered by some evidence marshaled by Bates and by Stiglitz. Contrary to popular rhetoric, Bates sees a 'race to the top' as poor countries strive to improve themselves, although usually with at least some unintended consequences, such as those documented by Nattrass and Seekings in the case of South Africa.

Commentators of diverse ideological persuasions recognize that governments of nation states where developmental imperatives loom large have relatively little influence over the international economic configurations and processes that determine the environment in which such transformation must be managed. Nonetheless, these nations on the periphery, and groups thereof, seeking to 'insert' themselves into the international economy, have to both understand the threats facing them, and seek viable means of recognizing and exploiting the opportunities offered by the wider forces of change. Are there particular ways by which leaders of developing countries in public and private roles can exploit the opportunities in the new world order and flip the threats into yet more opportunities? As the chapters in this book richly indicate, it is an exceptionally complex set of policy concerns that now face developing nations. These questions are often posed in the absence of a well-developed conceptual or empirical understanding of the precise nature of the crucial relationships, as is made especially clear in the chapters by Dezbakhsh, Hausman, Kincaid, and Laffont.

4 Institutions and incentives

Historically, the development of a community of interest regarding international political economy between the rich and the poor states has been hindered by the fact that each perceives a different set of problems to be most critical, a point emphasized in several of the chapters. With the developed and developing worlds perceiving different problems, having different priorities and domestic pressures, and enjoying vastly different influence capabilities, it is not surprising that the structure of incentives diverge, generating controversies. Examples of such controversies are the subject of discussions in the chapters by Rosenberg and Ross, one with respect to intellectual property rights and the other on the structure of and processes at the WTO.

Rosenberg's proposed solution to the intellectual property rights dilemma illustrates the claim that the existence of interconnections among the various aspects of transnational economic relations not only causes shocks to be transmitted worldwide, but as well presents special problems for those nations whose flexibility and control are most circumscribed. Unless the nature of these interconnections is fully understood, the cures chosen by leaders may be worse than the original diseases. For instance, Rosenberg's proposal requires restriction on the right of geographical movement of people. Human resource mobility (migration) is one of the key advantages from integration and is central to skills transfer, particularly for countries with dual economies. When there is a dual economy, the articulation between the formal and informal sectors complicates the relationships between the domestic and the international dimensions of an issue, and so in turn complicates the management of socio-economic issues, as Nattrass and Seekings make especially clear.

In broaching the question of the relative power of multinationals and governments, Ross reminds us that it is impossible to comprehend the dilemmas facing policy making in the developing world without examining the domestic as well as international linkages that give rise to them. Specifically, the role of aid, whether tied or not, and the international ethics of the entire assistance process need a careful examination. As Stiglitz cautions in his chapter, 'Finance is an important factor ... and if it is provided in the wrong way it can actually impede other factors.' We note two points raised by him that implicate the international ethical problems of concern here. One is the perverse circumstance of poor countries having to hold reserve currencies in dollars at rates of return far below the interest rate on their debt; this is like someone opening a savings account as collateral for high credit card debt, with this collateral earning near-zero nominal interest. In the same spirit of highlighting the appreciation of developed nations for 'foreign aid from poor African countries', Stiglitz cites the example of capital outflow from corrupt nations in Africa, aided by instrumentalities crafted by the developed nations. If the key to growth lies in stimulating domestic savings but not in an all-out race to attract foreign capital indiscriminately, then capital flight from developing nations must command the attention of the global community on its own merits, rather than as part of the global war on terrorism. At the same time, the discussions of Laffont, Ross, and Nattrass and Seekings remind us that the prevalence of this situation is partly due to domestic political dynamics in developing countries for which developed nations and their institutions are not responsible.

5 Development processes

Closely related to the issues raised by Ross with regard to the WTO and by Stiglitz with regard to the Bretton Woods institutions, we move from international ethics to the role of hybrid institutions. It is often noted that the role of non-governmental organizations (NGOs) has become increasingly central to the analysis of the international political economy. However, taking notice of this is one thing but carefully examining its implications for policy is another. The role of NGOs can be expected to assume greater importance as the world becomes more tightly knit, and as these organizations seek to secure advantage from direct participation in transnational economic relations. Yet how many people in the developed world are aware of a fact Ross points out in a endnote: that a large body of developing nations has petitioned the WTO for a *reduction* of the influence of NGOs in that institution?

The other major actors relevant for developing countries are multinational corporations (MNCs). Some MNCs can be considered truly transnational, not just in the sense that they do business in many countries, but also in the sense that their global activities require them to represent their policy interests on a global scale. This is certainly true of such icons as VISA, MasterCard, McDonald's, Coca-Cola, Toyota, Microsoft, Hilton, American Express, and Holiday Inn. However, the issue extends beyond questions about the balance of power such as Ross discusses, to the structure of incentives and the costs of commitment as raised by Rosenberg, Laffont, and Nattrass and Seekings. MNCs are considered important players in the task of creating jobs, attracting foreign direct investment, and achieving technology transfers. Laffont's chapter on liberalization of public utilities is relevant to examining this dimension of development in the context of MNCs, though Laffont himself does not explicitly draw the connection here. The link lies in the fact that power and telecommunications (often the most important sectors for actual or potential international investment) are highly technology-intensive sectors and primary sites for structural reforms, at least in the LDC context. The rationale is to modernize infrastructure through the equity participation of foreign investors, the so-called *strategic equity partners*. However, as Laffont points out, buyers have simply not been forthcoming in some instances where they have been sought. In focusing on the incentives required to attract investment – regulation and enforcement – Laffont highlights the problems of poor countries in attracting the 'right kind' of foreign capital, the same issues raised by Stiglitz. As well, the problem of corruption and the high cost of public funds, also raised by Stiglitz, reappears in Laffont's chapter. Ross describes some additional ways in which international integration leads some developing-world governments down new paths of collaboration in rent-seeking arrangements that imperil efficiency and growth.

The difficulties in attracting foreign investment and lowering the cost of capital are compounded by the fact that developing nations, particularly those in sub-Saharan Africa, can seldom rely on the benefit of the doubt from the international economic community. Critics regularly cite the quality of governance, for reasons Berger describes in detail. Perceptions associated with this concern are often self-reinforcing, to the extent that they affect *hurdle rates* for investment. All these complications limit the extent to which developmental difficulties can be understood through economic analysis alone. It is thus crucial to enhance the participation of developing countries in discussions and analyses – though, for reasons discussed by Ross, understanding *how* to do this in a working institutional context is at least as important as recognizing its importance. Participation as intended here transcends the various manifestations for voice and access such as protests, discussions on the future of the IMF and the World Bank, and strengthening of bargaining skills, to implicate philosophical problems of two kinds: questions about the fundamental ethics of mechanism choice, such as discussed by Ross and Hamilton, and epistemological questions about the appropriateness of different modeling alternatives and sources of data, as discussed by Hausman, Kincaid, and Dezhbakhsh.

6 Departing thoughts

To end, we return to the broadest question posed in the beginning, in light of what we find in the chapters. The first point to note is that nearly every contributor recommends against offering generic solutions to development dilemmas, particularly when those solutions are based on a single theoretical model or a policy program outcome. Do not blindly apply the 'Washington Consensus', cautions Stiglitz. Be hyper-critical of what you accept as data, caution Dezhbakhsh and Kincaid. As well, we hear from Berger, Kincaid, Laffont, and Nattrass and Seekings that one should pay deep attention to the specific nexus of institutions found in particular regions. Both Hausman and Ross recommend against policy prescriptions based on sweeping normative theses. Finally, according to Bates, Hamilton, Nattrass and Seekings, and Rosenberg, be ever-mindful that we face unavoidable trade-offs and cannot escape questions about how to decide on them democratically – *problems of social choice*. There is a vast research agenda.

Index

Abrevaya, J. 89
affiliative behaviour 223–4, 227, 231, 233
Africa *see also* South Africa: bio-cultural context 230–5; future prospects 235–6; markets and needs satisfaction 209–11; and popular perceptions of failure 215–17; readiness for democracy 232–5; telecommunications infrastructure 113, 120
agriculture: agrarian financial markets 74–7; OECD subsidies 165
aid, foreign *see* overseas development assistance
Aleem I. 76
antiretroviral drugs 125, 131–7
apartheid 172
Argentina 18, 110
Arndt, C. 183
Ashenfelter, O.A. 92
Ashmore, R.D. 227
assistance, overseas development *see* overseas development assistance
Atkinson, A.B. 83
auditing: costs 106, 116
augmented Solow model 64–5
Auriol, E. 112
Australia: utilities regulation 108
Australian Competition and Consumer Commission (ACCC) 108

Banaji, M.R. 227
banks and banking 17–18, 24
Bardhan, P. 73
Bargh, J.A. 216, 221, 226, 227
Barresi, J. 219
Barro, R.J. 66, 67, 83
Bates, Robert H. 2, 3, 4–5, 35, 48, 246, 247, 248

Baumeister, R.F. 221
behaviour: affected by context 229–30; biological basis 217–19; coalitional impulse 223–4; effect of mood and core affect 224; effect of personality and global orientation 224–6; emotional-cognitive apparatus 219–24; and identity 227–8; intrinsic heuristics and biases 226–7
Bell, T. 175
Bentham, Jeremy 49
Berger, Mike 3, 4, 10–11, 246, 247, 250, 251
best-response-to-market-failure argument pattern 75
Bhorat, H. 176
Bingham, R. 217
Binmore, K. 146, 161
Bodenhausen, G.V. 226
Boehm, C. 223, 229
Bolivia: utility regulation 110
Bound, J. 89
Boyd, R. 223, 229, 236
brain-drain 140
Brandolini, A. 83
Braybrooke, D. 146
Brock, G. 197
Brock, P. 35
Broome, J. 49, 58
Brown, D.E. 218, 223
Bugental, D.B. 225
Byrne, R. 218, 222

Camerer, C.F. 222
Cancun Ministerial Meeting 155
Canon, E. 33
Caporael, L.R. 222, 225
Carneiro, R.L. 229
Cartwright, N. 64, 70

Casley, D.J. 84, 85, 90, 91, 92
Cattaneo. N. 175
central planning 127, 208
Charlton, B.G. 223
Chartrand, T.L. 216, 221, 226, 227
China: economic growth 17; electricity 113–14; enforcement failures 120; telecommunications 114–15; utilities regulatory policies 118; utility regulation 110–11
Chow, G.C. 89
coalitional impulse 223–4, 227, 231, 233
coffee 34
cognition 216, 219–24
Cohen, P. 69
Colletta, N.J. 217
commons, global 25
communitarianism 145
competitiveness 15, 53–4, 128
computers see technology, new
convergence 1–2, 10–11
Cook, R.D. 90
corruption 7–8, 106, 116, 118–19
Cosmides, L. 217, 220, 221, 222, 224
cost-benefit analysis 44, 54–9, 134–7
Costa Rica 19
costs: of auditing 106, 116; monitoring 116; of public funds 105–6, 112, 115–16, 117
Côte d'Ivoire 117, 120;
cross-country regressions 66, 68, 69–72
culture 228–30; effects of relative prices 32; McDonaldization 30–1; value of local cultures 48–9

Damasio, A. 227
data see information and data
De la Fuente, A. 96
De Waal, F. 222
Delich, V. 150, 163, 164
democracy 153–5, 196, 228–30; vs. economic growth 247; needs and democratic sovereignty 206–7; readiness of African states 232–5
Dennett, D.C. 217
Devarajan, S. 95–6
development: global vision 247–8; importance of perspective 5; meaning of the term 9–10; measurement conventions 246–7; processes 249–51
'Development Issues in the New Economy' (conference) 4
Devos, T. 227
Dewald, W.G. 97

Dezhbakhsh, Hashem 3, 6–7, 96, 248, 251
Diamond, Jared 217
Diamond, L. 216
Dirwan, I. 174
Dispute Settlement Body (WTO) 147–8, 150–1, 163–4
Domenech, R. 96
Donald, M. 218, 219
Doxtader, E. 216, 230
Doyal, L. 197
dumping 149, 164
'Dutch disease,' 22

Earman, J. 64
East Asia 22–3, 33
East Asian Miracle, The (World Bank, 1993) 33
Easterly, W. 83
Economic Development and Cultural Change 93, 94(tab)
Edgerton, R.B. 218, 228
education 181, 231
Edwards, L. 174, 175
efficiency see Pareto efficiency
eflornithine 45
Ekman, P. 220, 222
electricity industry see also utilities: 111, 113–14
Ellemers, N. 231
Elster, J. 220, 223
emotions 216, 219–24
employment and unemployment: effect of trade liberalization 173–6, 179; 'high productivity now' (HPN) strategy 182–5
epistemiology 2–3
equilibrium, general 68
Esty, D. 166
ethical individualism 48–50
Etounga-Manguelle, D. 218, 228, 231
Evans, D. 224
exploitation 43–4
exports 175–6

FDI see foreign direct investment (FDI)
Fedderke, L. 174, 175
Fehr, E. 222
Finger, J.M. 164
Fiske, A.P. 225
Fisman, R. 96
Fleming, T. 70
Fleming Martin Securities 177

Index

foreign direct investment (FDI) 250; associated problems 21–4; South Africa 177; *vs.* portfolio flows 22
formal *vs.* informal economic sectors: effects of VAT 18–19
Fox, R. 231
Frank, R.H. 220
free market: and information transmission 127–8; and needs satisfaction 208
Freixas, X. 119
Fukuyama. F. 218, 228
Fuller, B. 181
Funder, D.C. 226
funds, public 105–6, 112, 115–17

Gachter, S. 222
GATT (General Agreement of Tariffs and Trade), 146–7
GEAR (Growth. Employment and Redistribution) strategy (South Africa), 178–9
Ghana 120
Gibson, B. 178
Gigerenzer, G. 226
Giles, D.E.A. 89
Gintis, H. 222
global commons 25
global greenbacks *see* Special Drawing Rights (SDRs)
globalization: associated conflicts 36, 37–8; and capital flows 177; and coffee-producing nations 34; and domestic policy 178–80, 181–2; and economic growth 19–20; effects on culture 30–2; effects on inequality 172–4, 180–1; effects on institutions 33–5; and political liberalism 33; predominance of rights discourse 196
Globalization, Growth and Poverty (World Bank, 2002) 19–20
Glover, D. 150
Goldgeier, J.M. 226, 236
Goldstein, D.G. 226
Gordon, Robert 170
Gough, I. 197
Gourieroux, C. 89
green room process (WTO) 156
greenbacks, global 25–7
Greenfield, S. 224
Greenwald, B. 120
Griffiths, P.E. 220, 221, 222
Griliches, Z. 82, 83, 89
Grossman, Sanford J. 35

group identification 223–4; in-group/out-group orientation 227–8
growth, economic: adverse effects of portfolio flows 22, 23–4; *vs.* democracy 247; effects of AIDS 183; and foreign banks 17–18; long-term keys 21; and trade liberalization 19–20;

Hadi, A.S. 90
Hahn, J. 89
Hamilton, Lawrence 2, 3, 10, 145–6, 246, 247, 251
Harrison, L.E. 228
Harvey, A.C. 89
Hausman, Daniel M. 2, 3, 5–6, 46, 58, 63, 74, 82, 87, 89, 146, 246, 248, 251
Hayek, F.A. 208
Heckman, J. 89
Heese, K. 177
Henley, A. 184
Henrich, J. 222
Herbert, H. 230
Hermalin, B.E. 221, 224
Heston, A. 83, 92, 96
Hicks, J. 55, 56
'high productivity now' (HPN) strategy 182–5
Hodge, J. 176
Hoekman, B.M. 162, 164
Hudec, R. 147
Human Rights Watch 216, 231
Huntington, S.P. 228

identification, group 223–4, 232
identity 227–8
import substitution strategies (ISS) 20, 147
individualism 194–5; ethical 48–50; explanatory (methodological), 45–8; ontological 45
inequality 172–4, 180–1
informal economic sector: agrarian lending and borrowing 74, 75–6; South Africa 173
information and data: econometric remedies for problem data 88–91; for evaluation of needs and institutions 203–6; institutional remedies for problem data 91–3; international trade data 85; microdata 83–5; policy effects of flawed data 95–7; price systems and information transmission 127–8;

problem data: journal survey 93–5; 'secondary' data sets 83; statistical inference with problematic data 85–8; types of data 81–2; types of data problems 82–3
innovation: and central planning 127; and cognition 219; funded by self-taxation 139; government reward schemes 129–31; and intellectual property rights 128–9; and quality of life 132–3; subsidized research 138; unpredictability 126–7; and welfarism 131–3
instincts: primary 221–2; social 222–4; tribal 223
institutions: evaluation 202–6; financial institutions and investment 17–18; and forms 33–4; incentives 248–9
intellectual property *see also* patents: alternative to patents 129–31; and innovation 128–9; political economy 137–41; welfarism as a basis for awarding rights 131–3
interest rates 16, 18
International Labor Organization 175, 177
International Trade Centre 162
investment *see also* foreign direct investment (FDI): importance of institutions 17–18; not assisted by Washington Consensus 16–17
Isen, A.M. 221, 224
Ivory Coast *see* Côte d'Ivoire

Jackson, J. 150, 163
Jones, L. 106
Jones, Ronald 158
Jost, J.T. 227

Kahneman, D. 226
Kaldor, N. 54–5, 56, 68
Kaplan, D. 179
Keeley, L.H. 228
Kenny, Charles 67
Kincaid, H. 2, 3, 4, 6, 9, 74, 246, 247, 248, 251
Kitcher, P. 70
Krueger, J.I. 226
Kruglanski, A.W. 226
Krugman, P. 68, 69
Kunda, Z. 227
Kurzban, R. 224

La Cerra, P. 217

Laffont, Jean-Jacques 2, 3, 7, 112, 116, 247, 248, 249, 250, 251
Lam, D. 172
Lancaster, K. 54
Landes, D. 218, 225, 228
Lange, O. 208
Latin America 20 109, 110, 174
law, rule of 107; undermined in Russia 16; weakness 121
Leamer, R. 70
Lee, J.W. 83
Leontief, W. 82
Lerner, A.P. 208
Leroy, A.M. 88
Levy, D. 96
Lewbel, A. 89
Lewis, J.D. 183
liberalization, trade 174–6; and capital inflow 16–17; and economic growth 19–20; effects on employment 175–6; and labour market rigidity 179; and size of government 34–5
limited liability: constraints 106
Lin, A. 89
Lipset, S.M. 229
Lipsey, R. 54
logrolling 155–6
lottery, global 25
Lucas, R. 67
Lury, D.A. 84, 85, 90, 91, 92

Macrae, C.N. 226
Malthus, Thomas Robert 126
Mankiw, N.G. 64, 67, 69, 82
Manning, R. 230
Manuel, Trevor 149
Marcus, G. 237
markets: and needs satisfaction 207–9
Martin, W. 162
Mason, D. 232
Masters, R.D. 226, 228
Mattes, R. 230, 231
Mavroidis, P.C. 164
Mbeki, Thabo (South African President), 234
McDonaldization 30–1
McGrath, M. 181
McGrew, W.C. 218
McPherson, M. 58
measurement: conventions 246–7; errors 82, 86–7, 89, 93
Messerlin, P. 150
Mill, John Stuart 49, 50, 51
Mills, G. 216, 233

Mischel, W. 225
models: augmented Solow 64–5; criteria 63–4; cross-country regressions 66, 68, 69–72; necessity of equations 68–73; Romer 65
Moll, P. 172, 176
Monfort, A. 89
monopolies, natural 115–16
Monterrey meeting (March, 2002) 24–5
mood 221, 224
Moore, C. 219
Moore, Mike 159
Moore's law 132–3
Morgenstern, Oskar 81–2, 85, 93
Morley, S. 174
Mukherjee, C. 93
Mule, H. 92
multinationals 158, 249, 250
Mung'omba, D. 230
Mwabu, G. 172

nationalism 145
Nattrass, Nicoli 2, 3, 9, 36, 37, 59, 77, 172, 173, 176, 178, 179, 182, 183, 205, 247, 248, 249, 250, 251
needs: African context 209–11; and democratic sovereignty 206–7; evaluation 202–6; formation and distortion 201–2; nature 201; need trajectories 204, 207; role of markets 207–9; vs. wants 197–200
neoclassical growth theory see growth, neoclassical theory
Nesse, R.M. 221, 224
'new economy' see globalization see technology, new
New Zealand: utilities regulation 107–8
Newey, W.K. 89
NGOs (non-governmental organizations) 249–50
Nigeria 22
normative economics: eflornithine example 45; pollution export example 41–5; vs. utilitarianism 50–2
Nugent, J.B. 96
Nussbaum, Martha 197–8

O'Brien, P. 70
OECD 174, 179; agricultural subsidies 165; limit on offshore banking secrecy 24; unfairness to non-members 149–51
Oliner, S. 170–1
On Liberty (J.S. Mill) 50, 51

One World (P. Singer) 144–5
outliers 87–8, 90
overseas development assistance 25, 163, 249

Panksepp, J. 220, 221, 227
Pareto efficiency 52–4, 129
Pareto improvements (Pareto superiority) 52, 54–9
patents 8 *see also* intellectual property; abrogation 133–7; South Africa 157–8; and welfare 125, 129
paternalism 145–6
Perry, L. 174
personality 224–6
Peru 113
Peters, P. 73
pharmaceuticals: antiretroviral drugs 125, 131–2, 157–8; consequences of abrogating patent rights 132, 133–7; eflornithine 45; political economy of property rights 137–41
Pierse, R.G. 89
pollution: as example to argue against liberalization 41–5
Popper, Karl 128
Porter, M.E. 218, 228
portfolio flow 22, 23–4
post-positivist philosophy 63, 64, 73–7
preferences: satisfaction 44, 49–50; and rationality 46–7; rights-preferences couple 193–7
Price, M.E. 223
prices: capping 120; coffee 34; effects on local culture 32; and information transmission 127–8
Prisoner's Dilemma 223
productivity: 'high productivity now' (HPN) strategy 182–5; impact of information technology 170–1
public funds 105–6, 112, 115–16; China 117

Quinn, N. 221

Rabin, M. 222
rationality: and explanatory individualism 46–8; general principle of human nature 48
Rawls, John 136
Rebelo, S. 83
Redding, S. 231
regressions, cross-country 66, 68, 69–72
regularities, universal 66–7, 70

regulation: agency structure 107–9; constraints 121; corruption 116, 118–19; enforcement failures 120; government commitment 119–20; policies 118
Richerson, R.J. 223, 229, 236
Roberts, J. 64
Rodriguez, F. 20
Rodrik, D. 20, 35
Romer, P. 65, 67, 127
Rose, R. 231
Rosenberg, Alexander 2, 3, 8, 59, 146, 247, 248–9, 250
Ross, Don 2, 3, 4, 8–9, 246, 247, 249, 250, 251
Rotberg, R.I. 216, 230
Rothgerber, H. 231
Rousseeuw, P.J. 88, 90
Rozanski, J. 85
Rubin, P.H. 229, 236
rural credit markets 74–7
Russia: portfolio flows 22; undermined rule of law 16
Ryan, K.F. 89

Sachs, Jeffrey 19, 217
Sala-I-Martin, X. 67, 70
Salmon, W. 70
Samuelson, P. 56, 71
Schott, J. 147
Schott, P.K. 231
Schrodinger, E. 217
Schultz, T.P. 172
scientists, freedom of 139–41
SDRs (Special Drawing Rights) 25–7
Seekings, Jeremy 2, 3, 9, 36, 37, 59, 77, 172, 205, 247, 248, 249, 250, 251
self-esteem 221, 227
Sen, A. 145, 146
Shapiro, M.D. 82
Shavell, S. 129
Siamwalla, A.C. 76
Sichel, D. 170–1
Sidanus, J. 224
significance, statistical 69–70
Simon, H.A. 226
Singer, Peter: on democracy in WTO 153; on environmental and labour standards 160; ethical charges against WTO 151–2; importance of WTO Dispute Settlement Body 147; on national sovereignty 157, 160–1; *One World* 144–5; on sentiency 146
Sloman, L. 221, 224

Smith, Adam 33
socialization 228–30
Solow, R. 64–5, 126
South Africa 9 *see also* Africa; domestic policy 178–80, 181–2; employment 175–6, 179; exports 175–6; foreign direct investment 177; future prospects 235–6; GEAR (Growth. Employment and Redistribution) strategy 178–9; 'high productivity now' (HPN) strategy 182–5; inequality 172–4, 180–1; pharmaceutical patent rights 125, 131–2, 157–8; post-independence policies 36–7; role in democratization of Africa 232–5; subliminal racism 215–16; xenophobia 231
sovereignty, democratic 206–7
sovereignty, national 157–61
Special Drawing Rights (SDRs), 25–7
Spencer, S.J. 227
Standing, G. 176, 178
Staples, B. 163
statistics: measurement error 86–7; problem data 87–91; statistical significance 69–70
Stiglitz, Joseph E. 2, 3, 4, 5, 9, 35, 74, 147, 152, 159, 177, 178, 247, 248, 249
Summers, Lawrence 24; on exporting pollution 41–5
Summers, R. 83, 92, 96
supply-and-demand argument pattern 74–5
Svensson, J. 96
Swarns, R.L. 233

technology, new: effects on employment and productivity 170–1, 175–6
telecommunications 113, 114–15, 117
Tetlock, P.E. 226, 236
Thagard, P. 227
Thailand: BAAC government loans 76
Tiefenthaler, J. 35
Tiger, L. 231
Tirole, J. 116
Tobin tax 25
Tomasello, M. 219
Tooby, J. 217, 220, 221, 222, 224
trade unions 172–3
Trebilcock, M. 106
TRIPS (WTO) 157–8
Tsikata, Y. 174, 176
Tskalotos, E. 184

Turk, D.J. 227
Tussie, D. 150
Tversky, A. 226
Tybout, J.R. 85, 96

Udry, C. 76
UNCTAD (United Nations Council on Trade and Development) 162
unemployment *see* employment and unemployment
United Nations: Development Programme 246; Monterrey meeting (March, 2002) 24–5; UNCTAD 162
Universal Declaration of Human Rights 195
universal regularities 66–7
Uruguay Agreement 158–9
utilitarianism 49, 50–2, 146
Utilitarianism (J.S. Mill) 51
utilities 250; agency-company collusion 116, 118–19; constraints to regulation 121; enforcement failures 120; industry structure 109, 112, 113–15; monitoring 116; and public funds 117; regulatory agency structure 107–9, 110–11; regulatory commitment 119–20; regulatory policies 118
utility 47, 50, 51

values, intrinsic 160–1
Van Seventer, D. 172, 178
van Zomeren, B.C. 90
Vanhanen, T. 229, 236
variables 67–8, 71
VAT 18–19
Villa-Vicencio, C. 216, 230
Vogel, Steven 158

wages 176, 184
Walton, M. 174
wants: *vs.* needs 197–200
Warner, Andrew 19
Washington Consensus 33, 74, 152, 178; shortcomings 15–17

Webster, D.M. 226
Weeks, J. 178–9
Weiss, L. 173
welfare: bias to preferences of the rich 45; as criterion for institutions 145; definition 49; *vs.* freedom of movement 140–1; of future generations 135–6; and intrinsic value 160–1; and patents 125, 129, 131–3; and preference satisfaction 44, 49–50; theorems 53–4; utilitarian viewpoint 49; utilitarianism *vs.* normative economics 50–2;
West Africa 32
Whiteford, A. 172
Whiten, A. 218, 222
Williams, David 67
Williamson, O.E. 33
willingness-to-pay 44, 58
Wilson, D.S. 222
Wood, A. 173, 174, 175, 176
Wooldridge, J.M. 89
World Bank 174 *see also* Summers, Lawrence; data errors 82; *The East Asian Miracle* 33; *Globalization, Growth and Poverty* (2002) 19–20
World Health Organization 231
World Trade Organization (WTO), 8–9; approach of Peter Singer 144–5; democracy 153–5; effects on individual countries 151–2; green room process 156; logrolling 155–6; and national sovereignty 157–61; as *prima facie* good 146–8; proposals for reform 162–6; role of Dispute Settlement Body 147–8, 150–1; Singer's ethical charges 151–2; and unfairness in world trade 150–1

xenophobia 231

Yeats, A. 85
Ypersele, T. van 129

eBooks – at www.eBookstore.tandf.co.uk

A library at your fingertips!

eBooks are electronic versions of printed books. You can store them on your PC/laptop or browse them online.

They have advantages for anyone needing rapid access to a wide variety of published, copyright information.

eBooks can help your research by enabling you to bookmark chapters, annotate text and use instant searches to find specific words or phrases. Several eBook files would fit on even a small laptop or PDA.

NEW: Save money by eSubscribing: cheap, online access to any eBook for as long as you need it.

Annual subscription packages

We now offer special low-cost bulk subscriptions to packages of eBooks in certain subject areas. These are available to libraries or to individuals.

For more information please contact webmaster.ebooks@tandf.co.uk

We're continually developing the eBook concept, so keep up to date by visiting the website.

www.eBookstore.tandf.co.uk